THE CONWAY HIS

SEAFARING

IN THE

TWENTIETH CENTURY

THE CONWAY HISTORY OF SEAFARING IN THE TWENTIETH CENTURY

With contributions by:

Alastair Couper
Philip Dawson
Ian Dear
Valerie Fenwick
Norman Friedman
Alison Gale
Eric Grove
Antony Preston
Peter Quartermaine
Ann Savours

CONWAY
MARITIME PRESS

Copyright © 2000 Conway Maritime Press

First published in Great Britain in 2000 by Conway Maritime Press,
9 Blenheim Court, Brewery Road, London N7 9NT
www.conwaymaritime.com

A member of the Chrysalis Group plc

British Library Cataloguing in Publication data
A record for this title is available upon request
from the British Library

ISBN 0 85177 759 7

Designed by Stephen Dent
Printed and bound in Spain by Bookprint, S.L. Barcelona.

CONTENTS

LIST OF PLATES

BIOGRAPHICAL NOTES

Alastair Couper is former head of department of Maritime Studies, Cardiff University. He was founding editor of the *International Journal of Maritime Policy and Management*, and is a Trustee of the National Maritime Museum, Greenwich.

Philip Dawson is the author of several books, including *Cruise Ships: An Evolution in Design*, and is contributing editor to a number of specialist and professional commercial shipping and global aviation periodicals in Europe and North America.

Ian Dear served in the Royal Marines, thereafter working in the publishing and film industries. Since 1979 he has worked as a writer of maritime and military books, and is the general editor of *The Oxford Companion to the Second World War*.

Valerie Fenwick is a maritime archaeologist, author and editor of the *International Journal of Nautical Archaeology*. For many years she has been actively involved at a national and international level to obtain better protection and management of shipwreck heritage.

Norman Friedman is probably America's leading naval analyst and author of many highly regarded warship studies, including *British Carrier Aviation* and *The Postwar Naval Revolution*.

Alison Gale specialises in maritime heritage management, pioneering Maritime Sites and Monuments Records at county and national level. She contributed to the Joint Nature Conservation Committee's series *Coasts and Seas of the United Kingdom*, and has written several books on shipwreck and coastal archaeology.

Eric Grove writes extensively on naval matters past and present. He is the author of the only major study of post-war British naval policy, *Vanguard to Trident* (1987), and Senior Lecturer in Politics and Acting Director of the Centre for Security Studies at the University of Hull.

Antony Preston is one of the world's best known writers on naval affairs. He is editor of the naval journals *Warship* and *Navint*, and has many books and articles to his credit.

Peter Quartermaine teaches postcolonial cultures. He has published *Building on the Sea* (1996) and *Port Architecture* (1999). His new book on the architecture and culture of modern cruise ships will be published in 2002.

Ann Savours writes and lectures on polar history. She has previously worked for Aberdeen University Library, the Scott Polar Research Institute, Cambridge, and the National Maritime Museum, London. She is the author of *The Voyages of the Discovery* (1992) and *The Search for the North West Passage* (1999).

FOREWORD

ETWEEN 1900 AND 2000 there were more exciting and greater changes in our use of the seas than in the entirety of the preceding two thousand five hundred years. Trade has expanded enormously, and more than 90% of this is still carried in ships. But whereas in 1900 an ancient Phoenician could have found the stowage and handling of cargo familiar, he would be bewildered by the changes to be seen at the end of the century. The liners that were establishing regular links for a much larger proportion of the world's population, enabling them to emigrate or move to other continents for work, reached their apogee during the century and are now gone, replaced by aircraft. Cruising has grown from nothing into one of the most important sources of relaxation, whilst yachting has grown from the preserve of a wealthy few to a mass sport available to millions. Naval power is no longer measured by quantity, power and the limited range of the guns of surface vessels, but by the missiles launched from aircraft and nuclear submarines.

In 1900 Britain controlled a greater proportion of world trade than does the United States one hundred years later. It was a maritime empire, maintained by the world's largest merchant fleet and a navy as strong as the next two most powerful nations put together. Whilst no longer the world leader in sheer numbers of vessels, no other country can claim such a wealth of experience and expertise in maritime matters as this book amply illustrates.

Sir Robin Knox-Johnston

They've got no colonies to speak of, and must have them, like us. They can't get them and keep them, and they can't protect their huge commerce without naval strength. The command of the seas is the thing nowadays, isn't it? . . . Well, the Germans have got a small fleet at present, but it's a thundering good one, and they're building hard.

Erskine Childers: *The Riddle of the Sands* (1903)

CHAPTER ONE

THE RACE FOR SEA SUPREMACY

Eric Grove

THE PERIOD FROM 1901 TO 1914 saw a complete revolution in naval warfare. Just as fleets seemed to have settled down into a definitive twentieth century form, everything was transformed yet again. A first class warship of the turn of the century was totally obsolete by the time war broke out almost a decade and a half later. These developments took place against a background of intensified naval competition as the traditional naval powers, Great Britain, France and Russia, were joined by the new and powerful fleets of the United States, Germany and Japan. Great Britain faced increasing problems in maintaining her traditional naval supremacy. She succeeded, but only through leading the process of radical technological change and using the new threat from Germany to create political support for the necessary naval programmes. The perception of a 'naval arms race' fuelled Anglo-German antagonism and helped lead to war in 1914.

The fleets of 1900 were based around battleships and armoured cruisers, which were the joint capital ships of the era. Both were products of developments in the 1890s, notably the introduction of face-hardened steel armour that allowed relatively thin plates to give protection comparable to the much thicker armour necessary in earlier ironclads. The armoured cruisers were probably the more powerful because of their superior speed, some 21 knots or more compared to the battleship's 16-18 knots. A British Drake class armoured cruiser laid down in 1899 displaced over 14,000 tons, was 500ft long and 70ft in beam, compared to a contemporary battleship's displacement of 14,500 tons, length of only 400ft and beam of 75ft. The cruiser was armed with sixteen 6in guns, eight on each beam, with a single 9.2in gun at each end. The battleship had twelve 6in guns, six on each beam, with twin 12in gun turrets at each end.

As well as being faster and more imposing in appearance with its four tall funnels, the armoured cruiser was effectively the more heavily armed as medium calibre guns were the main fighting power of the contemporary warship. The guns of the period had vastly outrun their capacity for accurate direction. Truly accurate fire was impossible beyond a nautical mile or so (2000 yards) and at greater ranges rapidity of fire was the key to success. The big 12in guns that adorned the ends of battleships could only fire one shot in the time it took a 9.2in (on the ends of an armoured cruiser) to fire three or four, and a 6in, the key weapon mounted in batteries on the sides of both kinds of capital ship, to fire up to a dozen. A 9.2in gun might have 85% the penetration of a 12in gun and four times the rate of fire; a 6in gun might have just over half the penetration and ten times the rate of fire. At 1000 yards a 6in gun might penetrate almost 12in of steel, the main belt armour of a battleship. In any case, shells with modern explosive fillings could cause serious fire and other damage. Ships of this period effectively pecked each other to death at close range and the extra speed of the less well protected but faster armoured cruisers was a real tactical and operational advantage. They also made excellent commerce raiders.

The other recent innovation had been the torpedo boat destroyer, a reflection of the increased power of the torpedo caused by the introduction of the gyroscope. This allowed torpedoes to be fired with a chance of hitting at a range of about 1-2000 yards, rather than 5-600 yards. The increased threat of torpedo boats had therefore encouraged the development of larger versions designed to neutralise them. Whether this was best done as escorts to the fleet or as blockading/hunting forces was a matter of debate but by 1900 the destroyer was a vital component of the fleet. Standard British destroyers of 1900 displaced about 400 tons, were about 200ft long and had a service speed of around 25 knots. They were armed with one 12pdr and five 6pdr guns plus two 18in torpedo tubes.

Increasing torpedo ranges also meant that fleets were likely to engage at longer gunnery ranges. During the Russo-Japanese war of 1904-5, fire was being opened at about 9500 yards, although effective results could only be obtained at 5000 yards or less and even this required new technique. The Japanese seem to have adopted the new British system of 'continuous aim' in which gunlayers tried to keep their guns on target all the time using telescopic sights. This allowed quite good results at ranges at which the Russians could make little effective reply but

ADMIRAL HEIHACHIRO TOGO

Admiral Togo plays much the same role in Japanese naval culture as Nelson does in British naval culture. He became the archetypal national naval hero, his status consummated in the annihilation of the Russian fleet at the Battle of the Sea of Japan (Tsushima) in 1905. His life straddled two very different eras. He was born in 1848 into a feudal pre-modern society, the son of a lesser Samurai in Kagoshima. In the 1860s the Satsuma domain established a navy which Togo and his brothers joined. Togo's ship supported the Emperor in the Boshin Civil war in 1868 that accompanied the Meiji Restoration, and in 1871 he began an extended visit to Britain to learn nautical science. Oriental officers were not welcome in Royal Navy training establishments, but Togo attended the merchant service training ship *Worcester* and went round the horn to Australia and back in a sailing ship. He also studied science and technology at Cambridge before overseeing the construction of warships being built for Japan, on board one of which he returned home in 1878. Togo had an active career in the new Japanese Navy, playing a prominent part in the Sino-Japanese War of 1894-5 and the Boxer Rebellion of 1900. At the end of 1903, as war with Russia was in the air, he was appointed Commander in Chief of the Combined Fleet, his blend of caution, decisiveness and considered courage suiting Japan's marginal strategic position admirably. Togo lived up to expectations and performed brilliantly, working jointly with the army to destroy the First Russian Pacific Squadron and annihilating the Second and Third sent from the Baltic to retrieve the situation. His Tsushima signal on 27 May 1905 read: 'The fate of the Empire depends on this one engagement: let each man do his fitting part.' Unlike Nelson, Togo did not die in his moment of triumph; he lived until 1934.

it put the more easily handled and rapid firing 6in guns still more at a premium.

The Russo-Japanese War was the great naval conflict of the period. Russia was an established naval power with a large force of both battleships and armoured cruisers but she had effectively to maintain three navies, one in the Baltic, one trapped by treaty in the Black Sea and a third in the Pacific, itself split between Port Arthur and Vladivostok. This allowed the Japanese to defeat the Russians in detail. Moreover Russian technological deficiencies coupled with the weaknesses of the design advice obtained from her French ally meant that Russian ships were inferior to the largely British-built fleet of her Japanese opponent. Russian gunnery was also poor.

At the outbreak of war at the beginning of 1904 the two fleets in the Far East were evenly matched numerically with about a dozen major units on either side. The Japanese began the war with a surprise torpedo attack on Port Arthur by ten destroyers. Hits were scored on the battleships *Tsesserevitch* and *Retvisan*, both of which were out of action for months. Japanese troops were landed in Korea and Port Arthur, which was increasingly surrounded by minefields laid by both sides. On 12 April Vice Admiral Makarov, probably the most able Russian admiral of the period, was killed when his flagship, the battleship *Petropavlovsk* blew up after being mined off the base; the battleship *Pobieda* also struck a mine but was able to limp back to Port Arthur.

Later in April, Japanese troops were landed in the Kwantung peninsula to besiege the Russian base, which forced the Russians to consider breaking out. Their chances were improved on 15 May when Togo lost *Yashima* and *Hatsuse*, a third of his battleships, in a minefield. In June the new Russian commander, Vitgeft, tried to break out twice but failed. Pressed by Japanese artillery fire he tried again on 10 August. His six battleships confronted four Japanese supported by two Japanese armoured cruisers. The Russians were able to leave harbour but were engaged by Togo in a long range gunnery duel. As the range closed, Vitgeft was killed by a shell splinter and shortly after his flagship *Tsessarevitch* suffered a hit on the conning tower, which killed the captain and many others and put the ship out of control. The Russian line was put into confusion, most turning back to Port Arthur to be destroyed by Japanese howitzers or scuttled by the time Port Arthur surrendered at the end of the year. *Tsessarevitch* took refuge in internment in German Tsingtao and was to fight more successfully in the Baltic 'another day' – during the First World War.

Four days after this Russian reverse, her three Vladivostok-based armoured cruisers *Rossiya*, *Gromoboi* and *Rurik* were finally cornered by the four Japanese armoured cruisers of Admiral Kamimura's Second Squadron. In a four hour battle *Rurik* was sunk and although the other two escaped they were deterred from their previously successful raiding activities in the Yellow Sea.

In October 1904 Vice Admiral Rozhdestvensky set sail from the Baltic with a Second Pacific Squadron designed to restore the situation in the Far East. It was based around four brand new Borodino class battleships. Already jumpy and fearing attack from imagined British-based Japanese destroyers (Great Britain and Japan had been formal allies since 1902) the Russian ships struck at the Hull fishing fleet in the North Sea; Britain and Russia came close to war. Eventually, after rendezvousing with a reinforcing Third Squadron Rozhdestvensky tried to break through the Tsushima Strait to Vladivostok. By ill luck his lighted hospital ship was sighted by a Japanese auxiliary cruiser and Togo sailed to intercept with his combined squadrons of four battleships and eight armoured cruisers. They faced an inferior force of four new battleships, two older battleships and five old ironclads together with three coast defence ships never intended for fleet action on the open ocean. In an action that lasted from 14.10 on 27 May to 12.00 the following day, the Russians lost all of their capital ships: ten sunk and four captured. They also lost two cruisers and all seven of their destroyers, one of the latter being captured with Rozhdestvensky on board. Only three cruisers and four auxiliaries escaped, the former to internment; one of them, *Aurora*, would obtain immortality by beginning the Bolshevik Revolution twelve-and-a-half years later. The Russians lost five thousand men, the Japanese only six hundred, in one of the most decisive engagements in naval history. No major Japanese units were sunk.

Even as the Japanese were annihilating the Russians with established technology, things were changing fundamentally. The British were experimenting with techniques of fire control that allowed the accurate delivery of salvos of heavy shells onto targets at ranges of 5000 yards or more. By 1904 gunnery experts such as Marine Officer Edward Harding were arguing that properly controlled salvos of flatter trajectory heavy shells could hit a target more effectively at these ranges and with much greater destructive power (this was shown in Russo-Japanese war by the few large shells that were lucky enough to hit their target). The 6in gun was now doomed as a major ship-killer, especially as rates of fire of 12in guns were improving.

What made longer ranges imperative as well as desirable were further torpedo improvements. In 1904-5 the leading torpedo manufacturers developed heaters that produced hot gas to drive torpedo engines rather than simple compressed air as used previously. A typical 18in torpedo of the old type had a range of only 800 yards at its maximum speed of 30 knots. The first heater torpedoes of similar size could travel 2000 yards at 34 knots and 4400 yards at 28 knots. By 1909 British 18in torpedoes could travel 3500 yards at 45 knots and 5000 yards at 35 knots. And a hit by even a single torpedo could be the end of a contemporary warship, as shown all too dramatically in trials.

These were the technological dynamics of a revolution in naval affairs that is encapsulated by the term 'Dreadnought'. In some ways this is a bad term as its major single architect, the British Admiral Sir John (Jackie) Fisher, British First Sea Lord from 1904, was no great enthusiast for the revolutionary battleship of that name that was built under his aegis. Nevertheless it provides a good shorthand term for an era in which naval warfare was completely transformed.

Fisher argued that a fast, all-big-gun armoured cruiser would be the key to future naval warfare. She would be able to destroy vessels of any size and thus deal with all threats posed by surface ships, both battleships and commerce raiders, in the open oceans. For sea denial duties in narrower seas, vulnerable big ships would be replaced by flotillas of destroyers and submarines utilising the new heater torpedoes.

Submarines had become practical propositions by the turn of the century because of the improvement of internal combustion engines for surface mobility and power generation and batteries for underwater propulsion. French and US developments at the end of the 1890s stimulated British development, and boats of US design were ordered from Vickers at the end of 1900. The first of these achieved its inaugural dive in 1902 and all were in commission by 1903. The design was enlarged and improved into the 'A' and 'B' classes, twenty-four of which were built over the next three years. In 1906 mass production began of thirty-eight more boats of the 320-ton 'C' class. By 1907 Fisher was boasting that the Royal Navy had forty submarines to add to a surface flotilla component of almost one hundred and twenty-five units. This he saw as dominating the narrow seas as the main barrier to invasion.

In order to provide resources for this flotilla, Fisher ruthlessly scrapped old and very obsolete larger warships, including fifty year old ironclads kept in reserve for anti-invasion duties. He also cut back on the numbers of older cruisers and gunboats on foreign stations to make up a more effective operational fleet and a readier reserve. Some one hundred and fifty-four ships were doomed under Fisher's plans.

The main aim of this radical policy was to continue British pre-eminence at sea in a more cost effective way. In 1889 Britain had declared the two power standard. Lord George Hamilton, the First Lord, stated that "Our establishment should be on such a scale that it should be equal to the naval strength of any two other countries . . . [in warships] . . . of the newest type and most approved design." The progress of the Franco-Russian navies both in battleships and the new armoured cruisers in the 1890s meant the maintenance of this principle became ever more expensive. Taxes were increased and naval policy began to be subsidised by special loans to be paid out of the Navy Estimates. The Boer War and its aftermath created a crisis that necessitated limitations on the naval estimates. Fisher was offering naval supremacy to the government for less money. The new Liberal government that came to office at the end of 1905 with an agenda of social reform was even keener than its Unionist predecessors were on these ideas.

The new armoured cruisers would provide the capital ships of Fisher's new fleet. An armoured cruiser capable of 24 knots and armed with eight 12in guns would be able to fight any major surface ship. Her thinner armour would be of little consequence as at even the longer ranges being experimented with at this time (around 9-10,000 yards) heavy armour could not protect from 12in salvos. But Fisher was no dictator at the Admiralty and he had to accept pressure from his colleagues that the first all-big-gun ship should be a more heavily armoured battleship, albeit turbine powered with the speed of most existing armoured cruisers (21 knots). She was completed in a very short space of time, being laid down on Trafalgar Day, 21 October 1905 and commissioned for trials at the beginning of September 1906. Trials before the end of the year showed that her main battery of ten 12in guns was indeed more accurate than the mixed batteries of 'pre-dreadnoughts'.

To Fisher, however, *Dreadnought* was an 'old testament' ship. He still pressed the case for his 'new testament' armoured cruisers. The design for these was approved in May 1905 and they were laid down in the spring of 1906. Significantly the first, of three, was called *Invincible*. Fisher hoped to move on to another generation of ships that would combine the speed of these ships with the resilience of the battleship but the probable expense of such fusion-armoured ships scared the Admiralty and the 1906-7 order were for three close copies of *Dreadnought*, *Bellerophon*, *Superb* and *Temeraire*.

In the circumstances the Admiralty were lucky to get these three. The new Liberal government came close to abandoning the Two Power standard in 1906. In any case, circumstances were changing. The old Franco-Russian threat seemed less pressing. France had been to an extent neutralised by an entente with Britain, forced by German belligerence; in any case her naval programme was in financial difficulties. The Russian Navy had been – for a time – wiped from the slate by Britain's Japanese ally. The armoured cruiser threat for which the Invincibles had been built was therefore rather less important.

Moreover, *Dreadnought* had created a real crisis for the other naval powers. No one could produce a similar ship for some time. France did not lay down new battleships until 1907-8 and these, though turbine powered, had mixed armaments and could not make even 20 knots. The all-big-gun Courbet class did not follow until 1910 and the first was not completed until 1913. Japan had begun to build her own battleships in 1905 but the intention to fit an all-big-gun armament was frustrated by production difficulties and *Satsuma* and *Aki* were completed as mixed armament ships in 1910-11. *Aki* had turbine propulsion but could only make 20 knots. True dreadnoughts, *Settsu* and *Kawachi* were not laid down until 1909, when Russia laid down her first four also. By that time, late 1909, the British had in service or under construction ten Dreadnought battleships and four Invincible battlecruisers.

By then all the above countries were either an ally of Britain (Japan) or in a state of diplomatic entente (France and Russia). This did not stop them being thought of as potential future enemies and factors in Admiralty planning but the main rivals to British naval power were now the USA and Germany.

America had begun to build a modern fleet in the 1880s, the decade that her steel production outstripped Britain's. At first she concentrated on cruisers and smaller second class battleships for coastal defence and commerce raiding but in the 1890s four sea going battleships and two first class armoured cruisers presaged a 'new navy' that defeated Spain in the war of 1898. This fuelled the USA's imperial and naval ambitions. Five more battleships were launched in 1898 and during the following seven years no less than sixteen battleships and thirteen armoured cruisers were laid down in American yards. Both types were clearly considered capital ships as all after 1900 were named after states of the Union. The USN decided to concentrate battleships in the Atlantic and the faster armoured cruisers in the Pacific.

The Dreadnought revolution created problems for the American naval build up. Gunnery enthusiasts in the USN supported the all-big-gun idea and the battleships *South Carolina* and *Michigan* laid down in 1905-6, were changed from mixed-calibre armament to eight 12in guns, although their limited displacement of 16,000 tons forced a slow pre-dreadnought speed of 18.5 knots. Neither were completed until 1910, the same year that the turbine-powered first American dreadnoughts proper, *Delaware* and *North Dakota* were commissioned. More similar ships followed in 1911, 1912 and 1914, giving a fleet of eight dreadnoughts by the summer of 1914.

The USN had first made its mark globally in 1907-9 when President Theodore

Roosevelt authorised the movement of the Atlantic fleet of pre-dreadnought battleships to the Pacific. Relations with Japan were uneasy because of American immigration policies and Roosevelt thought a show of force necessary. The US battlefleet, sixteen pre-dreadnoughts strong, called the 'Great White Fleet' because of its livery of white hulls with yellow funnels (the Royal Navy had gone to a more sombre and practical grey five years before), sailed round Cape Horn to the Pacific Coast and then moved across the Pacific to visit Australia and New Zealand, provocatively exploiting local doubts about the Anglo-Japanese alliance. Japan, however, also felt it necessary to extend an invitation as part of its policy of appeasing American opinion.

The fleet then moved westwards into the Indian Ocean and through the Suez Canal into the Mediterranean and then into the Atlantic where they met the four newest US battleships for a choreographed entry into Hampton Roads on 22 February 1909. The voyage was a major success in showing the flag but it also demonstrated the logistical weaknesses of the US fleet. Its movements had depended on foreign – essentially British – controlled coal supplies, and the British had also built up a considerable lead in the latest ships. The Great White Fleet was essentially obsolete. On the day it got home the British had in commission two Dreadnoughts and two Invincibles. The Americans had none; indeed they would never commission any Invincible-type ships, a major perceived weakness until the mid-1930s. The USA was an upcoming naval power; but it had yet to arrive.

The country in the most serious state was Germany. In 1898, masterminded by Alfred Tirpitz, the newly appointed Secretary of State for the Navy and with the enthusiastic support of naval enthusiast Kaiser Wilhelm II, she had made a self-conscious bid for sea power passing through the Reichstag a Navy Law that set in place a programme of nineteen battleships, eight coast defence ships, twelve armoured cruisers and thirty second-class cruisers by 1903. The aim was to create a 'Riskflotte', a fleet Britain could not take the risk of fighting and still confront her traditional Franco-Russian enemies. The Navy Law was strengthened by another act in 1902 that called for a fleet of no less than thirty-eight battleships, fourteen armoured cruisers, thirty-four light cruisers and ninety-six torpedo boats by 1920.

The Navy Law was expressed in classes of five battleships each laid down in 1899-1900 (the Wittelsbachs), 1901-2 (the Braunschweigs) and 1903-5 (the Deutschlands). Six armoured cruisers were also laid down one a year from 1900 to 1905. Germany's relative lack of interest in armoured cruisers was another argument against more Invincibles. By May 1905 Britain officially recognised Germany as the third-ranking naval power after France and thus the second of the powers against which she was building, albeit the one with whom war was after 1906 much the more plausible.

Germany's finely tuned programme was thrown into complete disarray by *Dreadnought*. Attempts to produce an eight 11in-gun ship no more expensive than an existing type proved impractical, and even when the first twelve 11in-gun Nassau-class ships were laid down in 1907 they had reciprocating engines as did all eight of Germany's first 'Dreadnoughts' completed between 1910-12. Their maximum speed was only 19-20 knots. Attempts to produce new armoured cruisers were marred by a false start with the 8.2in-gun *Blucher* and the first battlecruiser proper *Von Der Tann* was not laid down until 1908. Completed in 1911 she was a rather better ship than *Invincible* but she, and the next pair *Moltke* and *Goeben*, monopolised turbine production facilities. Not until 1912-13 were the first German Dreadnoughts proper completed in the shape of the Kaiser class. When war broke out in 1914 five were in commission along with four battlecruisers.

Germany intended to fight in the North Sea and this affected smaller craft also. She did not build destroyers proper but rather smaller and more economical 'high sea torpedo boats' optimised for operations in the Baltic and North Sea. There were not many of those either. Fisher gloated in 1907 that the German torpedo boat flotilla totalled forty-eight against Britain's one hundred and twenty-three torpedo boats and destroyers. There was but one submarine against Britain's forty, Germany not having laid down her first U-boat until 1906. This may seem odd given the importance of the U-boat to German naval strategy in two world wars but neither the submarine nor commerce raiding had much place in pre-war German naval thinking. The battlefleet was intended to offer a threat to Britain in the North Sea, a threat of casualties and attrition (to which submarines might contribute) – until perhaps at some very distant date it might be able to seek action with some chance of success. That would not be for some time.

The rise of the German battlefleet was taken more seriously outside Fisher's Admiralty than within it. It helped Fisher maintain warship building to sustain industrial infrastructure, but it made difficult the further cuts in old battleship strength to make economies as his flotilla defence ideas came on line. It also

THE DEVELOPMENT OF THE AIRCRAFT CARRIER

The first flight from the deck of a ship was achieved by Eugene Ely in a Curtiss biplane on 14 November 1910 from a platform built over the bows of the cruiser USS *Birmingham*. The following January, Ely's Curtiss landed on a flight deck built on the stern of the armoured cruiser *Pennsylvania* and then took off again. Little came of these experiments in the USA but the Royal Navy was already showing an interest in aircraft. On 10 January 1912 a Short seaplane took off from the forecastle of the battleship *Africa* and later in the year the feat was repeated from battleships underway. For the 1913 manoeuvres, the cruiser *Hermes* was fitted out as a specialist carrier for floatplanes with canvas hangars fore and aft and a flying-off platform, although her aircraft usually took off or came down on the water. She was the first carrier meant for fleet operations. During the First World War cross-channel ferries were converted along similar lines as seaplane carriers for use as air striking forces, and an old Cunard *Campania* was converted to support the main battlefleet. The Zeppelin threat forced the use of fighters flown from platforms, often temporary affairs built on gun turrets. Normally the aircraft ditched or flew ashore, but in 1917 a Sopwith Pup achieved a pioneering deck landing underway on the forecastle flight deck of the large cruiser *Furious* which had been completed partially as a carrier. This led to experiments with landing on ships, which showed the flight deck had to be clear of central superstructure. By the end of the war the Grand Fleet had a carrier with a totally clear flight deck. This ship was a converted liner, HMS *Argus*, with an air group of torpedo bombers intended for recovery after launch. Carriers with island superstructures were put under construction, the converted battleship *Eagle* and another *Hermes*, started at the beginning of 1918 as the first carrier to be laid down as such. She was commissioned in 1924 by which time both Japan and the USA had their first carriers in commission, *Hosho*, converted from a tanker, and *Langley*, converted from a collier.

forced the pace of new construction. In 1908 the passage of a second amendment to the 1900 German Navy Law called for more rapid replacement of German ships. This led to unfounded fears that Germany might, by secret building programmes, equal Great Britain in dreadnoughts as early as 1912. Agitation arose in Britain for eight new capital ships. The slogan was: "We want eight and we won't wait". The result as the decision to order the last 12in gun dreadnoughts *Colossus* and *Hercules* and six 13.5in gun 'super dreadnoughts', four Orion class battleships and two Lion class battlecruisers. This increased Britain's technological as well as numerical lead still further.

In order to pay for these ambitious programmes the Liberal Government had to increase the burden of taxation, especially on the aristocracy, which led to a constitutional crisis in Britain. The government remained committed to a Two Power standard, defined at the end of 1908 as a 10% superiority over the combined strength in capital ships of the next two largest navies (the USA and Germany). This, however, might not be enough given the conceivable increases in German strength. The second power plus 10% would not give sufficient superiority; hence the decision in 1909 to move to a more ambitious objective of One Power plus 60%, an objective announced by the First Lord of the Admiralty Winston Churchill in the House of Commons in 1912. In fact, this did not make much difference to British programmes that remained both ambitious and expensive.

The constitutional crisis precipitated Fisher's departure from the Admiralty at the beginning of 1910. This had the effect of diluting and reversing his radicalism. Then in 1911, when Britain confronted Germany in the Agadir crisis, the government became dissatisfied with the Navy's apparent lack of war readiness and Winston Churchill was moved into post as First Lord to remedy the situation. Churchill was traditionally an enemy of high naval expenditure but his ideas were mitigated by news of the latest German fleet expansion plan, the Novelle, that would raise the establishment of the German Navy from sixty-six thousand seven hundred men in 1912 to one hundred and one thousand five-hundred in 1920. These officers and men would man a fleet of twenty-five battleships and eight battlecruisers supported by eighteen light cruisers and a flotilla of one hundred and eleven torpedo boats and fifty-four submarines.

This led to Churchill's endorsement of the post-Fisherite thinking that argued for a powerful fleet of thirty-three capital ships in the North Sea, supported by light cruisers, destroyers and sea-going submarines. Ideas of setting up a system of battlecruiser-based 'fleet units' in the Pacific to safeguard British interests were abandoned after the creation of the Royal Australian Navy unit centred on the battlecruiser *Australia* laid down in 1910. Her sister *New Zealand*, subsidised by that dominion, was allocated to European waters rather than form the basis of another such Pacific-based unit. The growth of Austrian and Italian forces in the Mediterranean indeed advised the maintenance of a British battlecruiser force in this theatre to enhance the capability of British flotilla forces and the French Navy concentrated in the Mediterranean as an extension of the entente.

Building of super dreadnoughts went on to provide the cutting edge of this planned 'Grand Fleet' in the North Sea. The year 1911 saw the laying down of four King George V class battleships and the modified 'Lion', HMS *Queen Mary*. In 1912 four Iron Duke battleships were begun, together with the battlecruiser *Tiger*, a secondary armament of 6in guns in all these ships reflecting doubts about the whole long-range-firing logic of the Dreadnought revolution. Then in 1912-14 the Queen Elizabeth class battleships combined eight 15in guns with relatively heavy armour and a speed of 23 knots. This was less than *Tiger*'s 28 knots, but the new fast battleships were probably the best balanced ships of their time and a scale of capability that Germany was far from matching.

The period just before the First World War was one of relative conservatism in naval policy. The ambitions for very long range fire had been apparently mitigated by the abandonment by the Royal Navy of the ambitious analogue computer system invented by Arthur Pollen in favour of the inferior, bowdlerised product developed in-house. This was reinforced by apparently reliable intelligence that the Germans did not intend to fight other than at close range. Nevertheless when war did break out in 1914, Great Britain had a comfortable superiority over Germany in capital ships: ten dreadnoughts and ten super dreadnoughts to eight semi-dreadnoughts and five dreadnoughts. In battlecruisers the ratio was nine to four, with three of the British ships being armed equivalent to 'super dreadnoughts' with 13.5in guns. This was still a true Two Power standard, and also One Power plus 60%. Britain had won the race for sea supremacy.

The British also had a powerful supporting fleet of light cruisers and ocean-going destroyers. The light cruiser was reborn in 1909 to flesh out trade defence forces and to scout for the battlefleet. To some extent stimulated by German smaller cruiser concepts the new British ships were larger and more heavily armed, the Chatham class of 1911 being armed with eight 6in guns on a displacement of 6000 tons. The destroyer had grown to a high freeboard ship of over 1000 tons load displacement, armed with three 4in guns and four tubes for 21in heater torpedoes. It was effective both for flotilla defence and fleet support. The submarine flotilla had also been expanded with the larger sea-going vessels of the 'D' and 'E' classes. Germany had belatedly built up its submarine forces and had about thirty-five U-boats in service of which twenty were combat ready. These were intended for coast defence and fleet support duties. Few expected them to be unleashed on merchant ships.

Naval thinking was still very much battlefleet orientated. The main naval writers of the period, notably Alfred Thayer Mahan in the USA and Julian Corbett in Britain, stressed in their different ways the importance of main fleet units and fleet operations. Mahan in particular was quoted selectively by navalists in many countries to argue the case for large national navies based around battlefleets. These were both the symbols and the reality of naval power in the period 1901 to 1914. Although radicals like Fisher might advocate a move to smaller craft, the dynamics of the contemporary naval environment saw his name associated with the most spectacular battlefleet of all time. It was not 'the fleet that Jack intended' but it was 'the fleet that Jack built'. And most importantly to the security of the British Empire, it was a fleet that could not effectively be challenged.

The Titan of nature and the Titanic *of mechanical construction had met in mid-ocean. The iceberg ripped open the ship's side, exposing her boilers to the icy water, causing their explosion, plunging hundreds of people to their death within the short space of two hours.*

Marshall Everett: *Story of the Wreck of the Titanic* (1912)

CHAPTER TWO

THE GREAT LINERS

Philip Dawson

THE OCEAN LINER EMERGED from the nineteenth-century machine age to ultimately flourish as one of the great wonders of the twentieth century. Its development was significant not merely for its engineering and technological triumph and conquest of the elements, but also in its great human and social impact which brought the world's peoples together as never before.

Prior to the comparatively recent development of supertankers and other large modern specialised cargo vessels, the largest, mightiest, fastest and most prestigious ships were invariably the ocean liners which transported the world's inhabitants from one continent to another. These were powered by some of the largest and most powerful boilers, engines and propellers ever made. The grand accommodation in which the most prestigious of these carried and cosseted their human cargoes were created as veritable floating palaces. Their speed and performance, as rival steamship lines vied for supremacy, became matters of enormous corporate and even national pride, as well as sources of great popular fascination to ordinary people in all walks of life.

Philosophically, the ocean liner gets close to realising the human desire to create a complete microcosm of society in virtually every aspect of its contemporary domestic being. While today we aspire to create such capsules of human civilisation in outer space, the ocean-going passenger ship has for more than a hundred years now been accomplishing this at sea level. While the spacecraft or platform are but the preserve of scientists and explorers, and the cargo ship or naval vessel the domain of their own specially trained compliments, the liner was always something accessible to the ordinary citizen. Though steamship travel was at first but a privilege of the well heeled and famed, it was nonetheless greatly popularised. Even for those who could not muster the tourist-class fare for a crossing in the 1920s or 1930s, it was possible, if they were curious enough, in those days before anti-terrorist security measures became a necessity of our lives, to spend a few hours aboard a liner on sailing day as a visitor.

Human existence at sea was once as harsh as the natural elements themselves could inflict on the small and frail wooden sailing vessels that went to sea through most of the second millennium. Nobody other than hardened seafarers put to sea in a ship for any other reason than dire and absolute necessity. In the mid-eighteenth century, Doctor Samuel Johnson referred to the experience as being "like going to prison with the chance of being drowned."

The steam-powered wonders of the machine age first brought the reassuring predictability of scheduled sailings and the vestigial sea-going origins of shore-based human comfort and security to sea. The term liner was, in fact, originally coined late during the age of sail in reference to vessels which departed for scheduled crossings on a direct line between two ports, regardless of whether their holds had been filled to capacity or not. When Samuel Cunard put his first paddle steamer *Britannia* into service on the North Atlantic in 1840, he was able to stake his company motto of 'speed, comfort and safety' on the more predictable performance of machine power over the prevailing mercies of the winds. With sufficient allowances being made for the exigencies of storms and fog, Cunard was among the first to show that the steamship could be operated with something of the punctuality that the then new-fangled railways were boasting.

In the inevitable progression to larger, more powerful, and faster ships, which brought the switch from paddle wheels to propellers and introduction of iron and steel hulls, came vast improvements in the living conditions onboard. White Star Line's *Oceanic* of 1871 was one of the first to bring hotel-style living to sea. The majority of early paddle steamers were in essence sailing ships, whose entire mid-bodies were given over to their cumbersome mechanical workings. Passengers were berthed in the stern part of the hull entirely below the main deck.

In place of the sailing-ship style agglomeration of an all-purpose saloon flanked by double rows of small cabins, *Oceanic* offered midships-located corridor-accessed cabins, a bright and spacious dining room extending across the full width of the hull, a smoking room and ladies drawing room. However, it was Cunard's 1880s-built *Umbria* and *Etruria* which probably first inspired the truer notion of a 'floating hotel' idea with their lavishly appointed passenger accommodation, which also included a music room equipped with both a piano and an organ.

However, as greater numbers of people began to travel from one part of the world to another, and as countries such as Australia, Canada and the United States opened their frontiers to mass immigration, the steamship lines found themselves having to tend a complete cross-section of society. *Etruria* berthed only five hundred and fifty 'saloon' passengers and but a few dozen additional passengers astern in 'second cabin', yet ten years later the ocean-going societies of White Star Line's *Teutonic* and *Majestic* were deftly segregated into three hundred first class, one hundred and seventy-five second and eight hundred and fifty steerage. The divergent classes each had their own dining saloons, other public areas and deck spaces. First class was given pride of place amidships and on the uppermost decks, while second was generally relegated to the aft decks and steerage below.

The quintessential steamship plan began to emerge around its central core of funnel uptakes, engine room casings, ventilation shafts and cargo hatchways. These were lined up fore and aft along the ship's centre axis, as ordained by the locations of machinery, holds and other working spaces below. On the accommodation decks above, these vertical shafts were flanked by a pair of parallel cabin alleyways, with the intervening spaces along the centre line being used for stairways and deck vestibules, with other central spaces being extended outwards to the ships sides as needed for saloons and other public spaces.

The liner's interior has always presented a very special sense of scale and geometry. Constructed of steel, the hull and superstructure shell, along with internal bulkheads and walls, lacked the thickness of building materials used on land. This was most noticeable in the shallower door and window recesses as well as the lighter appearance to columns, beams and other supporting elements. The rounded corners of hatches and other openings and, perhaps most importantly, the very special lighting effects of that perfect circular marine window, the porthole, were all details unique to the shipboard experience. Above all, the uniquely symmetrical internal layout had to be balanced within the structure and dynamics of a strong and seaworthy tapered hull with a length some eight times its width.

Steamers of the late 1800s possessed the somewhat gangly stance of youthfulness and adolescence, with their tall stovepipe funnels standing atop their hulls and the low narrow deckhouses set well in from their bulwarks. The aptly named 'flying bridges' from which these ships were navigated were typically built atop towers that placed them high above the forward reaches of the deckhouse.

Despite the architectural grandeur and domestic comforts within, the exterior expression continued to solely express the art of the engineer. From the teak-planked decks there was an ever-present sense of the ship's real workings. The great funnels towered overhead, amid clusters of hooded ventilators and held in place by steel guy lines. From the uppermost deck it was possible to peer down the skylights of the engine-room casing to see the machinery being tended by its industrious keepers. There was the smell of coal fire in the air from the boiler room furnaces and underfoot the steady throb from the turn of the engines. The ocean liner's ultimate triumph and enduring legacy would be a phenomenon of the twentieth century. The form would fill out and become more enclosed and the lines become softened with a matured and cultured sense of style and fashion.

Among the first to bring forward a sense of twentieth-century styling were Cunard's *Caronia* and *Carmania* of 1905 and 1906. These introduced the sleeker modern liner appearance of the large, dominant and more fully enclosed superstructure. At its lowest level this was in reality an upwards continuation of the hull plating, with large portholes bringing daylight and fresh air to the spacious central dining saloon and cabins within. The first class accommodation and public rooms on the two decks above were surrounded by open promenades contained behind closed-in balustrades.

The deckhouse had, in effect, grown to incorporate a modern enclosed navigating bridge as part of its massif, while a near-full-length single row of lifeboats lent the attractive appearance of an architectural cornice topping off the smooth lines of the superstructure against the two evenly spaced funnels above. The altogether attractive, functional and modern lines of these ships quickly earned them the epithet 'The Pretty Sisters'.

While both ships outwardly appeared to be identical, hidden within the bowels of *Carmania* was a prototype installation of the steam-turbine machinery that would later be adopted in Cunard's famous record-breaking *Lusitania* and *Mauretania*. The marine turbine was a brainchild of Charles Algernon Parsons, who had demonstrated its remarkable performance by racing his tiny and agile turbine-powered yacht *Turbinia* through the procession of warships at the Jubilee Naval Review in 1897. Worldwide interest in this vast improvement over the reciprocating steam engine was immediate and urgent in naval and commercial circles. Steam turbines were fitted in a number of English Channel ferries, with

Allan Line also introducing it in their Atlantic liner *Victorian*.

The steam turbine was to marine engineering what the triumph of the jet engine over the propeller was later to realise in the aviation field. When completed in 1907, the speed of Cunard's turbine-engined *Lusitania* and *Mauretania* claimed, and for twenty-two years held, the long-contested Blue Riband of the North Atlantic. On her second westbound crossing in May 1907, *Lusitania* first took the honours from Hamburg America's *Deutschland*. The two Cunard sisters worked up from their design speed of 24.5 knots, with *Mauretania* ultimately achieving 26.35 knots after being converted from coal to oil firing after the Second World War, and finally conceding the Blue Riband to North German Lloyd's *Bremen* in 1929. The largest and fastest ships of their day, both *Lusitania* and *Mauretania* measured approximately 30,000 gross register tons and could accommodate some five hundred and sixty first-class passengers in the lap of Edwardian-era splendour, along with an additional one thousand six hundred or so in second and third classes.

Despite the great technical advance of their steam-turbine machinery, *Lusitania* and *Mauretania*'s outward appearance bore a likeness to the long and low profiles of the earlier *Campania* and *Lucania*, albeit in substantially larger proportions, with four funnels, rather than two. The new turbine ships also had a more closed-in forward superstructure, with its bowed forward end incorporating an enclosed navigating bridge. These distinguished sister ships had a unique expression of great power, strength and speed, belonging to them alone, and which ultimately gave way to other expressions and styles in the development of many still greater liners yet to follow.

The challenge of *Lusitania* and *Mauretania* was met in Britain by White Star Line's plans for three larger ships which, although not as fast as Cunard's Blue Riband holders, would instead offer such luxury as to make the extra time spent onboard worthwhile. These were to be liners with tall superstructures like 'The Pretty Sisters', but with the far greater measure at about 45,000 tons each. Bigger by a third than *Lusitania* and *Mauretania*, the new White Star ships were considered to be about the maximum size which building conventions of the day would sustain. Their great internal volumes were, above all else, to create a sense of spaciousness and luxury the likes of which had never before put to sea. The first of these was commissioned in 1911 as *Olympic*, with *Titanic* to follow a year later and *Britannic* due to debut in 1914.

Olympic's magnificent Louis XVI period-style first class dining room was one of

20TH-CENTURY DEVELOPMENTS IN NAVIGATION AND DISTRESS SIGNALLING

Peter Quartermaine

The 1998 Hollywood film based around RMS *Titanic* (a film whose cost equalled that of the liner itself) again focused popular attention on what has become the dominant maritime disaster image; this despite the fact that over four thousand troops died on the *Lancastria* on 17 June, 1940 (not to mention other world shipping disasters). The sinking of the *Titanic* on 15 April 1912, on her maiden voyage from Southampton to New York, and especially the findings of two committee of enquiry that, for example, this modern and prestigious ship carried lifeboats sufficient for only one thousand one hundred and seventy-eight of the two thousand two hundred and one persons on board, also made very clear the urgent need for international agreement on maritime safety, including navigational and distress procedures. The *Titanic* did send out radio distress signals, but the closest ship did not have a radio officer on watch at the time; by the time the more distant *Carpathia* reached the scene many lives had been lost in the icy waters. In all, nine hundred and sixteen passengers and six hundred and seventy-three crew died in the tragedy, which made headline news around the world.

The compelling simplicity of the *Titanic*'s sinking, in which state-of-the-art maritime technology was destroyed by a large block of ice, contrasts with the dramatic changes since brought about by radio and other technologies. Radio was invented by the Italian scientist Gugliemo Marconi in 1895, and within

several remarkable interiors which conveyed a sense of palatial seagoing grandeur. There were no double-height spaces, as had been featured in the dining rooms of the *Lusitania* and *Mauretania*, but rather an expression of a habitable horizontal dimension that could be enjoyed for its roominess rather than merely being admired for its vastness overhead. The same sense of dimension was also given to the generous expanses of covered deck space. However, as was the usual case with Victorian- and Edwardian-era liners, other key public areas such as the smoking room, lounge and drawing room tended to be comparatively small, any one of which could only seat a small part of the first class population.

Although *Olympic* did offer the added, and predominantly male, diversions of Turkish baths, a gymnasium, squash court and one of the first ocean-going indoor swimming pools, the decks themselves still played a key role in daily shipboard ten years was already recognised as offering a breakthrough in maritime safety. The first radio message across the Atlantic was sent in 1901, and during the next five years two conferences met in Berlin to consider its effective international regulation. The Convention for the Safety of Life at Sea (SOLAS) was first adopted at a 1914 conference held in London on the initiative of the British government and was attended by representatives of thirteen governments; one section of it required ships carrying more than fifty passengers to carry radio equipment with a range of at least 100 nautical miles. This Convention would have come into effect in 1915, but the outbreak of war delayed this until a further meeting in London in 1929, by which time the radiotelephone had made possible direct transmission of the human voice. Since then SOLAS has been regularly reviewed and upgraded by the International Maritime Organisation, a United Nations body which was established in 1948 and came into being ten years later (originally as the Inter-Governmental Maritime Consultative Organisation, or IMCO); this body is based in London and today co-ordinates a range of detailed agreements to which some one hundred and sixty nations are signatories. These agreements cover everything from the technical design of vessels to basic hygiene and safety regulations for both crews and passengers, as well as for all types of cargo from livestock and vehicles to wine and liquid gas. The main threat to life at sea remains, as in the case of the *Titanic*, death from drowning or exposure after abandoning ship, and modern safety equipment is designed both to protect the individual and to signal automatically to both shore stations and to other vessels, which under SOLAS have an obligation to respond with all possible speed.

life. Many daytime hours would be spent in ritual promenading around the 'block' of the promenade decks or reclined under a steamer rug in the comfort of a deck chair where the on-going social parade of shipboard life could be enjoyed and partaken of. Apart from meal times and evening dancing in the main lounge, the promenade deck was one of the few public areas where passengers of both sexes could mix socially. Ladies were then categorically barred from ships smoking rooms and gentlemen regarded the drawing room as an exclusively feminine preserve.

While neither *Titanic* nor *Britannic* ever completed a commercial voyage, their plans nonetheless showed some concession towards a more homogeneous shipboard lifestyle. The two ships were registered at slightly higher tonnages by virtue of their lower promenade deck spaces being appropriated for additional cabins. Apart from giving *Titanic* and *Britannic* each two spacious veranda suites and some very attractive and spacious outer staterooms with large windows, this change put a greater emphasis on the main Promenade deck above as the centre of daytime social activity. To make this higher-deck space more habitable, its forward half was enclosed by large sliding windows of the type fitted in the 1909-built Holland America ship *Rotterdam*.

The small à-la-carte restaurant aft on *Olympic*'s Bridge deck was enlarged and augmented by a reception hall and Parisian-style café in *Titanic*, providing more opportunity for passengers to socialise in mixed company. *Britannic* featured a yet again enlarged rendition of the restaurant and reception lounge as well as the addition of a children's playroom.

Titanic's tragic sinking after hitting an iceberg whilst bound for New York on her maiden voyage was one of the greatest marine disasters of the twentieth century; some one thousand five hundred lives were lost. It was one of the first world calamities to be communicated instantaneously to both sides of the Atlantic by wireless, which was still an infant prodigy of twentieth-century technology in 1912. The ship's inadequate lifeboat capacity, mandated by arbitrary regulations which did not take into account the actual number of passengers aboard, focused world-wide attention on civilisation's complacent faith in the integrity of its engineering accomplishments against the might of the natural elements. *Britannic* was immediately taken into government service at the outbreak of the First World War, later meeting a more ignominious end inflicted by an enemy torpedo with but a small loss of life. The ocean liner's conquest of the world has, fortunately, been marred by very few such disasters involving heavy loss of lives.

The three White Star ships nonetheless set the standard of elegance for Cunard's magnificent *Aquitania*, which was likewise designed more for luxury than speed. Her oak-panelled smoking room and ornate plastered main lounge were two of the most enduring classic ship's public interiors from the period. Although not fully double-height, the ceilings of these were higher than the surrounding enclosed promenades, allowing light from the boat deck above to be admitted by way of their ceiling vaults.

The layout of *Aquitania*'s first-class public spaces, with the smoking room aft, main lounge amidships and quieter areas such as the drawing room forward, was to form the quintessential scheme of later Cunard developments which would include a second *Mauretania*, the *Queens*, the second *Caronia*, as well as various adaptations of it in smaller intermediate-class liners.

These great British liners, were rivalled from across the channel by, most notably, the French Line's exquisitely old-world style *France* and *Hamburg*, and America's vast *Imperator* and *Vaterland* with their lofty, skylighted social halls, and the remarkable axial layout made possible in *Vaterland* by parting her funnel uptakes towards either side of the hull. These, the last ships of their kind, were to close out the opulent and carefree grand-luxe pre-First World War era known as La Belle Époque.

After the First World War, the mass emigration that had greatly sustained the livelihood of the ocean liner trade was drastically curtailed. However, the steamship lines found new opportunities that the war itself had brought their way. Thousands of American doughboys who had crossed the Atlantic to fight in the trenches would be eager to return to Europe with their wives and young families to experience its wonders in peacetime. Likewise there would be the families of war brides and battle comrades in Europe who would want to visit the New World. As liners were restored to peacetime operations their former emigrant accommodation was spruced up and offered as inexpensive tourist or tourist-third.

These changes brought a whole new mobility to the travelling public, with liner travel no longer being either a luxury of the privileged and wealthy or the hardship of steerage-class emigration where families were split up with men and women sleeping in separate parts of the ship. With the basic comforts of its minimalist two- and four-berth cabins, tourist-third even became fashionable, attracting also many students and other young people wanting to make the grand tour during their summer holidays.

In May 1927 Charles Lindbergh made his historic non-stop flight from New York to Paris. Although few at the time could realistically foresee the likelihood of frail flying contraptions such as his posing any serious challenge to the mighty ocean liner, many nevertheless cast their eyes to the heavens, and part of that sense of wonder which belonged to the great machine-age mystique of the steamship went aloft. However, for the time being at least, the ocean liner would still be the only viable way to cross, and competing owners and nations were eager to provide the best standards of comfort and luxury, the highest speeds and the latest in design and style.

Aviation-inspired streamlining quickly became the crusade of contemporary industrial design as the ultimate expression of modernity and efficiency. Its first

DOCTOR DIESEL'S REMARKABLE OIL ENGINE

In 1912 the East Asiatic Company's *Selandia* and *Jutlandia* started their lives as the world's first successful ocean-going 'motor ships'. Described then also as being 'steamless' ships, they did away with the need to separately produce steam as an engine power source by using oil engines which produced their own power by internal combustion. The modernity of the dawning automobile age was expressed in the very appearance of these ships that were built without conventional funnels. Like the 'horseless carriages' beginning to appear ashore, these only needed exhaust pipes, which were carried up through the mast. Although at first no doubt regarded with some scepticism by some, especially in coal-rich countries such as Britain and Germany, there was nonetheless eager early speculation that this could well be the way of the future.

The motor ship owes its origins largely to the German engineer Doctor Rudolf Diesel, who first developed the compression oil engine named after him as an alternative to the electric-spark-ignition principle that has ultimately flourished in automotive engineering. The low-speed running of Doctor Diesel's invention soon proved to be also ideally suited to its use in the far larger sizes and much higher power ratings needed for marine use. The first diesel-engined ships appeared on coastal and inland waterways in Russia, France and Switzerland at about the time *Carmania* and *Victoria* introduced the steam turbine on the North Atlantic.

However, large passenger motor ships only began to appear on the high seas in the 1920s. Among the most notable of large-scale manifestation at sea came in the form of North German Lloyd's *Bremen* and *Europa*. The long low lines of these ships with their squat twin funnels, semi-circular superstructure fronts, cut away bows and fully glassed-in promenades were for their time the ultimate expression of streamlined ocean-going luxury and high technology.

Within their fast seaworthy hulls and aerodynamically formed superstructures these modern ships each featured a magnificent suite of modern double-height public rooms arranged along an uninterrupted central axis almost the full length of the superstructure itself. Each ship also featured a bright, à-la-carte restaurant sited between the funnels high above the lifeboat line with commanding views out to sea.

In planning the sleeping accommodation, North German Lloyd took into account the lifestyle standards of modern American hotel and apartment design.

these were Swedish American Line's trend-setting *Gripsholm* and *Kungsholm*, as well as *Asturias* and *Alcantara* of Royal Mail Lines. The following decade brought speed and power, including the stylish quadruple-propeller *Victoria* of Lloyd Triestino, with a comparatively high service speed of 21 knots. Holland's *Oranje* and *Willem Ruys* were engined for the 26.5 knots needed for fast passage of their long routes to the Dutch East Indies. Of these, *Willem Ruys*, only completed long after the Second World War in 1947, was particularly notable for her aggregate of eight engines geared to twin propellers. Until *Queen Elizabeth 2* was re-engined in 1986, *Willem Ruys'* 28,310kW installations made her the world's most powerful passenger motor ship.

Steam propulsion remained the preserve of the truly large and fast north Atlantic liners, including *Normandie*, the *Queens*, *United States*, and finally *Queen Elizabeth 2*, as built in 1969. A number of others, among them the 1960s-built *Oriana*, *Canberra*, *Raffaello* and *Michelangelo* were also turbine powered. The vast majority of new passenger tonnage being built in the 1950s and 1960s, including many car and passenger ferries and eventually cruise ships, was diesel. The final and decisive conquest of the little oil engine which Doctor Diesel built at his workshop in 1897 came when, exactly ninety years later, *Queen Elizabeth 2's* original steam machinery was replaced with a nine-engine diesel-electric power plant of the type now in virtually universal use throughout the world's cruise fleets.

Some of the latest developments offer the possibility that, by the time *Selandia's* centenary is marked, there will be diesel or diesel-electric liners speeding cruise passengers across the seven seas at up to 40 knots. Doctor Diesel would indeed be very pleased.

Cabins were laid out on several standard plans, each of which had modern hotel amenities, bright and spacious rectangular living spaces, en-suite bathrooms, and built-in closets. Third and tourist classes were also provided with spacious, well-planned and comfortable cabins, no longer relegated to the least desirable parts of the ship, but rather arranged along the full length of the decks beneath the higher-priced accommodation.

Bremen and *Europa* were followed by a veritable spate of new liners flying the flags of the world's leading seafaring nations. The prestige and speed records of the new German liners were soon challenged by Italy's *Rex* and *Conte di Savoia*, with *Rex* briefly taking the Blue Riband from 1933 to 1935. Of the two ships, her more angular superstructure shape had a far less modern appearance than *Conte di Savoia*, whose clean lines of form made her one of the most admired liners of the early 1930s. The two ships had, in fact, been ordered by different owners from separate yards before the lines were merged as Italian Line prior to their completion.

Liners of great significance were also built for services other than the North Atlantic. Hamburg South America Line's 1927-delivered *Cap Arcona* brought an unprecedented standard of comfort and luxury to the Line's Brazilian and Argentinean line services. One of the most popular features of this elegant three-funnelled liner was her spacious double-height dining room located aft on her Promenade deck, affording views out to sea from its wide windows and the natural coolness offered by its height in those days before air conditioning.

Inaugurated in 1931 as flagship of French Line affiliate, Compagnie Générale Sudatlantique, *L'Atlantique* appeared as a modern ship of such structural daring as had yet to be seen on the North Atlantic. Glimpsed for the first time at a distance she immediately appeared different. Instead of the course of sheer that traditionally arc a ship's hull lines slightly upwards towards the bow and stern, her decks were absolutely flat from end-to-end. Here too, a remarkable interior plan was devised. *L'Atlantique* had the unusual feature of a wide two-deck-high galleria extending along the centre of the two uppermost cabin decks, incorporating the ship's main entrance hall with its various shops and other services. The impressive suite of public rooms also included a double-height dining room, which in the truly French Line fashion was entered at its upper level by way of a wide processional staircase.

Orient Line's Far Eastern services *Orion*, was one of the most exquisitely designed British liners of the 1930s. Her entire suite of Promenade-deck first-class public rooms was arranged on a remarkably open plan that encouraged passengers to move about freely in their enjoyment of a far less formal shipboard lifestyle. The idea behind these bright and modern interiors was that their various connected spaces could be used for different functions as needed throughout the daytime and evening hours and reflect the mood and character of their various uses. One of the deck's more unusual features was a ballroom with glass sides which could be swung out of the way, effectively turning the whole area into an open-sided covered deck for parties or dancing in tropical latitudes. *Orion*'s functional décor set the modern design standards which Orient line was to follow in the building of *Oriana* in 1960.

From the Netherlands came Holland America's timelessly elegant *Nieuw Amsterdam*. Built for the Line's Rotterdam to New York service, she was considered by many to be the perfect Atlantic liner. Smaller than her British,

French and German counterparts, *Nieuw Amsterdam* possessed a remarkably human scale which was never too overwhelming or overpowering, offering her passengers an easily acquired sense of orientation and a comfortable familiarity with the ship's amenities and services. *Nieuw Amsterdam's* memorable interior architecture and decoration was a tableau of the very best in contemporary Dutch and European design and craftsmanship.

The greatest triumph of the classic ocean liner was to emerge as French Line flagship *Normandie* and Cunard's *Queen Mary* and *Queen Elizabeth*. At a register of around 80,000 tons each, these still stand as the mightiest, fastest and most celebrated manifestations of the floating cosmopolis that were ever created. Though their measure of size has been eclipsed by some recently built cruise ships, their wide sailing ranges, great structural stamina, the completeness of services and facilities needed for long periods at sea, and, above all, their inimitable image, remain largely unchallenged.

Their vast black hulls, whose fineness of line and form belies their size and strength, the towering white superstructures and their great oval funnels combined to form one of the most compelling icons of modern civilisation. While it has been more than half a century since the last of these, *Queen Elizabeth*, was built, it is their image which still flourishes to this day, as the defacto visualisation of the idea 'ocean liner', 'steamer' or 'passenger ship', illustrated in encyclopaedias, dictionaries, children's books, business and computer graphics.

Normandie was the most outstanding, progressive and excessive of the three. When she made her debut in 1935 the world marvelled at her streamlined exterior greatness and the modern magnificence of her interiors. Her passenger spaces brought to the prestigious North Atlantic trade some of the innovation her builders had introduced four years earlier in *L'Atlantique*. The new French Line flagship featured a vast three-deck-high dining room which lay the length of nearly 100m along the centre of her hull. Above, her suite of first-class public rooms was arranged on a remarkably open plan, with a sliding wall that allowed the high-ceilinged main lounge and smoking room to be combined as a central focus of social activity.

Normandie was also the first liner to be outfitted with a full-fledged theatre, equipped both for stage productions and as a cinema. This, along with the Upper Hall amidships and the Grill Room, at the top of a spectacular stairway ascending from the aft end of the smoking room, formed a memorable sequence of spaces which flowed one into the other as a boulevard along the ship's centre. The whole scheme, with its emphasis on light moveable furniture and its adaptability of function and mood offered a sense of comfortable informality despite its grand proportions. However, comparison of *Normandie*'s deck plans with those of *Queen Mary* and *Queen Elizabeth* suggests that, apart from some very elaborate suites aboard the French ship, the cubic excesses of her public rooms were gained to some degree at the expense of her average cabin sizes.

Although as remarkable in their own right, the *Queens* were more traditional in character, stressing a British North Atlantic preference for the 'solid' comfort of a less informal atmosphere. For whatever those Empire interiors, with their multitudes of shimmering polished veneers assembled from every corner of the Crown's dominions and territories, vivid chintzes, boldly geometrical carpet patterns, and their outrageous lighting schemes, may have lacked in the higher flights of architectural and artistic canescence, they made up for in their eternal popular appeal. The public at large simply fell in love with these great ships, which in their own minds were what the inside of an ocean liner really ought to be like.

The *Queens* had a sense of comfortable, liveable homeliness that survived the rigors of the Second World War intact and which mellowed as the two ships gently aged through the 1950s and 1960s. *Queen Mary* and *Queen Elizabeth* were each duly withdrawn after long and distinguished careers as two of the grandest and most loved ships the world has ever known. Alas, *Normandie* was a femme fatale whose commercial service life lasted but five years before she was laid up at the outbreak of the Second World War and eventually gutted by fire in 1942 while being converted in New York harbour for trooping as the USS *Lafayette*.

The exteriors of modern ships such as these were the ultimate expression of classic naval architecture and marine engineering. Yet in the pursuit of public appeal the onboard milieu was becoming ever farther removed from any expression of the ship's inner workings and more an expression of architectural splendour in its own right. Twentieth-century lifestyles were becoming increasingly varied and steamship passengers wanted ever more diversions to help them while away the days at sea. *Normandie* and the *Queens* offered so much in contemporary lifestyle pleasures, that the wonders of their existence as the world's greatest ocean liners started to be taken for granted.

The Second World War brought with it not only the plotting of long-haul intercontinental and overseas air routes, but also the aircraft, electronics and other advanced technologies which would shape the post-war world. People's imaginations were beginning to be stimulated by the emerging wonders of an altogether new age. Through the 1950s and 1960s the Comet and Boeing 707 airliners, transistorised electronics, integrated-circuit chips and space craft such as Sputnik and Mercury became what the railways, steamships and other great engineering works of the machine age had been to earlier generations.

This was also a period of growth and liberalisation which produced phenomenal increases in personal wealth and freedom. The populous of the Western World in particular attained mobility and the free time to travel. The private automobile came of age, with vast new highway networks being built in Britain, Europe and America. Long distance and international travel, whether by land, sea or air was within the reach of virtually anyone who wanted it.

United States, *France* and, finally, *Queen Elizabeth 2*, were designed and built in the spirit of this technological age as the last elite-class express ocean liners. These were smaller, more compact and offered greater efficiencies than their forebears of the 1930s. In 1952 *United States* decisively claimed the Blue Riband for America on her maiden crossings, made at average speeds of 35.59 knots eastbound and 34.51 knots westbound. Technical information released by the United States Navy, after the ship was declassified from her never-exercised alternative role as a troop transport, revealed that she would have been capable of speeds approaching 40 knots in calm sea and wind conditions.

Ten years later, French Line's elegant new *France* made her debut as an appropriate successor to *Normandie*, revitalising something of the spirit of her great predecessor, but doing so in the more restrained and rationalised character of the jet age. At 66,348 tons, her design was more compact than *Normandie*. Yet *France* offered accommodation of very high modern standards for two thousand and forty-four passengers as compared with the earlier ship's capacity of 1972. This was achieved largely through a far better use of space, thanks in part to a change from three to two passenger classes. Also there were great advances in the cabin design, which had progressed from a multiplicity of individual plans and bulky shipwright-made fittings towards the modern Pullman-style efficiencies of standardised layouts with compact built-in furniture and fittings.

However, the two-deck-high first-class main lounge, the elegant circular library, domed forward dining room and the spacious theatre all reflected a contemporary interpretation of the same sense of French pride that had once rendered *Normandie*. *France* and her interiors were perhaps best summed up at the time of her completion in the British trade journal, The Shipping World as: ". . . a 'never-never' land, and perhaps sadly enough a 'never-again' land."

Holland America's *Rotterdam* along with the P&O liner *Canberra* introduced a radically new look for the 1960s with the aft location of their slender side-by-side tanker-style funnels. Both ships had been designed with their machinery as far aft as possible, so as to make the best use of their midships spaces for passenger accommodations. *Canberra* also had the benefit of her lifeboats being recessed into the sides of her superstructure, allowing the upper decks to be almost entirely devoted to the passenger recreation facilities needed for her long tropical voyages to Australia, New Zealand and onward to the American West Coast.

Both ships were created with alternative cruising roles in mind, and ultimately made the transition to full-time cruising with great success. The advantages of their straightforward and unobstructed internal layouts have been influential in the development of the modern cruise ship. Although the actual funnel styles have largely remained unique to *Rotterdam* and *Canberra*, these liners have nonetheless asserted a contemporary aft-engined passenger vessel image. While this has been rendered in many variations through the last three decades, it has never fully displaced the liner-era image. As recently as 1994 The Disney Corporation, which trades heavily on its vision of tradition, asked the designers of their first two cruise ships for 'a modern classic'. These have proportionally balanced dark-blue hulls, streamlined white superstructures and twin funnels amidships as renditions of the enduring storybook ocean liner image.

In 1969 Cunard's *Queen Elizabeth 2* asserted her own unique variation of the classic image as the last great ocean liner to be built for regular service on the North Atlantic. Her design was also conceived from the keel up to take her throughout the world during the winter months as one of the most sophisticated and luxurious cruise ships on earth. She was designed around a compact twin-screw propulsion plant which offered optimised modes of operation at 28.5 knots for the Atlantic crossing and long open sea passages on world cruises and at 16 knots for shorter spells of tropical island hopping.

The conception of *Queen Elizabeth 2*'s passenger facilities was shifted from the notion of an express vessel with hotel facilities added, to that of a modern ocean-going urban resort with mobility and, when needed, North Atlantic express speed added. As such, she would provide equally for worldwide cruise passengers as for those whose travels would include an Atlantic crossing as part of a holiday or business trip.

The ship was given a remarkably high proportion of outside-facing cabins that would be suitable for long cruises, and throughout her three principal superstructure decks an extensive array of public rooms, including the restaurants. The traditional enclosed promenade decks were revitalised and brought into the fully climate-controlled realm of her interior layout as the main means of circulating among the various lounges, bars and other places. Those rooms which would be used for entertainment were equipped with production lighting and sound systems, and their seating was terraced to provide proper sight lines. Perhaps most significantly of all, *Queen Elizabeth 2* was essentially planned as a single class ship with a wide range of facilities, which on North Atlantic services could be loosely divided between her first and tourist classes.

Queen Elizabeth 2 was not merely another great Cunard ship cast in the traditional mould of her famed predecessors, but an entirely modern ship designed with an image and identity all her own. The interiors were created by some of Britain's leading contemporary architects and designers of the 1960s. Her exterior profile, fashioned by architect James Gardner featured modern flowing lines, and, as originally built, a single tall black funnel rising from an ingeniously designed white cowl, visually balanced against the massif of her main mast above the bridge. *Queen Elizabeth 2* was created as a modern yet timeless classic.

At the end of the twentieth century, *Queen Elizabeth 2* was the only ocean liner that still made regular crossings of the North Atlantic. She was completely re-engined with a modern diesel-electric power plant, and her accommodation was extensively altered to keep pace with the latest trends in cruising, although recent work has restored some of the clarity of her original plan. At the end of the century, *France* was sailing as the cruise ship *Norway*, with her forward engine room decommissioned and her outer two propellers removed. Despite the addition of two cabin decks atop her superstructure and various other changes, her profile with its distinctive winged funnels remained clearly recognisable. Her original first-class lounge, library and forward dining room, along with many of her cabins retained much of their original character. *United States* continued to languish in a tenuous state of limbo, laid up for more years than she was in ever in service for, as one scheme to revitalise her after another failed to materialise, while *Queen Mary* remained as a tourist attraction and hotel in Long Beach, California.

The age of the great ocean liners has come and gone. The vibrant new era of cruise shipping is a somewhat different phenomenon, rooted in an entirely different image. For those of us who have been around long enough to have experienced the great ocean liners and those who can but speculate, fantasise and dream of the wonders that they once were, they are still wonders which will live forever in our hearts and minds.

The 12-inch shells had blasted away great holes in the unarmoured upper work; one had blown a gap in the horizontal protective deck. The Gunnery Commander saw her lurching through the waves, smoke – furnace smoke, and shell fumes, and smoke from fires – pouring from every crevice; but she was still a ship; she still moved, she still floated; she might still fire her guns.

C. S. Forester: *Brown on Resolution* (1929)

CHAPTER THREE

UNSEEN ENEMIES: THE FIRST WORLD WAR

Antony Preston

IN 1914 THE ROYAL NAVY could look back with pride on two centuries as the most powerful naval force in the world. For the previous hundred years that supremacy had not been seriously tested in battle, but now a new enemy was ready for just such a trial of strength. Rapid advances in technology had, it seemed, totally changed the basic assumptions of naval warfare, but there had been little or no practical evaluation of these developments, nor of the doctrines which had evolved around them. It is against that background that the relative performance of the two major players, the Royal Navy and the Imperial German Navy must be judged.

Neither of the two major navies lacked allies when war broke out. The French Navy, although handicapped by a decade of neglect and muddle, and possessing relatively few modern ships, was far from negligible, and played a major rôle in the Mediterranean. The Russian Navy was also part of the alliance, and although brought to a new state of efficiency after its disasters in the war against Japan a decade earlier, its forces were largely penned in the Black Sea and Baltic. The Japanese, on the other hand, had a modern fleet built up and trained largely with British technical assistance, and had shown in 1904 that it could beat a first class European battle fleet decisively.

The Imperial German Navy had one relatively powerful ally, the Imperial and Royal (KuK) Austro-Hungarian Navy, intended to fight the Italian Navy in the Adriatic. It also gained an unexpected ally shortly after the outbreak of war, the tiny Turkish Navy, which controlled the strategically vital Dardanelles.

In one important respect the 'Entente' navies differed from those of the Central Powers: the Royal Navy would be the 'motor' of the Allies' war effort, whereas the German Army would fulfil that role for its allies. Britain's allies might be defeated individually on land, but for Germany to win, the Royal Navy would have to be defeated. That simple truth was to dictate the pattern of naval warfare from 1914 to 1918.

In a simple headcount of ships the Royal Navy had an overwhelming margin of strength: twenty-nine modern 'dreadnought' battleships and battlecruisers, as well a forty older ships, the largest fleet of submarines (seventy-three), one hundred and fourteen cruisers and one hundred and fifty modern destroyers. The nation also benefited from the most efficient and powerful naval shipbuilding industry as well as most of the world's greatest armament manufacturers. Germany had twenty dreadnoughts and thirty-two older ships (some fit only for coast defence), forty-seven cruisers and eighty modern destroyers. Although only thirty submarines had been completed these 'U-boats' were seagoing, rather than the preponderance of coastal boats built for the Royal Navy, and they were to prove formidable adversaries. The British Empire relied on world-wide trade, through its huge merchant fleet, and a chain of bases existed to protect this national asset. But it was also vulnerable to attack by enemy cruisers on distant trade routes, a problem which had been a source of worry to the Admiralty for many years.

Faced with such overwhelming strength, the pre-war German Navy planners could do little beyond pinning their hopes on a war of attrition, whittling down British strength by mines, surface forces and submarines to a point at which they could be brought to battle on favourable terms. Unfortunately, the geography of the North Sea also favoured the Royal Navy, for the only exits from the North Sea were around the north of Scotland or through the narrow Dover Straits to the south. For many years the Germans based their war plans on the assumption that the Royal Navy would maintain a classic 'close blockade' of its North Sea bases, where it could all too easily suffer losses to surface and submarine torpedo attacks and mines. But in 1913 this strategy was outflanked when the Admiralty formally abandoned close blockade in favour of a 'distant blockade', stationing the main fleet in the Orkneys and leaving the task of challenging German light forces with the Royal Navy's own light cruisers, destroyers and submarines.

The Royal Navy also had an amazing piece of luck. A full mobilisation of the

THE CRUISE OF THE EMDEN

The German light cruiser SMS *Emden* was commissioned in 1910 and assigned to the East Asia Cruiser Squadron, stationed at Tsingtao; the day before war broke out, Captain Karl von Müller, sailed from Tsingtao, and captured a Russian mail boat on 4 August.

Together with her supply vessel, *Emden* cruised into the Indian Ocean, and captured further shipping between Burma and India – sometimes achieving a rate of two ships a day. *Emden* shelled the Burma Oil Company gas tanks at Madras on 21 September, and then avoided contact with HMS *Hampshire*. Entering Penang a month later, *Emden* torpedoed the Russian cruiser *Yemtschuk*, and sunk the French destroyer *Mousquet* later the same day.

Von Müller's next move was to land a detachment of fifty men at the Cocos-Keeling Islands, to destroy the radio transmitters of the transoceanic cable. Whilst there, the crew learnt that the Kaiser had awarded the ship's crew Iron Crosses – so far, the *Emden* had captured or sunk sixteen enemy ships, and was being searched for by more than seventy five Allied warships. Whilst the landing party was still ashore, the light cruiser HMAS *Sydney* cornered the *Emden* and after a battle of more than an hour in which the Australian cruiser gained the upper hand, von Müller intentionally ran his ship aground on North Keeling Island. The *Emden's* landing party, stranded when *Sydney* approached, stole the schooner *Ayesha* and eventually arrived in Istanbul.

Fleet was planned for July 1914 to test the efficiency of the reserve. When the tension generated by the assassination of Archduke Franz Ferdinand in Sarajevo showed no sign of abating, the First Lord of the Admiralty, Winston Churchill, ordered the reserve crews to remain with their ships, avoiding the chaos of a second mobilisation as well as frustrating any surprise attack by German light squadrons. The former Home Fleet became the Grand Fleet under the command of Vice Admiral Sir John Jellicoe, and left for its new base at Scapa Flow in the Orkneys.

The risk of small detachments of ships being defeated piecemeal by superior enemy formations was all too real, but the first such setback suffered by the Royal Navy took place off the coast of Chile. The German East Asiatic Squadron under Admiral Graf von Spee destroyed a weak Royal Navy squadron off Coronel on 1 November. But Spee had little time to enjoy the fruits of victory, for the Admiralty sent two modern battlecruisers to the Falklands and assembled a powerful force of cruisers to bring him to action. Spee obliged by trying to attack the coaling station at Stanley, and on 8 December his force was virtually wiped out in the Battle of the Falklands. On 9 November the Australian light cruiser HMAS *Sydney* destroyed the light cruiser SMS *Emden* at Cocos-Keeling Island in the Pacific, bringing to an end a remarkably destructive cruise. Only five days earlier the cruiser *Karlsruhe* had been destroyed by an internal explosion east of Trinidad, and the month before, the cruiser *Königsberg* was driven into hiding in the Rufiji River in east Africa. The brief phase of classic cruiser warfare was over, and although many British and allied warships had been tied up in hunting for raiders, the damage to the British merchant marine was negligible.

Both the British public and the Navy had expected a decisive clash of the main fleets in the North Sea, a 'new Trafalgar', but the conditions of early twentieth century naval warfare were so novel that neither side was prepared to take unnecessary risks. For the first time radio played a major role, allowing the headquarters staff to alter orders in the light of fresh intelligence. Cryptography and what is known today as communications intelligence (COMINT) was in its infancy, but the Royal Navy's Grand Fleet practised tight 'radio discipline' at sea, unlike the German High Seas Fleet. As a result the Admiralty's codebreakers began to assume a dominance over their opposite numbers in Germany, although it was to take three years before such high-grade intelligence was used to maximum efficiency.

The U-boat made its presence felt in the North Sea. In a single attack on 22 September 1914, *U-9* torpedoed three large armoured cruisers with apparently ludicrous ease. Casualties among their largely reservist crews were heavy, but the real culprit was the relatively inexperienced Admiralty Staff, which had failed to provide an escort of destroyers for these vulnerable ships. But these losses, and other casualties inflicted were virtually all obsolete ships, whose loss did not affect the balance of power, and the Royal Navy did not accept them passively. On 28 August, just over three weeks after the outbreak of war, the Harwich Force of light cruisers and destroyers entered the Heligoland Bight with the intention of destroying the light forces patrolling the approaches to the main German bases. In a series of confused actions the Harwich Force began to be overwhelmed by superior numbers, but the Admiralty had ordered Rear Admiral Beatty and his battlecruisers to reinforce the lighter cruisers and destroyers. Just as the German forces seemed about to score a significant victory, Beatty's battlecruisers appeared out of the mist, turning the tables dramatically. Three German light cruisers were sunk, while their supporting capital ships were still trying to get to sea. The battle was confused, not least because of very poor Admiralty staffwork, but for the Germans it was seen as a disaster; ships had been sunk close their main bases, apparently with impunity. It was clear that the British would not hesitate to act aggressively and would not be deterred by the risk of losses.

German mines were also effective. The first shot of the war at sea was fired by the destroyer HMS *Lance* at the converted North Sea steamer *Konigin Luise* when she was caught laying mines off Harwich a day after the outbreak of war. The next morning, however, the flotilla's leader, the light cruiser HMS *Amphion*, ran into the minefield and sank. On 27 October the dreadnought battleship HMS *Audacious* was sunk off the coast of Northern Ireland; this was a serious loss which prompted the Admiralty to attempt a ludicrous cover-up which was not admitted until after the Armistice four years later.

Late in 1914 the High Seas Fleet began a series of 'pinprick' raids on the east coast of England – such as the shelling of Scarborough. Physical damage and casualties were light, but the public and press demanded to know why the Royal Navy could not protect its own homeland. In January 1915 a further raid was planned on the fishing fleet working on the Dogger Bank, but this time cryptanalysis gave timely warning. Beatty's battlecruisers were able to intercept the First Scouting Group of German battlecruisers on 24 January, but it proved to less of a triumph than it might have been. The Germans fled, leaving the slower armoured cruiser *Blücher* to fend for herself, and a combination of signalling errors and damage to the flagship HMS *Lion* caused the rest of the pursuing British force to break off the chase and concentrate on the doomed *Blücher*. By the time the mix-up was sorted out the Germans were out of range, and a chance to inflict a major defeat had slipped away.

By the late spring of 1916 all hopes of a short war had faded. The Grand Fleet had not brought the High Sea Fleet to action, and the blockade had so far failed to bring Germany to its knees. The Grand Fleet seemed doomed to make an endless series of sweeps, or to remain at anchor in Scapa Flow. Then on 31 May the two fleets met at Jutland (Skagerrak to the Germans). Once again the British had first class intelligence, whereas the Germans had no idea that the whole Grand Fleet was at sea. The two battlecruiser forces met in the afternoon, and Beatty skilfully fell back on Jellicoe's main battle fleet, but at the cost of losing two of his ships to catastrophic magazine explosions. It was an unpleasant moment to learn that British cordite propellant was unstable, and that the shell rooms and magazines were not properly flashproof. However, Beatty achieved what he had been intended to achieve, and delivered not only Hipper's battlecruisers but also Scheer's High Seas Fleet into the arms of the Grand Fleet, in an unfavourable position for the German forces. Jellicoe's deployment was brilliant, although another battlecruiser was sunk by German gunfire. But once again, poor communications prevented Jutland from being that 'second Trafalgar', which the Royal Navy yearned for so much. The Admiralty failed to pass on vital decrypts, and nearly all Jellicoe's subordinates failed to keep him informed of events. When darkness fell, the sorely battered High Seas Fleet forced its way through the screen of harrying light forces at the rear of the Grand Fleet, heading for the security of home waters.

The inquest was acrimonious. On paper the British had the worst of the encounter, with three battlecruisers and three armoured cruisers sunk, as against only one German battlecruiser and an old battleship, but Scheer was well aware that his fleet had been very lucky to escape a massive defeat, if not annihilation. Although the High Seas Fleet did put to sea again, its sorties were insignificant, and were terminated as soon as the Germans suspected that British heavy ships were at sea.

The fight to dominate the North Sea obscured the struggle between the Germans and the Russians in the Baltic, where the Russians conducted a skilful war of attrition, using their powerful new dreadnoughts and mine fields to prevent the Germans from reinforcing their land forces. But by early 1917 sedition was seriously undermining the Russian Baltic Fleet's efficiency, and the October Revolution completed the process.

The Germans' initial attempts to use U-boats against merchant ships were largely ineffective because of the provisions of International Law. A ship had to be stopped, inspected and the prisoners had to be taken on board the U-boat or put in lifeboats and towed to safety. As U-boats lacked space for confining prisoners they would have to tow the lifeboats to safety, during which time a hostile warship could all too easily arrive on the scene. Nor were U-boats fast enough to catch the bigger merchantmen such as cargo liners, and when the British started to arm their merchant ships the Germans felt justified in abandoning their legal obligations.

In 1915 the German High Command gave approval for an 'unrestricted' U-boat campaign, declaring a 'war zone' around the British Isles in which merchant ships could be sunk 'at sight'. Although it caused heavy losses, this strategy was ultimately a failure. There were insufficient U-boats to sustain the tempo of

⚛ THE BEATTY VS JELLICOE ARGUMENT ⚛

Long after Jutland the debate continued between the partisans of Jellicoe, the Commander in Chief of the Grand Fleet, and his subordinate (and later successor) Beatty, commander of the Battle Cruiser Force. The two admirals were exact opposites in temperament, Jellicoe being quiet and reserved, as opposed to the flamboyant Beatty, with his rich American wife and colourful private life. Their leadership styles were also very different, Jellicoe stressing the highest level of training and planning in all procedures, whereas Beatty was very inclined to favour 'dash' over detail. When accused of neglecting gunnery practice, his officers were happy to say that the battlecruisers "practised their gunnery in action".

Beatty lost no time in trying to exculpate himself as the post-Jutland debate grew ever more heated, even trying to influence the official account. But he cannot avoid criticism for retaining the services of his inept signals officer Ralph Seymour, who was responsible for the muddled signals from the flagship *Lion* at the Dogger Bank. At Jutland his ineptitude had even more serious consequences, but still he enjoyed Beatty's favour.

Although Beatty knew that Jellicoe and the Grand Fleet had saved his battlecruisers from even heavier losses and possible destruction, he intrigued to ensure that the Grand Fleet got no credit for its part in the battle. To his great credit Jellicoe never stooped to such tactics, and maintained a dignified silence for the rest of his life. Beatty's behaviour at the internment of the High Seas Fleet after the Armistice showed a vulgar theatricality by all accounts, with no hint of magnanimity to the defeated. Despite the fact that the German ships were only to be interned pending the outcome of the peace conference at Versailles, Beatty made the event into an abject surrender and humiliated the senior German officers at every turn.

Perhaps the last word on the argument can be left to Andrew Gordon, author of the latest analysis of Jutland – a hybrid with the dash and imagination of Beatty but lacking his slipshod attitude, combined with the attention to detail of Jellicoe without his caution might have produced a very different battle. However, one must also remember Churchill's verdict that "Jellicoe was the only man on either side who could have lost the war in an afternoon."

attacks, and by sinking such contentious targets as the liner *Lusitania*, the U-boats aroused a very unfavourable reaction in neutral countries, particularly the United States. In 1916 the German Navy once again approached the High Command with plans for a second unrestricted campaign. Despairing of a breakthrough on the Western Front, the generals overrode the diplomats' objections, and gave its approval. The omens were propitious – the shipyards had stepped up construction of U-boats, and the designs were now greatly improved. Nor were British countermeasures effective – 'offensive' patrols and disguised decoys (Q-ships) could only hope to stumble on U-boats by accident, while the U-boats merely had to lie in wait until solitary, unescorted targets arrived. Jellicoe, now moved to the Admiralty as First Sea Lord, had been worn down by his stint as Commander in Chief of the Grand Fleet, and could only think in terms of more of the same countermeasures, and when these failed he lobbied for a land campaign to capture the U-boat bases on the Flanders coast. This led to the appallingly heavy casualties of the Passchendaele offensive late in 1917.

By the spring of 1917 defeat for the Allies was a very real prospect, for if the armies in France could not be supplied and the home population faced starvation, Britain would have had to sue for peace. Fortunately there was a solution which had been used in the eighteenth and early nineteenth centuries – the use of the convoy. The sailing of merchant ships in compact groups under the protection of warships had been rejected as too 'defensive' for the Royal Navy of the twentieth century, and Jellicoe's advisors told him it could not be done. But junior officers in the Trade Division believed otherwise, and enlisted the support of the Cabinet Secretary. He in turn persuaded the Prime Minister Lloyd George, who claimed it as his own idea, but what mattered was that he told the Admiralty to adopt convoy or make way for officers who would do what they were told. The statistics of sailings used by Jellicoe's staff were shown to be false, and sufficient escorts were found among the many vessels of the useless Auxiliary Patrol and the numerous destroyer flotillas attached to the Grand Fleet.

The results were remarkable. Shipping losses began to fall rapidly and sinkings of U-boats went up. The reasons were simple – U-boats now had to attack defended groups of ships, risking counter-attack, and instead of submerging only when a tell-tale plume of smoke indicated a target, they now spent much of their time submerged. Convoy also eliminated the use of U-boat deck guns to sink small vessels such as schooners. At the same time the Admiralty was beginning to harness science, with methods of detecting submerged submarines and more destructive weapons, notably the depth-charge. Other measures helped in less obvious ways. Until well into 1916 there were virtually no replacements for the merchant ships lost, and no salvage organisation to get damaged ships into port where they could be repaired. New programmes of standardised merchant ship designs were put in hand, not only in British yards but as far afield as Canada and

⟿ NAVAL AVIATION ⟾

Aviation made great strides in 1914-18, but the greatest exponent was the Royal Naval Air Service. The first aircraft carrier strike in history was launched on Christmas Day 1914, when converted seaplane carriers were used to get seaplanes within range of the Zeppelin sheds at Cuxhaven. On 31 May 1916 a seaplane spotted the High Sea Fleet but could not get a message to the flagship because her radio was faulty. Determined efforts were made to get higher-performance wheeled aircraft to sea, using takeoff platforms on deck or on the roofs of gun turrets, and even from platforms towed by destroyers. In 1917 the first efforts were put in hand to get true aircraft carriers to sea. The Grand Fleet's interest was primarily to deal with the ubiquitous German Zeppelin rigid airships, which always warned German surface forces of the proximity of British forces, but reconnaissance and spotting for long-range gunfire were also priorities. Large numbers of relatively cheap non-rigid airships ('blimps') were built, and they proved very useful as convoy escorts.

In 1918 the large light battlecruiser HMS *Furious* emerged from a lengthy reconstruction with a large landing deck, and shortly before the Armistice the flush-decked converted liner HMS *Argus* was at sea. Earlier in the year the keel of the first purpose-built carrier had been laid, and she was to emerge in the post-war years as HMS *Hermes*. Had the war lasted until 1919, a massive strike against the High Seas Fleet in harbour was planned, using Sopwith Cuckoo torpedo-bombers – a foretaste of Taranto and Pearl Harbor.

The Americans, French, Germans, Italians, Japanese and Russians also experimented with shipborne aircraft, the Germans following a British lead in taking light seaplanes to sea in submarines to provide reconnaissance.

Japan. The Admiralty set up a salvage organisation and built large numbers of oceangoing tugs for the job. The entry of the United States into the war in April 1917 also released one million tons of interned German shipping for the use of the Allies, and American yards started their own programme of standard ships, the 'Hog Islanders'. By the summer of 1918 the U-boat menace was not eliminated, but it had been contained, and the replacement building programmes outstripped the losses. The German Navy's gamble had failed, and enormous numbers of American troops were pouring into France.

Although pre-war planning had envisaged the French Fleet as containing the Austro-Hungarian forces and leaving the British to protect the coast of Northern France and Brittany, the presence of the German battlecruiser *Goeben* and the light cruiser *Breslau* in the Mediterranean in 1914 upset these calculations. As the French had no ships fast enough to catch the *Goeben* the Royal Navy had to maintain two battlecruisers and a squadron of armoured cruisers on station to guard against an attack on French troopships passing between Algeria and Marseilles or Toulon.

It was these forces which managed to lose the *Goeben* and *Breslau* at a critical moment, when the British ultimatum to Germany had not expired. By a combination of bad luck and timidity the German ships were allowed to escape and seek refuge in Turkish waters. There they were welcomed and nominally recommissioned into the Ottoman Navy, helping the pro-German elements in the government to gain the upper hand. When the British government seized two dreadnought battleships building for Turkey on the Tyne, this provided the pretext for Turkey to join the Central Powers and declare war on the Allies. Thus was set in train the disastrous course which led to the Dardanelles Campaign, although modern research in Turkish archives suggests that the Turkish 'war party' had every intention of joining Germany in any event, and would even have sold the two battleships to her after delivery.

The Dardanelles campaign is one of the great 'what ifs?' of history. It is conceivable that the purely naval attack on the Narrows in March 1915 could have succeeded if losses had been ignored. The appearance of an Anglo-French squadron in the Bosporus might have toppled the war party in Istanbul, but it seems certain that a better co-ordinated amphibious landing on the Gallipoli Peninsula might have proved successful. As things turned out, the troop landings were delayed until the Turks had time to strengthen the defences, and the landings were in any case badly co-ordinated. A secondary landing petered out when the land forces failed to press ahead, and thereafter the Navy could do little more than enable the hard-pressed Anzac and British troops to cling to their precarious footholds on the peninsula. By far the most successful parts of the campaign were the two final evacuations, the skill of which astonished the German and Turkish forces. Had as much time been devoted to preparation for the landings of the year before as was devoted to these evacuations, the campaign might have succeeded.

British, French and Australian submarines penetrated the minefields in the Narrows and succeeded in reaching the Sea of Marmora, but losses were heavy for somewhat meagre results. The Dardanelles campaign saw the first aerial torpedo attacks ever to take place, and aircraft also provided the first primitive spotting for long-range naval gunfire.

Although sympathetic to the Central Powers before 1914, the Italians decided that they had more to gain by joining the Allies, and after a period of indecision declared war on 24 May 1915. In theory the large Italian forces should have proved of great value to their allies, but in practice the fleet was not handled with any great élan, and the British were frequently called on to reinforce a navy which heavily outnumbered the Austro-Hungarians.

Specialised ships were developed to support the Italian Army in the north, and great attention was paid to the development of motor torpedo boats (MAS) and other even more exotic special assault craft. In June 1918 the dreadnought *Szent Istvan* was sunk of Premuda Island by *MAS-15*, the only case of a large warships being sunk in daylight by such a small combatant. On 1 November 1918 the Austro-Hungarian dreadnought *Viribus Unitis* was sunk at Pola by a *Mignatta* self-propelled mine piloted by two Italian officers, but the achievement was slightly sullied by the fact that the KuK Navy had ceased to exist, and a day earlier the ship had been commissioned as the flagship of the new (neutral) Yugoslav Navy.

Much was expected of the large Italian submarine fleet in the Adriatic, but its operations were a byword for reluctance to go to sea. Even the Royal Navy submarines sent to Brindisi after the Dardanelles campaign had been brought to its conclusion did not achieve as much as they had hoped. Instead the laurels of the Adriatic campaign go the French and the Austro-Hungarians for aggressive patrolling, despite both having obsolescent and unreliable boats. Casualties in the clear waters of the Adriatic were heavy, but the enemy losses were proportionate.

"The ascent was gradual and as we slowly gained height the wind rose too, so that it became very cold in spite of the sun being out. But in defiance of wind and sun a thick cloud clung persistently to the ice-cap, a fact which we noted with misgiving since in such conditions the crossing of it would be both perplexing and unrewarding."

H. W. Tilman: *Mischief Among the Penguins* (1961)

CHAPTER FOUR

ICY WATERS

Ann Savours

AT THE BEGINNING OF THE TWENTIETH CENTURY, there were still unknown areas of the world, one of which was a whole continent, the Antarctic, far to the south of Australia, New Zealand, South Africa and South America. Another blank space on the globe was part of the Arctic Ocean, the icy sea surrounding the North Pole, which is bordered by the north coasts of America, Greenland, Europe and Asia. Who was to say that a large stretch of land did not lie there? No one had yet reached either the North or the South Pole, nor had a ship ever navigated the whole of the long-sought North West Passage, the sea way connecting the Atlantic Ocean with the Pacific Ocean. The early twentieth century was to see all these goals attained, while by mid-century, submarines had surfaced at the North Pole and in the 1970s, a nuclear icebreaker, the *Arktika*, had battled her way through the ice floes to the North Pole. Dog teams and sledges gave way to mechanical vehicles, while the use of aircraft and radio lessened both time and distance in the polar regions. Scientific studies of the sea, ice and the publication of atlases showing its distribution increased our knowledge of this hindrance to navigation, while modern technology and ship design have made polar voyages less hazardous, even encouraging wealthy tourists to venture to hitherto remote and unfrequented islands, lands and seas, and even to the North Pole itself. Let us turn to the Antarctic first.

The Antarctic continent is the highest, driest, coldest and most remote of all the continents. At only a few places do its underlying rocks pierce the thickness of the great ice sheet that covers it. Generally circular in shape and following the line of the Antarctic Circle, it has a mountainous tail (the Antarctic Peninsula) whose tip is nearest to another continent: South America. This lies to the north across Drake Passage, named after Sir Francis Drake, who was blown south of Cape Horn during his 'great voyage' – the second circumnavigation of the globe in the time of Queen Elizabeth I. This passage is the narrowest part of the great Southern Ocean, which surrounds the Antarctic land mass and whose great waters rush ever onwards in the forties and fifties of south latitude. Near to the continent, the surface of the sea freezes during the continuous darkness of the Antarctic winter. The fragmented pack ice is the home of seals, whales and penguins, through the long light days and nights of summer. A ship's track has to be broken through it and travelling icebergs avoided – a hazardous passage, where fog and snow storms can cloak visibility and gales can whip the floes into a fury of crashing blocks.

It is not surprising that little was known of this distant supposed southern continent, even in 1900. The great Yorkshire navigator, Captain James Cook in the eighteenth century, followed by the Russian Captain Bellingshausen in the nineteenth century had circumnavigated Antarctica, roughly defining its limits, but without claiming to have sighted it. British and American sealers, and the national expeditions of France, the United States and Great Britain made certain discoveries in the first half of the nineteenth century, touching the mainland for the first time. The greatest advance was made in the 1840s by Sir James Clark Ross, the most experienced of all the nineteenth century 'Arctic officers' of the Royal Navy. He was the first to penetrate the belt of pack ice and enter the Ross Sea, discovering the 'Great Icy Barrier' or Ross Ice Shelf and mountainous 'South Victoria Land', claiming it for the young Queen Victoria – one of the first acquisitions of her long reign and said to be 'the whitest, if not the brightest jewel in her crown'. By the end of the nineteenth century the blank space at the bottom of the globe had become a reproach to geographers and they resolved at an international congress in London that something should be done.

The result was that a number of national expeditions departed for the Antarctic from Belgium, Germany, Great Britain, Sweden and France. The stage was set for the 'Heroic Age' of Antarctic exploration – when, during the early years of the twentieth century, puny man, with muscle power alone, pitted himself against the might and fury of the unknown southern continent, making the first inland journeys. The ships that transported these expeditions were wooden sailing vessels, with auxiliary steam engines. They were strengthened for use in ice and usually adapted from a previous occupation. However, both the *Gauss* (Germany) and the *Discovery* (United Kingdom) were specially designed and constructed for their Antarctic voyages of 1901-3 and 1901-4 respectively. Their scientific programmes were co-ordinated, but their geographical results turned out to be very different. The *Gauss*, built on similar rounded lines to Nansen's *Fram*, spent fourteen months in the pack, at some distance from the mainland, but journeys were successfully made across the sea ice to the land, where an extinct volcano, the Gaussberg, was discovered. An amusing and ingenious solution to the problem of passing a line under the keel of the vessel when icebound, was to get a penguin to swim from a hole on one side to one on the other, with the rope attached to its foot. The leader of this first German South Polar Expedition was Dr Erich von Drygalski. The *Gauss* became a scientific station on the continental shelf of Antarctica – a particularly interesting location. After nearly a year beset in the sea ice, the vessel was carried towards open water, locked in a huge ice floe, over a mile wide and around twenty miles long, which eventually broke up, leaving her free for the voyage home. The expedition results were published in twenty-two heavy volumes.

The men of the *Discovery* had an even more tantalising time. Locked in the ice at the head of the Ross Sea, much further south than the other expeditions taking part in this international assault on Antarctica, they were still beset a year after their arrival and the little relief ship, *Morning* (Captain William Colbeck), sailed home leaving the *Discovery* to another winter and a further useful summer season of inland sledge journeys and scientific work. This National Antarctic Expedition of 1901-04 was organised jointly by the Royal Geographical Society (owners of the *Discovery*) and the Royal Society of London. Its leader was Commander Robert Falcon Scott, RN who was to lose his life on what became known as Scott's Last Expedition of 1910-13. He proved to have a wonderful gift for words and his book, *The Voyage of the Discovery* is still very much worth reading today. Through it we meet the members of the expedition and learn how they coped by trial and error with wintering in the far south and with making the first extensive sledge journeys into the icebound interior of the Antarctic. The water-colours and drawings by the junior surgeon, Dr Edward Wilson, the photographs by Engineering Lieutenant Reginald Skelton and the monthly magazine produced on board the *Discovery* also provide a fine record. Perhaps the most remarkable scientific results were, firstly, the evidence in the shape of fossils that the continent, had once been green, and secondly, the discovery of a rookery of that extraordinary bird, the Emperor Penguin, which lays its eggs in the depths of the Antarctic winter.

By early February 1904, there were still several miles of ice between the *Discovery* and open water. Many of the scientific instruments, the library and the scientific collections were sledged over the ice to the relief ships, *Morning* (Captain Colbeck) and *Terra Nova* (Captain H MacKay). Explosives were used in an attempt to break up the ice, to little apparent effect. A restless and despondent Captain Scott had made arrangements for abandoning the *Discovery*. However, on 14 February, whilst dinner was in progress, there was a shout on deck, and, in Scott's words, 'a voice sang out down the hatchway, "The ships are coming sir!".' Dinner was abandoned, as they all rushed to witness the 'glorious sight' of the ice streaming northwards. The wind was calm and there was not a sound.

> Yet in the midst of this peaceful silence was an awful unseen agency rending that great ice-sheet as though it had been naught but the thinnest paper. We knew well by this time the nature of our prison bars; we had not plodded again and again over those long dreary miles of snow without realising the formidable strength of the great barrier which held us bound; we knew that the heaviest battleship would have shattered itself ineffectually against it, and we had seen a million ton iceberg brought to rest at its edge . . . But now without a word, without an effort on our part, it was all melting away, and we knew that in an hour or two the open sea would be lapping on the black rocks of Hut Point.[1]

The two relief ships crashed into the floes and splintered them. 'Meanwhile our small community in their nondescript tattered garments stood breathlessly watching this wonderful scene', silent and spellbound. Then 'a burst of frenzied cheering broke out'. The more powerful *Terra Nova* had won the contest first to break through to the *Discovery*, but the stout little *Morning* followed very soon afterwards.

Everyone dashed about madly from ship to ship, shaking everyone else by the hand. The *Discovery*'s little bay became 'a scene of wild revelry', with some reaching 'that state which places them in doubt as to which ship they really belong to', something, thought Scott, that could be excused on such a night. The *Discovery* was free to sail the high seas again. She returned to England after completing a circumnavigation of the Antarctic, carrying a harvest of scientific results and the first surveys of the interior of the icy continent.

A Swedish expedition led by Dr Otto Nordenskjöld in a vessel called *Antarctic*, and the Scottish National Antarctic Expedition in the *Scotia* also took part in the Antarctic campaign, between 1902 and 1904, operating in the far South Atlantic on either side of the Weddell Sea. The Swedish expedition encountered an

1 Scott, R F, *The Voyage of the Discovery*, 1905, pages 347-48.

extraordinary mixture of good and bad luck – bad in that the *Antarctic* sank after being crushed in the ice, but good in that three groups of men, the crew, two scientists and the main scientific party were reunited and rescued from Snow Hill Island by the Argentine frigate *Uruguay*. The scientists lived, collected and observed on two small islands off the east coast, at the tip of the Antarctic Peninsula. Here they found two fossil floras – one of them related to the Upper Gondwana series in India – showing that at one time the vegetation in both continents had been the same.

The Scottish National Antarctic Expedition was more fortunate. The *Scotia* made the first oceanographical exploration of the Weddell Sea, under the direction of the Scottish scientist, Dr William Speirs Bruce, discovering Coats Land, named after his benefactors. This expedition wintered on Laurie Island, one of the South Orkneys. The meteorological station which they set up was transferred on departure to the Argentine weather service, which has operated it ever since. We are told that Bruce was 'a man of high ideals and strong passions', dedicating most of his life to the scholarly pursuit of polar science, 'and yet he nurtured a Scottish patriotism which grew in his later years to a positive xenophobia for all things English'.[2] When writing about the Scottish National Antarctic Expedition, he observed that 'while *Science* was the talisman of the Expedition, *Scotland* was emblazoned on its flag'.[3] Bruce was a retiring man, who shunned the limelight, so that while the *Scotia* expedition was very successful scientifically, it met with little public acclaim, partly perhaps because its proceedings lacked the perils, dangers and difficulties experienced by other expeditions.

Looking back on the men and the ships which joined to make this assault on the Antarctic at the dawn of the twentieth century, one is struck by their common characteristics: the importance of leadership; the importance of science, survey and the art of navigation; the hazards of sailing in wooden vessels with engines of low horse power among ice floes and icebergs, in uncharted waters, amid fog, gales and snowstorms. Much still remained to be learnt and vast regions to be explored.

Before proceeding any further with Antarctica's 'Heroic Age', let us turn to the far North – the lands and seas beyond the Arctic Circle. Because there are towns, villages and settlements, especially in northern Russia and Siberia, as well as great

2 Speak, P, in Bruce, W S, *The Log of the Scotia Expedition 1902-4, 1992*, page 3.
3 ibid.

rivers flowing northwards, the Arctic regions began to be known far earlier than the far distant Antarctic. During the reign of Queen Elizabeth I of England, the English and the Dutch had already searched for a northern passage – either northeast beyond northern Scandinavia and Russia, or northwest through what we now know as the Canadian Arctic archipelago, that maze of islands beyond the mainland of North America.

Although the coastline of northern Russia and Siberia had been charted in the eighteenth century, it was not until 1878-79 that a Swedish expedition organised by A E Nordenskiöld in the *Vega* (commanded by Captain L Palander) actually navigated the North East Passage. This achievement left two other geographical prizes still to be won in the twentieth century: firstly, the traverse of the North West Passage and secondly, the attainment of the North Pole. The approach to the latter through Nares Channel between Greenland and Ellesmere Island had been navigated by British and American expeditions in the late nineteenth century. F A Cook and Robert Peary both claimed to have reached the North Pole early in the twentieth century. Even today there are still arguments as to whether Peary did so in 1909, despite official recognition by Congress and prominent organisations in the United States and elsewhere.

The first navigation of the North West Passage was achieved by the Norwegian, Roald Amundsen during the years 1903 to 1905. In the *Gjøa* of 47 tons, he entered Lancaster Sound from the Atlantic side of the Passage, wintered on King William Island (where Franklin's men had met their fate in 1847-48), eventually passing through Bering Strait into the Pacific, after another winter spent on the north coast of Canada. The *Gjøa* spent some years in a park in San Francisco, but is now on show at the Norwegian Maritime Museum, Oslo.

The Norwegian Maritime Museum also houses the *Fram*, a far larger wooden vessel, famous for Dr Fridtjof Nansen's attempted drift in the sea ice to the North Pole towards the end of the nineteenth century. Amundsen sailed south in this same *Fram* on his expedition of 1910-12 to reach the South Pole. He attained this point in December 1911 with a small party. They travelled by dog sledge from the Bay of Whales at the eastern side of the Ross Ice Shelf and up an unknown glacier – the Axel Heiberg – onto the plateau of the Antarctic ice sheet. At the South Pole, the Norwegian flag and a tent containing written records and a letter for the King of Norway were found by the British party, led by Captain R F Scott, RN a month later in January 1912, who had set out from the western edge of the ice shelf. All perished on the return journey. Amundsen attributed his success to

⟿ SHACKLETON'S ANTARCTIC EXPEDITIONS ⟼

During 1907-09, Ernest Shackleton, who had served in the *Discovery*, sailed in the *Nimrod* aiming to reach the South Pole. He made a magnificent sledge journey, but had to turn back when only ninety-seven miles away, not having enough food and fuel to go further. This expedition reached the summit of Mount Erebus, the active volcano on Ross Island, as well as the South Magnetic Pole. Shackleton returned to the Antarctic in 1914, this time to the Weddell Sea, in the *Endurance*, a wooden barquentine, built in Norway as the *Polaris*. His aim was to cross the Antarctic from Weddell Sea to Ross Sea, where another party of men was laying depots to the south. The *Endurance* was beset in the ice of the Weddell Sea and was eventually crushed and sunk, leaving the members of the Imperial Trans-Antarctic Expedition on the ice floes, drifting fortunately northwards. They escaped in three boats to desolate Elephant Island, where they managed to survive under Frank Wild's leadership. Shackleton himself departed in the *James Caird* (one of the three boats named after his sponsors) for South Georgia, where Norwegian whalers were operating. After a heroic voyage of eight hundred miles across the Southern Ocean, Shackleton and his companions eventually arrived at the whaling station, to the astonishment of the manager. The larger party, marooned on Elephant Island, was rescued, after several other attempts, by the Chilean vessel *Yelcho* in August 1916. Shackleton, known as 'The Boss', proved his greatness as a leader during this expedition and the photographs and film taken by Frank Hurley still enthral people today. The *James Caird* was brought back to England and is now displayed at Shackleton's old school, Dulwich College, south London. 'The Boss' was to sail again for the Antarctic in the sealer *Quest* in 1921-22. He died suddenly on board and was buried on South Georgia.

his use of dogs in relation to the building of food depots. 'In making my calculations,' he wrote, 'for the distances between these stations and the amount of provisions which should be left in each, I was able to reduce the weight of provisions to be carried by calculating the flesh of the dogs which carried it as a part of the food supply of us men.' He added that as 'there are about fifty pounds of edible food in the carcass of an Eskimo dog, it was quite probable that every dog we took south with us meant fifty pounds less food to be carried and cached'. He even calculated the precise day on which each dog should be killed. This schedule, above all, 'was the essential factor in our successful trip to the Pole and our safe return to the base camp'.[4] Although Amundsen made such a fine journey, the scientific work of his 1910-12 expedition was meagre. The *Fram* made an oceanographic survey in warmer waters. In comparison, the numerous volumes resulting from Scott's Last Expedition, 1910-13, provide a splendid record. Like the *Fram*, Scott's ship, the Dundee whaler *Terra Nova* did not act as a base for the Antarctic journeys. Oates Land was discovered from the *Terra Nova* in 1911. Herbert Ponting, the 'camera artist' filmed and took splendid photographs still treasured today. Scott's *Message to the Public*, written in the tent while dying on the 'Great Ice Barrier' in March 1912 has never been forgotten.

We need to note the four other expeditions to the Antarctic of the 'Heroic Age'. Ernest Shackleton's expeditions are dealt with in his biographical feature within this chapter; he made three journeys, in 1907-09, 1914-16 and finally in 1921-22.

The *Endurance*, which carried Shackleton's Imperial Trans-Antarctic Expedition in 1914, had in fact been preceded into the Weddell Sea by the *Deutschland*, transporting the second German South Polar Expedition, led by Wilhelm Filchner, of 1910-12. Its aim was to extend W S Bruce's discovery of Coats Land to the head of the Weddell Sea, where winter quarters would be established and sledge journeys sent further south. This expedition was not so unfortunate as Shackleton's had been. It duly discovered the ice shelf at the head of the Weddell Sea, which was named after its leader. A large hut had been almost completely constructed on the ice shelf, when that part of it broke away to form a tabular berg, with the builders of the hut still sound asleep inside. Fortunately they, the ponies, much of the timber, and all the dogs but one were brought off safely to the ship. The despairing howls of the abandoned dog were answered with a mournful chorus from the deck. Like the *Endurance*, the *Deutschland* was beset in the sea ice, but emerged at the end of her nine months' drift, able to reach South Georgia and then Germany. The scientific observations from these unknown and icebound waters were of great importance, yet the leaders' narratives of both German South Polar expeditions have only recently been translated into English. That of the Japanese South Polar expedition of 1911-12 in the *Kainan Maru* is in preparation. Its members sledged for some miles across the Ross Ice Shelf and landed on King Edward VII Land.

Of the ships and men ploughing the icy seas of the Southern Ocean during the so-called 'Heroic Age' of Antarctic exploration, it remains to feature Sir Douglas

4 Amundsen, R, *My Life as an Explorer*, 1927, pages 69-70.

Mawson, the son of Yorkshire emigrants to Australia, and the barquentine *Aurora* (Captain John King Davis). Mawson had taken part in Shackleton's *Nimrod* expedition of 1907-09, while Davis in the *Aurora* later rescued the surviving members of Shackleton's Ross Sea party in January 1917. The foremost achievement of Mawson, Davis and the *Aurora* was Mawson's Australasian Antarctic Expedition of 1911-14. Its members were divided into three groups: one to operate on Macquarie Island, half way to the Antarctic from Australia, one to winter as the main party at Cape Denison in Commonwealth Bay on the Antarctic mainland and the third, led by Frank Wild, to winter on the Shackleton Ice Shelf, to the west of the main party. King George V Land and Queen Mary Land were discovered and explored, while a sledge party reached the region of the South Magnetic Pole. Mawson's main base at Cape Denison proved to be one of the windiest places in the world – he called his book *The Home of the Blizzard*.

With two companions, Mawson set off on a long sledge journey to the east of Commonwealth Bay. When Davis arrived in the *Aurora* to relieve the main base, Mawson had not returned. He did so a few hours after the ship had sailed to relieve Wild and the Western Party. Six men had been left at Cape Denison to wait for Mawson's return and to face a further winter there, when Davis received a wireless message from Mawson after departure, which read, 'Arrived safely at hut. Mertz and Ninnis dead. Return and pick up all hands'. Davis endeavoured to do so but a coastal blizzard sprang up in which a boat could not be launched. He wrote in his memoirs, *High Latitude*:

> As the hours went by I saw the outlines of the terrible choice that must confront me if the blizzard showed no signs of abating – whether to wait and perhaps jeopardise the eight men on the floating Barrier on the coast of Queen Mary Land, or whether to abandon my leader and his companions to the awful wind-ridden solitude for another year of exile.[5]

He rightly decided that he must relieve Wild's party whose ice shelf had fortunately not 'calved' and floated out to sea. The *Aurora*'s westward passage on this mission, was a constant battle against headwinds, fog, gales, pack ice, blizzards and icebergs, which lay 'silent and menacing athwart our track'. In order to reach the Western Party before the sea froze for the winter, heavy risks had to be taken. At a time like that, wrote Davis:

> one learns to regard one's ship with a degree of affection and trust that deepens with every

5 *High Latitude*, page 215-16.

new danger met and surmounted. As, repeatedly, I asked of the old *Aurora* more, perhaps, than I had the right to ask, and as without fail she performed whatever was asked of her, I began to rely on her in much the same instinctive way . . . that an athlete or a mountaineer relies on his arm or his leg. She was a magnificent ship.[6]

Sir Douglas Mawson was to return to the Antarctic as leader of the British, Australian and New Zealand Antarctic Research Expedition (BANZARE) of 1929-31, this time in Captain Scott's old *Discovery*, with Davis as Master for the first voyage of 1929-30 and K N MacKenzie for the second. A Gypsy Moth sea plane was the eyes of the ship. A vast arc of the Antarctic coast was charted, new discoveries were made and claimed for King George V, while oceanographic and other scientific work was done. Relations between Mawson, as leader, and Davis, as Master of the *Discovery*, became very strained, as can happen during exploring voyages, when the leader usually wants to go further and the captain has to think, not only of the safety of the ship and those on board in uncharted waters, but also of his own career. Both Mawson's and Davis's diaries have recently been published, so that one can see both sides of the story. Once home in Adelaide, Mawson had great difficulty in finding the funds to publish the scientific results of both his expeditions, which were considerable.

An Arctic voyage made at roughly the same time and in the same style as the Antarctic expeditions of the 'Heroic Era' was that of the *Karluk*, during Vilhjalmur Stefansson's Canadian Arctic Expedition of 1913-18. The Canadian government financed the expedition. Stefansson, described by Roland Huntford as a flamboyant and persuasive man, was an anthropologist by profession. He had made two expeditions to the Arctic in 1906-07 and 1908-13, during which he learnt the Inuit way of life, and afterwards published *My Life with the Eskimos* (1913). His discovery of the so-called 'Blond Eskimos' created something of a sensation. Stefansson's great theory, which he put into practice to an extent, was that parties could live off the land (or the ice floes) in remote regions, where even the Eskimos did not venture. It is interesting that that foremost of polar travellers, Roald Amundsen, decried this theory of the 'friendly Arctic' in the pages of his autobiography.

The *Karluk*, a small square-rigged fishing vessel adapted for whaling, had been laid up for several years before being bought by Stefansson. In the words of her Master, Captain Robert (Bob) Bartlett, 'she had neither the strength to sustain

---

6 *High Latitude*, pages 220-221.

pressure, nor the engine power to force herself through loose ice'. Bartlett had been skipper of the *Roosevelt* transporting Peary's north polar expeditions to their starting place, north Greenland. He came from a seafaring family in Newfoundland and in 1916 published a book about the voyage of the *Karluk*, and his autobiography in 1928.

The title of Stefansson's narrative of the Canadian Arctic Expedition's five years in the North, *The Friendly Arctic* (1921) has an ironic ring to it when considered in conjunction with the tragic and haunting story of the *Karluk*. She was the principal vessel, together with the *Mary Sachs* and the *Alaska* of this expedition (1913-18). The expedition's aims were a geographical and oceanographic survey of the Beaufort Sea and adjoining islands by the Northern Division, led by Stefansson and later Storker Storkersen and scientific, ethnological and survey work by the Southern Division, led by Dr R M Anderson. The *Karluk* was able to round Point Barrow, Alaska on 7 August 1913 and to sail eastward, bound for Herschel Island. However, she was beset, and began drifting westward. Stefansson and a small party travelled over the ice to the Alaskan shore, in order to hunt caribou, leaving Captain Bartlett with a letter of instructions, saying Stefansson would return in ten days, provided no accident happened. Bartlett's wry comment on this was as follows:

> You can make all the plans you want in the Far North and write them out on hundreds and hundreds of pages, using all the words in the dictionary. But the finer the plan you have the worse it will go smash when wind and ice and drifting snow take charge. That's exactly what happened to Stefansson's plan.[7]

Stefansson never rejoined the *Karluk* and she met the same fate as Shackleton's *Endurance* – crushed on 10 January 1914 by the massive ice of the Chukchi Sea, north of Bering Strait, between Alaska and Siberia. However, whereas Shackleton lost not a man, eleven from the *Karluk* died out of a party consisting of twenty scientists and mariners, plus five Eskimos. Camped at first on the sea ice, and then from 12 March on desolate Wrangel Island, the heterogeneous and largely inexperienced group spent a terrible six months marooned there. Three men died. Captain Bartlett, like Shackleton, left to summon help by sledging with an Eskimo companion to the Siberian mainland and thence to Alaska, where relief expeditions were organised. The little trading schooner *King and Winge* rescued

7 *Autobiography*, page 260.

the dazed survivors from Wrangel Island on 7 September. They returned south with Captain Bartlett in the US revenue cutter *Bear*. The members of two missing sledge parties were never seen again. Among them perished Mackay and Murray, who had been members of Shackleton's *Nimrod* expedition, 1907-09 in the Antarctic. The Eskimo husband and wife, skilled in Arctic survival, proved of great help to the party left on Wrangel Island, the Inuk by hunting and the wife, known as 'Auntie', by making clothes from skins, and as cook. Unlike 'Mrs Chippy', McNeish's cat in the *Endurance*, Nigeraurak, the *Karluk*'s cat, survived unscathed – the only member of the expedition to do so, according to W L McKinlay. Not until 1976 was the full story of the *Karluk* published by McKinlay, a young Scottish school teacher who joined the expedition as magnetician and meteorologist in 1913.

The First World War, 1914-18 provides a dividing line between the early years of the century and the 1920s, when effective radio communication and reliable aircraft became additional aids to the explorer. No longer was he so isolated as before. During the war, an Arctic Squadron of the Royal Navy operated between Murmansk and Archangel to safeguard the Allied and neutral cargo vessels carrying supplies and munitions to feed the Russian Bear, and to keep the Russians on the Eastern Front fighting the Germans, the Baltic being closed to the Allies. In 1915 *Discovery* was one of those vessels. During the Second World War, similar but much larger convoys braved the German U-boats, warships and aircraft to reach Murmansk. The story of PQ 17 and other convoys, of German meteorological stations on Spitsbergen and Greenland cannot be told in this chapter.

Between the two wars, the exploration of the Southern Ocean and of the Antarctic continent was resumed. Whaling moved from the Arctic to the Antarctic because the whales had been over-fished in the North. Even as early as 1913, the British Colonial Office sent a biologist to work on South Georgia, which by the 1920s became the centre of the greatest whaling industry the world had ever known, the whalers being mainly Norwegians from the Oslofjord. In an effort to conserve the great whales and to enable the industry to continue, the Colonial Office issued licences to the whalers and also set up a committee which (after the purchase of Captain Scott's old ship) became known as the Discovery Committee. A shore party, housed in the marine station near the installations at Grytviken, South Georgia, worked on the carcasses pulled on to the platform or 'plan' for rendering down into oil and meal. The *Discovery* Expedition of 1925-

27 investigated the oceanography of the South Atlantic between South Georgia and the Antarctic Peninsula, concentrating on the waters surrounding South Georgia in order to study the krill – shrimp-like creatures, which occur in swarms – and which are the food of the baleen whales. *Discovery* was joined by the *William Scoresby* during the second season. As a result of their voyages, the data collected and analysed yielded a very detailed picture of the whole living community of the whaling grounds and its physical and chemical background, thus linking the tiny plants and animals of the plankton, through its predator the krill, with the great whales themselves.

The *Discovery* rolled a great deal, making laboratory work difficult, while her heavy spars and rigging caught the wind and made it hazardous to keep on station, when thermometers and nets were being used. The *Discovery* was the first Royal Research Ship of the Royal Navy, but she was superseded in 1929 by *Discovery II*, specially designed for oceanographic investigations, working the Southern Ocean together with the *William Scoresby* in order to study the whole watery environment of the great whales, to chart some sub-Antarctic (peri-Antarctic) islands that ring the continent and to plot the Antarctic Convergence, where cold and warm waters meet. Two circumnavigations of the continent were made, one in the winter time. The RRS *William Scoresby* carried out whale-marking, in the same way that ornithologists ring birds. The results of the twelve inter-war commissions can be found in the celebrated volumes of *Discovery Reports*.

Expeditions from Oxford and Cambridge universities were a feature of the inter-war years in the Arctic, some of the more notable being led by H G ('Gino') Watkins. Members of his parties learnt to roll their kayaks on the River Cam in Cambridge; this was a very difficult skill, previously known only to the Eskimos. A forerunner of submarine voyages later in the twentieth century was Sir Hurbert Wilkins' attempt in 1931 to reach the North Pole under the ice in the *Nautilus*. In contrast to these individual expeditions, the supply ships of the venerable Hudson's Bay Company, which was given a royal charter in 1670, made their annual voyages to Hudson Bay. During the years 1905-11 and again in 1918, one of those vessels was Captain Scott's *Discovery*. Ice in Hudson Strait and in Hudson Bay had to be navigated before reaching the Company posts, where supplies were unloaded and the 'returns' – furs, goose feathers, oil, together with passengers for home, were taken on board. That these voyages were by no means only a matter of routine after two hundred and fifty years was shown by the sinking of the

Nascopie in 1947. During the Second World War, the schooner *St Roch*, commanded by Sergeant Henry Larsen of the Royal Canadian Mounted Police, sheathed with iron bark, made the first traverse of the North West Passage from west to east in 1940-42 and returned in a single season, 1944. Designed for use in ice, she had spent the previous decade patrolling the Arctic for the Royal Canadian Mounted Police. She is now preserved at the Vancouver Maritime Museum, being the first vessel to navigate the Passage both ways and to complete it in one season.

The sixteen members of the British Graham Land Expedition to the Antarctic of 1934-37 maintained that theirs gave the greatest value for money of any. Fitted out on a shoestring and led by the South Australian, John Rymill, half its members were Cambridge men. The skipper of their topsail schooner, *Penola*, was R E D ('Bob') Ryder, who won the Victoria Cross during the Second World War at St Nazaire. Sailing at 4 knots – a speed less than a man can walk – across hundreds of miles of sea from the Thames to the Antarctic Peninsula, those who started as landlubbers became competent seamen *en route*. Some had learnt dog driving and sledge techniques in Greenland. They did a lot of this on coastal sea ice in the Antarctic and at one time had about a hundred dogs. They might be placed mid-way between the 'Heroic Age' and the modern one, in that they had the benefit of vitamin pills, better clothing, planned food rations, radio and a Fox Moth aircraft. They were able to feed themselves and the dogs partly on seals, (like many an earlier expedition). Besides carrying out survey, geological, biological and other work, the BGLE had the satisfaction of converting (through its explorations) what was thought to be the Antarctic Archipelago into the Antarctic Peninsula and of discovering George VI Sound. It was the last expedition to reach Antarctica under sail, in the old tradition. In the words of its zoologist, Colin Bertram, 'it quietly achieved a great deal and was the direct and immediate forerunner in leadership and technique of, successively, the British 'Operation Tabarin', the Falkland Islands Dependencies Survey, and the British Antarctic Survey.'[8] They all returned safely, but with only a few of their splendid dogs. Rymill and Bertram wept as they shot the rest, one by one, and tumbled their bodies down a cliff. As with the *Karluk*, the *Penola's* cat came home.

Operation 'Tabarin', to which Bertram refers, was the code name for the wartime British naval expeditions to the Antarctic in 1943-44 and 1944-45. The

8 *A Biologist's Story*, page 56.

FRENCH POLAR EXPLORATION COMMANDANT J B CHARCOT

The French were not far behind the British in polar exploration, but have often been ignored by history. Like the British, they had some tradition of Antarctic exploration, in that J S C Dumont d'Urville had discovered Terre Adélie in the 1840s. His successor, sixty years later, was Commandant J B Charcot (son of the eminent neurologist J M Charcot who became known as 'le polar gentleman'). He spent most of his inheritance in building (at Saint Malo) first the schooner *Français* and secondly a larger vessel, the celebrated *Pourquoi Pas?*, a barque with an auxiliary engine. In the years 1903-05 and 1908-10, he explored and charted much of the west coast of Graham Land (part of the Antarctic Peninsula) as far south as Alexander Island, so named by Bellingshausen nearly a century before,

after the Czar of Russia. He also carried out a comprehensive scientific programme on both voyages. After the First World War, *Pourquoi Pas?* continued her polar researches in the northern hemisphere, particularly off east Greenland, but sank near Iceland in September 1936, with only one survivor. A medical man by training, in the footsteps and at the wish of his famous father, Charcot could not resist the call of the sea. He maintained a doctor's care for his crew and earned the respect of scientific colleagues, in the field, in France and abroad. To later Frenchmen of Expéditions Polaires Françaises, who were continuing his work in Greenland and the Antarctic after the Second World War, Charcot was always, in the words of their leader, Paul-Emile Victor, 'Le Patron'.

name is said to have come from that of a Paris night club. The vessels transporting its members were the *Fitzroy* and HMS *William Scoresby*. At the end of the war, the administrative responsibility for the stations established by 'Tabarin' was transferred from the Admiralty to the Colonial Office and in 1948 to the Governor of the Falkland Islands. A Scientific Bureau was established in London in 1949 to co-ordinate the work on data and specimens. Its head was Dr (later Sir) Vivian Fuchs, who was to make the first crossing of Antarctica in the 1950s. Members of the Survey became known as 'Fids' and the term is still used for members of the British Antarctic Survey, the successor to the FIDS. Only in recent years were the last dogs evacuated from the British Antarctic Territory, in accordance with an international agreement. Sadly, they could not stand up to infection in the North and nearly all have died. In the previous five decades, many notable long distance dog-sledge journeys had been made to survey the Peninsula and to make scientific observations. Sir Vivian Fuchs' *Of Ice and Men* tells the story. He makes the point that the men were all 'ordinary chaps.' Their work has been published in numerous scientific reports. The first of the red-hulled ice-strengthened supply ships, *John Biscoe*, formerly HMS *Pretext*, was acquired in 1947; her successors were RRS *John Biscoe* in 1955 and RRS *Bransfield* in 1971. Sir Vivian Fuchs has paid tribute to the officers and men serving in these ships, some over a period of many years, in the hazardous waters of the Antarctic, encountering:

> . . . the ice floes that suddenly close on a ship and hold her fast, the unstable iceberg that turns over, or the unexpected rapid freezing of the sea in which ships are so often beset. On these vessels and the supplies they carry, the bases depend. Rarely have the ships failed them, and then only in circumstances when even an icebreaker could not have fought a way through to a station. Only skilful handling and a long experience of the ways of ice can sail them safely through to their destinations – our Captains have indeed served us well.[9]

The name of Richard Evelyn Byrd is well known in the annals of both polar regions – in the Arctic for his pioneering flights and in the Antarctic for expeditions based on the Ross Ice Shelf, near Amundsen's old winter quarters in the Bay of Whales. Byrd organised and led four large-scale Antarctic expeditions. Their headquarters were known as 'Little America' and the first expedition took place in 1928-30, the second in 1933-35, the third in 1939-41 (the United States Antarctic Service Expedition) and the fourth in 1946-47 (Operation 'High Jump' of the US Navy) in which thirteen ships participated, but left no wintering parties. A member of an old Virginia family, Byrd was a Commander in the United States Navy when he began planning the first of these expeditions. 'Somebody has to explore' [the Antarctic], he said, 'and it is the job I have picked out for myself'.[10] He was primarily interested in exploring the continent from the air, with the benefit of effective radio communications. There is a photograph of 'Little America' showing the tall aerials rimmed with ice. Byrd also took advantage of new knowledge of nutrition and fresh designs for clothing, tents and other equipment. However, his surface transport would still be dogs. His first ships would be the *City of New York*, formerly the *Samson*, a Norwegian barque, which was re-rigged as a barquentine, and the freighter *Eleanor Bolling*, formerly the British mine-sweeper *Chelsea*.

9 *Of Ice and Men*, page 162.
10 Quoted in Rodgers, E, *Beyond the Barrier*, page 13.

The enterprise grew and grew until it cost more than a million dollars, raised with great difficulty and persistence by Byrd. In the words of the historian of this first venture, 'Because necessity had made Byrd into a media personality and his expedition into a media event, his accomplishments had to be of more than academic interest. He knew that they must create headlines'.[11] The continent was indeed explored from the air (including a flight to the Pole) and on sledge journeys. A large portion of the continent was called 'Marie Byrd Land', after Byrd's wife. His narrative *Little America* was published in 1930.

Byrd's second Antarctic expedition of 1933-35 created a more extensive base by adding ten new buildings to the 1929 base. A great deal of exploring, as well as a scientific programme, was accomplished. It had been thought that the Weddell Sea and the Ross Sea might be connected; this was proved almost certainly not to be so. A weather station one hundred miles south of 'Little America II' was manned for seven months. The vessels transporting the expedition were the *Jacob Ruppert*, a steel freighter of about 9000 tons and the celebrated barquentine *Bear*, whose keel was laid in Dundee in 1873. Built for the Newfoundland seal fishery, she had sailed in 1884 to rescue the Greely expedition and in 1914, to rescue the survivors of the *Karluk*. She had spent years in the US Revenue Cutter Service and years with the US Coast Guard, on the Alaska patrol. The *Bear*'s main achievement in exploration during the second Byrd expedition was to navigate and take echo soundings beyond King Edward VII Land at the eastern side of the Ross Sea in February 1934. There was, according to Byrd, 'a fine and indestructible courage in her oak timbering with its sheathing of iron bark, which age and rot could not corrupt'.[12] Late that season, she made a rendezvous with *Discovery II* and took on board a surgeon to replace another who had left 'Little America' for home. The *Bear* delivered the new surgeon and departed on 26 February 1934, hidden by the sea smoke until only her topmasts were visible to the onlookers ashore. She had an extremely rough passage north to New Zealand, making handling the sails aloft an icy and daunting task.

The following summer the voyage of the *Bear* along the Ross Ice Front early in 1935 appeared to show that the ice shelf had advanced fourteen miles since the survey by Scott's *Terra Nova* in 1911. 'Little America II' was evacuated from the Bay of Whales, with tractors hauling material to the limit of safe ice, dog teams taking it then to the *Bear* alongside the ice shelf and then transferring it to the

---

11 Rodgers, E, *Beyond the Barrier*, page 43.
12 Quoted in Bixby, *Track of the Bear*, page 259.

vulnerable *Ruppert* with her thin steel hull. The *Ruppert*, carrying four planes, steamed well ahead of the little *Bear*, with her sixty-year-old engines but both arrived safely in New Zealand. Byrd had christened the old sealer the *Bear of Oakland*, because she had been a museum ship since May 1929 and was taken out of retirement on her purchase by Byrd from the City of Oakland. She was to return to the Antarctic again, together with the *North Star*, a large cargo carrier, as part of the United States Antarctic Service Expedition of 1939-41. She served during the war with the United States Greenland Patrol and even towed a prize – a German weather ship – into Boston harbour. At the age of eighty-nine, the *Bear* sank in March 1963 off Nova Scotia, taking with her, in the words of one of her three biographers 'all the long forgotten days, the history, and all the vanished men'.[13]

There were many more ships, for instance the whale catchers and whale factory ships, venturing into the icy waters of the Antarctic than have been mentioned in this short survey of exploration mostly in the first half of the twentieth century, which saw so many changes in the world, including the near extinction of the great whales and the approaching end of the industry which they were so unfortunate as to support. Yet, because of their thick wooden hulls and ability to use wind power rather than rely on coal (where there were no depots), the *Discovery*, the *Bear* and other sailing vessels made hazardous exploring voyages into the ice and usually survived. Those who sailed in these old fashioned ships seem to have developed a great affection for and strong ties with them. Dr Edward Wilson expressed some of these feelings in his diary of 26 July 1904, written aboard the *Discovery* in the South Atlantic:

> There is nothing made by man more wonderful than a sailing ship and to realise this fully one must spend some hours at night under more sail than appears quite safe in a sou'westerly gale in the roaring forties with squalls of force 10 and 11 by Beaufort's scale. And then, one must spend eight hours bumping and grinding the very soul out of her on the rocks, in the ice and the fury of an Antarctic southerly blizzard. One may see her gripped in ice and half buried in snow drift and she waits patiently, one may see her smiling fresh with new paint in the tropics and she looks beautiful, one may have felt her punching her way in the face of head winds when all else fails, by steam, or rolling till she creaks and groans again in a flat calm on a long and heavy swell. She may look obstinate, she may be trying, but wait till you see her tried to the utmost and when she has to bend or break she is like a really perfect

13 Bixby, *Track of the Bear*, page 286.

human being and she bends double first. Then you can realise how instinct with life and therefore loveable is the work of man, if only he has done his best.[14]

The political situation in the Arctic and in the Antarctic diverged greatly during the second half of the century. Because of the Cold War, the strategic importance of the Arctic Ocean increased enormously, while in the southern hemisphere, the signing of the Antarctic Treaty in 1959 by twelve nations – including the United States and the Soviet Union – ensured the continuation of peaceful co-operation in the pursuit of science, which had proved effective during the International Geophysical Year of 1957-58. Earlier still, the Norwegian-British-Swedish Antarctic Expedition of 1949-52 had shown that such co-operation could be both practical and successful.

The long Arctic coastline of Russia and Siberia, linking the Atlantic with the Pacific (the old North East Passage), was known about in the eighteenth century, but not navigated from end to end until the close of the nineteenth century. Efforts were subsequently made, largely by foreign merchants, to establish a sea route at the western end of the passage, but it was the crushing defeat of the Russians by Japan at the Battle of Tsushima in 1905 which led the Imperial Russian Navy to undertake a hydrographic survey. This lasted for six summer seasons between 1910 and 1915, in the icebreakers *Taymyr* and *Vaygach*. Had it been possible to send ships and men along this route to the Pacific, it was believed that the disaster at Tsushima could have been averted.

The Imperial Russian Government were given a number of British-built icebreakers early in the First World War. The first of these was the powerful *Yermak*, which was in service in the Arctic until the mid-1960s. However, it was the Soviet Government which set up the Chief Administration of the Northern Sea Route ('Glavsvemorput') in 1932, encouraged by the hydrological and meteorlogical results of the voyages of the *Krasin* and two other icebreakers going to rescue the airship *Italia* in 1928. Further encouragement came from the *Sibiryakov*'s voyage in one season from the Atlantic to the Pacific, carrying out extensive scientific work along the way, despite untoward events:

The ship sailed round the north end of Severnaya Zemlya – she was the first ship to do so ñ and lost a propeller blade in heavy ice as she came south again in the Laptev Sea. Off Kolyuchinskaya Guba heavy ice was met, one propeller blade was lost and the remaining three were badly damaged. By jettisoning much coal and fuel, the stern was raised sufficiently

14 Wilson, E, (ed. Savours, A), *Diary of the Discovery Expedition to the Antarctic Regions 1901-1904*, page 390.

to allow repairs to be carried out. The voyage was continued. On the next day, the thrust-bearing went, and on the following day, the propeller shaft broke and the screw fell to the bottom of the sea. The ship drifted towards Bering Strait in heavy ice, and with the aid of improvised sails she reached the neighbourhood of Mys Deshneva where a trawler took her in tow.[15]

The voyage of the newly built, ice-strengthened freighter *Chelyuskin* the following year ended with her being crushed by ice and sunk in 1934. In 1940, the German raider *Komet* navigated the sea route.

Through their successes and failures, the Russians gained unrivalled experience of ice navigation in northern waters, and unique knowledge of the types and strengths of icebreakers and cargo vessels for use in ice. This resulted in the construction of ships for specific tasks, whether as convoy escorts, in convoy, or as transports for scientific expeditions. A number of later polar icebreakers were built in the Finnish yards, for example, the *Vladivostok*, *Murmansk*, *Moskva*, *Leningrad* and *Kiev*, which were delivered in the 1960s. Nuclear icebreakers came into use during the later decades of the twentieth century. So-called 'global warming' led scientists to assess the feasibility of the Russian Northern Sea Route being navigated by ice-strengthened freighters, unescorted by icebreakers, sailing between Europe and the Far East in some twenty-two days. This compares favourably with the Suez Canal route (thirty-five days), the Panama Canal (forty days) and the Cape of Good Hope (forty-six days).

The dream of Sir Hubert Wilkins was realised when the first submarine reached the North Pole under the ice in 1958. The submarine that achieved this was the USS *Nautilus*. The first actually to surface there was the USS *Skate*, the following year. In 1971, the British nuclear submarine HMS *Dreadnought* followed suit. The exploitation of oil and minerals in the North American Arctic during the later decades of the twentieth century led to more shipping movement, mainly in the eastern Arctic, and to the voyage of the American supertanker SS *Manhattan*. She was the first merchant ship to navigate the North West Passage (north of Canada and Alaska) in 1969, returning in 1970 for further trials in ice. However, the building of a pipeline across Alaska meant that tanker traffic through these ice-infested waters became unnecessary, besides being an environmental hazard. Both Canadian and US Coastguard icebreakers have operated for many years in the seas north of the North American mainland. During the later twentieth

15 Armstrong, T, *The Northern Sea Route: Soviet Exploration of the North East Passage*, 1952 (Cambridge), p32.

century, a number of the American vessels have also been employed in the Southern Ocean as part of the United States Antarctic scientific programme – a very large scale operation.

Scientific investigations, charting and mapping have been under way in the Antarctic regions from the 1950s. They have been carried out by countries other than just the original signatories of the Antarctic Treaty, including China. Some of the signatories acquired their own ice-strengthened ships (such as Germany), while others, like the Australians, who have maintained the Australian National Antarctic Research Expeditions since 1947, have chartered from Lauritzen and other owners. The *Sir James Clark Ross* was built for the British Antarctic Survey, commissioned towards the end of the twentieth century. As for the Russians, the *Ob* and other icebreakers operated in both hemispheres during the Cold War. Since the end of the Cold War, some have carried tourists into the icy seas, north and south.

"Bismarck *lay, a shattered, burning, sinking hulk as* Dorsetshire *approached. At two miles she fired two torpedoes which burst on* Bismarck's *starboard side. At a mile and a half she fired another which burst on the port side of the wreck. She rolled over and sank, leaving the surface covered with debris and struggling men.*"

C. S. Forester: *Hunting the Bismarck* (1959)

CHAPTER FIVE

THE WORLD AT WAR

Antony Preston

THE SECOND WORLD WAR was, above all else, a maritime war. Without sea power Japan could not have overrun the Pacific, and the United States could never have projected power across the Atlantic to defeat Nazi Germany. Without diminishing the role of air and land power, it was maritime power in its widest sense, warships, merchantmen and aircraft operating over the sea which determined the nature of the war.

When the Anglo-French ultimatum to Germany expired at midnight on 3 September 1939 the naval balance was heavily in favour of the Allies. The Royal Navy was still the largest in the world, but only two battleships had been built since the end of the First World War twenty years earlier. Only one of the carriers was modern, and half the cruisers and destroyers were of similar vintage, although most of the submarines were modern. A massive building programme had begun in 1936, to build nine battleships, six large aircraft carriers, twenty-four light cruisers, twenty-four destroyers and twelve submarines, but none would be ready until 1940 at the earliest. The state of naval aviation was parlous because it had only recently been returned to naval control from the Royal Air Force, and was saddled with obsolete aircraft and a shortage of personnel.

The French Navy was smaller, and it too had weaknesses. The solitary aircraft carrier was a slow conversion from a battleship, and the Popular Front government of Leon Blum had reduced the efficiency of the shipyards and ordnance factories. The cruisers and destroyers had been designed to operate against the Italian Fleet, emphasizing speed at the expense of range. Four powerful new battleships had been ordered, of which the first would be ready in 1940, and two new carriers were under construction, along with four cruisers, twenty-seven destroyers and thirty escorts.

Fortunately for the Allies the German Navy – the *Kriegsmarine* – had insufficient time to build up to parity with the Royal Navy, and could muster only two fast battleships, three armoured ships ('pocket battleships'), eight cruisers, twenty-two destroyers, twenty escorts and fifty-nine submarines ('U-boats'). But they were all modern ships, built since the late 1920s. A huge expansion programme was in hand, eleven battleships, nine cruisers, twenty-five destroyers and fifty U-boats.

The main burden of the maritime war would rest on the Royal Navy. At the heart of its sprawling maritime empire, Great Britain relied heavily on imports of foods and raw materials, so the Royal Navy's responsibilities included the protection of a huge Merchant Navy as well as preserving the nation and its imperial possessions from direct enemy attack. Geography dictated the same basic strategy as that followed in 1914-18 – blocking the exits from the North Sea to confine the German Fleet to the Baltic approaches and its coastal waters. Further afield, control of the Mediterranean guaranteed access to the Suez Canal and Middle East oil. Britain had huge investments in India, the Far East, Australia, Canada and South Africa and strategic possessions around the world. The government was well aware of the threat posed by Japanese expansionism, and hoped somehow to avoid the insupportable burden of a simultaneous war in Europe and the Far East.

The biggest threats to the Royal Navy were posed by the land-based *Luftwaffe* and the *Kriegsmarine*'s U-boats. Technical advances since 1918 had given the Royal Navy a 'secret weapon', the Asdic active underwater sensor (now known as Sonar). Some two hundred warships had been fitted with the device, but pre-war exercises had not shown up its operational limitations, and although a powerful weapon in the forthcoming battle it did not render the U-boat ineffective as some of its ardent exponents had claimed. Above water, radar (then known as radio direction finding or RDF) had been at sea in limited numbers since 1936, and it was to revolutionize sea warfare.

First blood went to the U-boats, which sank the aircraft carrier *Courageous* in the Western Approaches two weeks after the outbreak of war. Then came a second disaster, when on 8 October *U47* penetrated the defences of the Home Fleet base at Scapa Flow, torpedoing the old battleship *Royal Oak*. The Home Fleet's attempts to intercept German surface units were frustrated by German penetration of the Admiralty ciphers. The naval war seemed to be going badly for the Allies; the Germans were not winning, but they seemed to be able to evade all countermoves. The British press called it the 'Phoney War' but it was hardly phoney at sea, with mounting U-boat sinkings of merchant ships. Then in December 1939 came some very welcome news. The 'pocket battleship' *Admiral Graf Spee* was brought to bay off the River Plate estuary by three British cruisers. Although nominally capable of sinking all three, the *Admiral Graf Spee* took refuge in the neutral port of Montevideo to repair battle damage. Hitler ordered her captain to scuttle his ship, and three days later she left harbour to find a resting place in Uruguayan territorial waters.

The Battle of the River Plate raised British morale, but 1940 was to see a catastrophic reversal of fortunes. First came the poorly executed Norwegian Campaign in April, undertaken with the French in a vain attempt to forestall a German invasion. Once again German reading of the Home Fleet ciphers enabled the heavy units to avoid being brought to action, and allowed six divisions to reach southern Norway undetected. Criticism of the Admiralty was widespread, but the German destroyer-force was severely depleted in the two Battles of Narvik, and several major units were sunk or damaged. During the withdrawal the British lost another aircraft carrier, HMS *Glorious*, but the Germans had suffered proportionately more casualties.

There was little time for post-mortems on Norway. On 10 May the *Wehrmacht* launched its *blitzkrieg* against the Allies in Belgium and France. Only nine days later the Admiralty was asked by the War Cabinet to advise on the possibility of evacuating the British Expeditionary Force, and the result was Operation 'Dynamo', the evacuation of some three hundred and thirty-eight thousand troops from Dunkirk, and Operations 'Ariel' and 'Cycle' to get another one hundred and ninety-one thousand out from other ports down to the Bay of Biscay. These huge and complex events, virtually an amphibious operation in reverse, robbed the Germans of the full fruits of victory, but the five hundred thousand troops taken back to England had left behind virtually all their equipment, and well over three hundred warships and mercantile vessels of all sizes had been sunk or damaged.

Although hardly a British victory, it was a strategic defeat for Germany, for the British were still in the war, free to make mischief. The causes of that missed chance can be put down to the *Wehrmacht*'s lack of any plans for an amphibious assault and the *Kriegsmarine*'s patent inability to cover such an operation. The losses of ships in Norway were keenly felt, but the failure to inflict serious damage

⟜ GROSSADMIRAL KARL DÖNITZ ⟞

The life of Karl Dönitz spanned ninety years (1891-1981), during which he went from being the head of state to a prisoner of the War Crimes Tribunal at Nuremberg in a matter of months. Demonised by the Allies as the head of the merciless onslaught on Allied shipping, and indisputably a dedicated Nazi, to the day he died he remained a hero to the officers and men who survived the slaughter of the U-boats in 1943-45.

One of a number of surface fleet officers transferred to the expanding U-boat Arm, Dönitz entered the U-boat School in 1916. Once qualified he was posted to *U39*, operating in the Mediterranean under the command of Kapitän Leutnant Walter Forstmann, one of the First World War 'aces'. After a period in command of *UC25* he transferred to *UB68* but his final commission came to an abrupt halt in October 1918, when his boat was sunk by Royal Navy escorts.

Dönitz was one of the lucky few to be retained by the truncated post-war *Reichsmarine*. His appointment to run the reborn U-boat Arm in 1935 was tackled with characteristic determination. Only four years later his force was ready for war, and as *Führer der Uboote* he waged unremitting war against Allied shipping wherever it could be attacked.

on the Dunkirk evacuation showed poor planning as well. U-boat bases were quickly set up on the Atlantic coast down to Brest and Lorient in Brittany. At a stroke the British strategy had been outflanked, cutting the time needed to reach the Western Approaches.

With the failure of the *Luftwaffe*'s assault on the Royal Air Force, Hitler soon dropped any pretence of sticking to the Prize Regulations, and the Battle of the Atlantic can be said to start in the late summer of 1940. It was to last until the German surrender in 1945, a remorseless struggle in which no quarter was given. To the British the Atlantic Battle meant survival, but in the broader strategic sense it was also essential for the Americans, for without the British Isles as an 'unsinkable aircraft carrier' the task of expelling the Germans from Western Europe would have been immeasurably greater.

American neutrality was laxly enforced where Britain was concerned. In September 1940 a 'bases for destroyers' deal was arranged, whereby fifty old destroyers were lent to the Royal Navy in exchange for a ninety-nine year lease on bases in the West Indies, the Western Atlantic and elsewhere. The repeal of the Cash and Carry Act also enabled the British to acquire war material without paying in hard currency. In practice this meant that British warships could be

He very nearly made good his boast of destroying the Atlantic convoy system with his 'wolf packs', when the last of his brilliant pre-war 'ace' commanders was lost, but his insistence on centralised control and excessive use of radio proved to be the weak link. When he succeeded Raeder as Commander in Chief in January 1943 he appeared to have reached the pinnacle of success. But time was running out for the U-boats and the *Kriegsmarine*. In the spring of 1943 the Atlantic U-boats suffered such disastrous losses that Dönitz was forced to withdraw them for 'regrouping', and they never regained the initiative. When they were equipped with new weapons and sensors the Allies' countermeasures had also made big strides and the American shipyards were now able to build merchant ships faster than they could be torpedoed. The final act in the drama was pure farce, when Hitler designated the Admiral as his successor. Reichsmarschall Hermann Göring underscored the comic element by calling him the 'Weekend Führer'. After his release from prison he lived quietly in retirement and wrote his memoirs. The final humiliation was almost accidental, when the massive Allied penetration of his Enigma cipher messages was revealed to him in old age. Until then he had been unaware of the ease with which Bletchley Park had been reading his orders since May 1941.

repaired and refitted in US Navy shipyards, a process which also gave the US Navy invaluable experience in battle-damage repairs. By September 1941 the US Navy was getting drawn into the Atlantic battle by allowing its destroyers to escort supply ships to Iceland, taken into 'protective custody' for the duration of the war. So freely did US Navy commanders interpret their rules of engagement that a destroyer was torpedoed and another was severely damaged, in both cases by U-boats that were defending themselves. Even so, the mood of isolationism was strong that deaths and injuries to US Navy sailors were insufficient to bring the United States into the war.

In May 1941 the *Kriegsmarine* launched its most powerful assault on the North Atlantic convoy system, sending the new battleship *Bismarck* and the heavy cruiser *Prinz Eugen* out via Norway to prey on shipping. Intercepted by the old battlecruiser HMS *Hood* and the new battleship HMS *Prince of Wales*, the Germans scored a resounding victory, sinking the *Hood* and forcing the *Prince of Wales* to withdraw damaged. But it was a hollow victory, for the *Bismarck* had suffered underwater hits from the *Prince of Wales*, and during the next two days suffered torpedo damage from Fleet Air Arm Swordfish aircraft launched by the carriers HMS *Victorious* and HMS *Ark Royal*. Steering on her propellers and leaking oil, the *Bismarck* could only head for Brest on the French Atlantic coast, in the hope that she might get cover from shore-based aircraft. Early on the morning of 27 May she was brought to bay by the Home Fleet flagship, the battleship HMS *King George V* and her consort HMS *Rodney*, and was reduced to impotence in only twenty minutes. The Home Fleet left the stricken hulk to be torpedoed by a heavy cruiser and headed back to Scapa Flow. No Atlantic foray was ever attempted by her sister *Tirpitz*.

The Battle of the Atlantic became a race between the Allied shipyards and Admiral Dönitz and his U-boats. If they could turn out merchant ships and convoy escorts faster than the U-boats could sink them, the superior industrial resources of the Allies would give them victory. In 1942 the tide began to turn, with new weapons and sensors such as radar and high-frequency direction finding to give the escorts a vital edge in the battle. The German scientists responded, and the scientific battle became as important as the sea battle. Known only to a few was the priceless asset of the cryptographers at Bletchley Park. Breaking into the German Enigma ciphers could not avoid defeat in the dark days of 1941-42, but at the very least it allowed countermeasures to be applied where they were most effective. At its best it enabled Allied planners to know the innermost secrets of their opponents and to have advance warning of new tactics.

After a long wrangle with the Royal Air Force strategic bombing advocates, American-built Liberator four-engined bombers were released for long-range anti-submarine patrol work. These very long-range (VLR) Liberators began to play a key role in the fight against the U-boats. The so-called 'Black Gap' in mid-Atlantic could not be covered by any other shore-based aircraft, and here the U-boats could find rich pickings. As a counterpart to the VLR Liberators the Royal Navy introduced small carriers converted from mercantile hulls, some carrying a cargo of grain or oil (MAC-Ships) and others undergoing a full conversion (escort carriers). These ships sailed with the convoys, providing them with constant air cover across the Atlantic.

War is always a matter of conflicting priorities, and the decision at the highest level to mount an Allied assault on North Africa (Operation 'Torch') meant that escort forces had to be diverted from the Atlantic to convoy the troopships and transports from the United States and Britain. Dönitz was quick to sense the weakening of the Allied effort in the Atlantic, and despite all the advances achieved in 1942, shipping losses climbed alarmingly to 500,000 tons in the first twenty days of March 1943. The Admiralty was admitting the possibility of defeat, and there was talk of abandoning the convoy system. Yet in that same month the tide suddenly turned. In part it was the Bletchley Park cryptographers getting into a new U-boat cipher after a long struggle, in part the return of the powerful escort groups from the 'Torch' landings, and a range of new tactics and weapons in better-trained escorts. In April the tonnage sunk fell to half the March figure. The U-boats were also taking heavy losses: six in January, fifteen in March, fifteen in April and forty-one in May.

The U-boats were not yet beaten outright, but they had suffered a crushing defeat. Morale remained high to the end, but never again did they show the determination that they had in 1942-43. In 1941 the virtual elimination of the 'aces' had forced Dönitz to resuscitate an idea which had been tried in 1918, the *rudeltaktik* or 'wolfpack'. It used a complex system of shore-based command and control (opening the system to attack by the Allied cryptographers). The first U-boat to sight a convoy was ordered not to attack but to signal to U-boat HQ number of ships, estimated course and speed etc, trailing the convoy until HQ could direct more U-boats to join her. Once the 'pack' was assembled it could in theory swamp the convoy defences and sink ships at will. In practice it was never quite so easy. The Admiralty used Bletchley Park decrypts to re-route convoys clear of U-boat concentrations, and escorts and aircraft could force the 'reporting' U-boat down, cutting off communications. From the spring of 1941 a growing number of escorts had radar, which put an end to attacks on the surface, and by the end of 1942 the new ASV III airborne radar could spot a periscope.

In July 1943 the total of new shipbuilding finally overtook the total of ships sunk, enabling the Allies to move to the offensive. The need to keep the Soviet Union from collapse forced the Allies to run convoys to Murmansk, but even that grim ordeal became less dangerous by early 1943. In December 1942 a force of eight Royal Navy destroyers fought off the heavy cruiser *Admiral Hipper* and the 'pocket battleship' *Lützow*. Hitler was so angry that he threatened to scrap the surface fleet, prompting the resignation of *Grossadmiral* Erich Raeder, the Commander in Chief. Although Dönitz had previously criticized the resources allocated to surface ships, he persuaded Hitler to reprieve the heavy units because they played a useful role in tying down Allied forces. On 26 December 1943, the Royal Navy's Home Fleet fought the last major surface action against the battlecruiser *Scharnhorst*, the last operational capital ship in the *Kriegsmarine*. In the past Dönitz had complained about interference by the Führer in naval operations and this time he insisted on planning it himself. As a result of poor

THE 'LIBERTY' SHIP

If any ship-type was crucial to the Battle of the Atlantic it was the 'Liberty' standard cargo ship built in huge numbers. The speed with which these very basic ships were built enabled the Allies to offset the hideous losses inflicted by the German Navy's U-boats.

There was nothing new about the idea of standard merchant ships. In the First World War huge numbers were built in Great Britain, Canada, Japan and the United States to replace losses, and many survived to serve again in 1939-1945. British and Canadian yards followed suit from 1939, with a range of 'Empire', 'Fort' and 'Park' designs, and the 'Liberty' itself originated in a British Doxford design passed to the United States to expedite the shipbuilding effort. U-boats sank 2828 merchantmen, totalling 14,687,231dwt tons, and it was not only necessary to replace them but to add sufficient to meet Allied needs for the support of offensive operations around the world.

What made the 'Liberty' different was the approach of the contractor. Henry J Kaiser was a civil engineer who had never built a ship, and when his company won the contract his rivals could scarcely conceal their contempt. Kaiser use prefabrication on a scale never attempted before, with sections built in factories well away from the sea. The simplicity of the 10,500dwt tons, 11 knot design helped, and when Kaiser learned that diesels and turbines were earmarked for naval construction and high-priority mercantile types he chose the older but robust vertical triple-expansion reciprocating steam engine and steam-powered auxiliary machinery. To cut time he used welding on a large scale, setting up schools to train welders.

The scale of his achievement is measured by the staggering statistics: 2770 'Liberties' built, totalling 29,292,000dwt tons, of which a number were converted to naval use.

Although they were sturdy and reliable, their mild steel hulls were prone to brittle fractures in sub-zero temperatures. Ships affected sank so rapidly that survivors usually assumed they had been torpedoed. Despite this they survived long after the end of the War.

liaison between the *Luftwaffe* and the Navy the hapless Admiral Bey in the *Scharnhorst* had no inkling that he was facing the battleship HMS *Duke of York* and a powerful force of cruisers and destroyers, until a salvo of 14in shells hit his flagship. The weather was so bad that nobody on the British side saw their adversary sink.

With the *Scharnhorst* went the last serious surface threat to Allied shipping. The *Tirpitz* had been disabled in 1943 by midget submarines (X-craft) and in April

1944 she was hit in a massive air strike, Operation 'Tungsten', launched from the carriers HMS *Victorious*, HMS *Furious*, HMS *Emperor*, HMS *Searcher*, HMS *Fencer* and HMS *Pursuer*. Finally, she left the security of the northern Norwegian fjords and was sent south to Tromsö to serve as a floating battery to deter an invasion. Here she was at last in range of bombers based in Britain, and on 12 November 1944 she was sunk by 12,000lb 'earthquake' bombs dropped by Royal Air Force Lancasters.

With convoys now crossing the Atlantic with relatively light losses it was at last possible to implement the plan to invade France. The Allies' grand strategy had been based on the liberation of Occupied Europe to bring the main German ground and air forces to battle, but apart from pinprick commando raids and the unsuccessful raid on Dieppe in 1942, lack of resources prevented any serious large-scale planning until 1942. The build up of American troops and supplies and the assembly of specialized landing craft delayed took until the spring of 1944. Operation 'Overlord' and its naval element Operation 'Neptune' were ready.

Space does not permit a detailed account of the D-Day landings in Normandy on 6 June 1944, but they were the outcome of three years experience. The armada assembled numbered some five thousand ships, ranging from battleships down to minor landing craft. A combination of luck and very detailed planning made the largest amphibious operation in history a brilliant success, fooling the Germans about the landing beaches and suffering relatively low casualties in ships and troops. Although a long, hard fight remained before the Germans surrendered at Lüneburg Heath the following spring, the Normandy landings were the beginning of the end of the war in Europe. They also brought about the total eclipse of the *Kriegsmarine* outside German coastal waters and the Baltic.

In the Mediterranean, the position of the British and their French allies had been good up to the moment of the French surrender in June 1940, and the Italian Fleet was not regarded as a great danger. All this changed with the fall of France, and when Italy joined the war as an ally of Germany, the whole Mediterranean threatened to become an Axis lake. The British took the controversial decision to knock out the French Fleet at Mers-el-Kebir to prevent it from being taken over by an Italian *coup de main*. Although the fleet was not sunk outright, heavy French casualties were suffered, and even to this day the attack has never been forgiven by the French Navy.

The reinforcements sent to the Mediterranean to fight the Italians soon made their mark. Admiral Cunningham, Commander in Chief of the Mediterranean Fleet, and Admiral Somerville's Force 'H' at Gibraltar were not overawed by the numerical superiority of the Italians, and soon dominated the Mediterranean. When it was clear the Italians were reluctant to leave their main base at Taranto, Cunningham launched an air strike from the carriers *Illustrious* and *Eagle*, putting Italian battleships and heavy cruisers out of action for many months. The situation became so bad for the Italians that their German allies took a hand, sending the Afrika Korps to North Africa to defeat or contain the Eighth Army; Germany also sent the anti-shipping strike force Flieger Korps X and a dozen precious U-boats. As a result the carrier *Illustrious* was nearly sunk off Malta by dive-bombers, and Malta became almost untenable as a naval base, reducing the threat to the convoys supplying German and Italian forces in North Africa. To complete the tale of woe, a British expeditionary force was expelled from Greece and Crete in turn, and the Navy suffered terrible losses while evacuating Crete. Fortunately Cunningham was never daunted by heavy odds, and on the night of 28 March 1941 his fleet had sunk three Italian heavy cruisers off Cape Matapan. This disaster made the Italians very reluctant to support the German airborne assault on Crete in May, missing an opportunity to crush the British. However, they recovered their nerve and staged a brilliant attack on Alexandria in December, using 'human torpedoes' to immobilize the battleships HMS *Queen Elizabeth* and HMS *Valiant*. The Navy also lost the old battleship HMS *Barham* and the carrier HMS *Ark Royal* to U-boat attack.

Despite these reverses, Cunningham's bold handling of his remaining forces frustrated the Italian Navy's hopes of victory. Malta was not finally saved until August 1942, but thereafter the tide turned. The 'Torch' landings in North Africa in November 1942 were followed by the 'Husky' landings in Sicily and the 'Avalanche' landings at Salerno. When Italy tried to sue for a separate peace on the eve of the Salerno landings, the Germans turned on their reluctant allies, sinking the battleship *Roma* with a radio-controlled bomb. Cunningham and his fleet could savour the magnitude of their victory on 10 September, when four battleships filed into Malta's Grand Harbour to surrender. But the Germans were determined to fight on, and they were not finally expelled from northern Italy until late in 1944. The Allies' attempt to 'leapfrog' by landing behind the German defensive line at Anzio ran into very heavy opposition, and remained bogged down for three months. The final act of the drama was the largely American invasion of southern France.

In the Pacific the Japanese, the third partner in the Axis, had decided to strike at South East Asia to expel the Americans, British and Dutch. The key was oil, the Japanese High Command reasoning that the American embargo on oil exports, imposed to penalize Japan for its aggression in China, would become critical in 1942. With frightening rapidity the Japanese attacked almost simultaneously against the US Pacific Fleet at its main base, Pearl Harbor in Hawaii with a carrier air strike, invaded the Philippines and Malaya and wiped out the Western 'treaty ports' in China. By April 1942 the Japanese Army took Singapore, intended to be the 'Gibraltar of the Far East', and was fighting its way through the former Dutch colonial empire from Java down to New Guinea. The attack on Pearl Harbor on Sunday 7 December 1941 was devastating. The two waves of air attacks sank four battleships at their moorings and inflicted severe damage on two more. Two of them were wrecked beyond repair, but the other six were repairable. That, combined with other factors, mitigated the worst effects of the attack. First, the three American carriers were not in harbour as they were carrying out flying training at sea. Second, the vital tank farms were not attacked, leaving the Pacific Fleet's fuel reserves intact. Third, the Japanese hope that the destruction of the Pacific Fleet would cow the Americans into conceding mastery of the Pacific was not fulfilled. An outraged public demanded vengeance, making isolationism a dead letter. Much to the relief of the hard-pressed British, Hitler chose the moment to declare war on the United States, saving President Roosevelt from having to argue for war against Germany as well as Japan, and linking the struggle for Europe with the campaign against Japan.

That said, the months after Pearl Harbor were deeply worrying. Replacements for the major losses could be brought through the Panama Canal, with the virtual elimination of the German surface threat by the Royal Navy. Major warships like aircraft carriers take a long time to build, and new aircraft and pilots had to be integrated before they could face the Japanese. Inept reactions to U-boat attacks on east coast shipping led to six months of 'Happy Time' for the Germans and deprived the Allies of yet more mercantile tonnage. In Malaya the British had suffered a series of disasters. The new battleship HMS *Prince of Wales* and the old battlecruiser HMS *Repulse* succumbed to torpedo-attack by shore-based bombers three days after the attack on Pearl Harbor. After a brilliant drive down the Malayan Peninsula, a Japanese Army took the surrender of Singapore and its 80,000-strong garrison. Losses continued, with vain attempts to delay the Japanese advance through Java and Sumatra. The Battle of the Java Sea resulted in the virtual destruction of the American-British-Dutch-Australian (ABDA) cruiser force hurriedly cobbled together at the start of hostilities.

Although the Japanese seemed unstoppable, they had already succumbed to a common yet fatal 'victory disease', in which they became over-extended. On 6-7 May 1942 the Battle of the Coral Sea became the first carrier versus carrier battle, in which the fleets never sighted each other. It was a tactical setback for the Americans because their losses were heavier, but it halted the Japanese drive into the South West Pacific against Australia and New Zealand. Three days later a task force of three carriers based at Pearl Harbor clashed with the main Japanese Combined Fleet in the Battle of Midway. An over-complex plan by the Japanese resulted in the loss of four carrier veterans of Pearl Harbor, the *Akagi*, *Hiryu*, *Kaga* and *Soryu*, and most of their aircrews, in exchange for only one American carrier, the USS *Yorktown*. Once again it was carrier versus carrier, and the Combined Fleet was unable to exert its strength against the Americans. The American counterpart to Bletchley Park's 'Ultra' activities, the US Navy's 'Magic' cryptographic offensive, had cracked the Japanese Navy's ciphers, enabling the carriers to stay out of trouble and making their own air strikes more effective.

The vast distances of the Pacific called for radically new tactics, the use of fast carrier task forces capable of launching heavy air strikes and then withdrawing to refuel and re-arm. It also called for a massive support operation, using remote anchorages to establish temporary bases, a fleet train of oilers and supply ships to bring fuel, ordnance and food from the United States. It was the underpinning for the strategy devised by Admiral Nimitz, Commander in Chief of the Pacific Fleet. By 'island-hopping' the fast carrier groups could bypass the Japanese strong points and cut them off. Great use was made of submarines to attack Japanese shipping and a number of other tasks, including reconnaissance and rescue of downed aircrew. The huge Japanese submarine fleet, in contrast, achieved few results. Its tactical doctrines were faulty, and the prodigality of the High Command resulted in many of them being used to supply island garrisons with food and ammunition. The long lifeline between the west coast of the United States and the front line in the Central Pacific was never seriously threatened, and the few successes against heavily defended warships were achieved at great cost. There was an equivalent of the Battle of the Atlantic, but it was a highly successful onslaught on Japanese shipping. Unlike the Allies, the Imperial Japanese Navy devoted only slender resources to the development of sonar and radar, and countermeasures were poor.

The news via 'Magic' that the Japanese were about to occupy Guadalcanal in the Solomon Islands set in train a long battle of attrition which would strain the Americans and their allies near to breaking point, but would ultimately weaken the Japanese fatally. The US Chiefs of Staff had already decided to occupy the Santa Cruz Islands, giving them a vital base near Tulagi. This made a rapid response possible, and an amphibious force of US Marines was able to capture a vital airstrip that the Japanese had started to build on Guadalcanal. Renamed Henderson Field, it was to be the prize over which the Japanese and the Americans were to fight to the bitter end.

The Japanese reaction was typically rapid and devastating. Admiral Mikawa's force of seven cruisers set out from Rabaul, 550 miles away, and succeeded in getting close to the amphibious landing force without being detected. An Australian bomber sighted Mikawa's force on the morning of 9 August, but Admiral Turner did not receive the message for another eight hours, in garbled form. The Battle of Savo Island was a frightening demonstration of the Japanese skill in night fighting. The Allied screening cruisers were unaware of the Japanese presence until 01.30 the following morning, when they rounded the southern end of Savo Island. In the confusion that followed the Australian heavy cruiser HMAS *Canberra* was riddled by 8in shellfire and hit by two torpedoes. Next to be destroyed were the heavy cruisers USS *Astoria*, *Quincy* and *Vincennes*. All that saved the amphibious force from annihilation was an unexplained withdrawal by Mikawa.

Despite this close shave the fight to hold Henderson Field continued. On the night of 19 August the Japanese tried to rush in one thousand five hundred troops to reinforce their garrison, but the Allies were better prepared. In the ensuing Battle of the Eastern Solomons the light carrier *Ryujo* was sunk by American carrier aircraft, but the American carrier *Enterprise* was badly damaged. Thereafter the Japanese repeatedly ran fast convoys, the so-called 'Tokyo Express', down the 'Slot' between the Eastern and Western Solomons. By day the Allies controlled the seas around the Solomons, but by night the Japanese were the masters. The defenders were roughly handled, and only their possession of radar prevented losses from being heavier.

Attrition was heavy. On 31 August the big carrier *Saratoga* was torpedoed and put out of action. Three weeks later the carrier *Wasp* was torpedoed and sunk. On 15 September the battleship *North Carolina* was damaged by a submarine torpedo, leaving only one carrier and a battleship to protect Guadalcanal. On 26

October the Battle of the Santa Cruz Islands saw the loss of the carriers *Zuiho* and USS *Hornet* and damage to two other carriers (one on either side). The US Navy was now so hard-pressed that it had to borrow HMS *Victorious* for a few months until the first of the big Essex class carriers ordered in 1940 could make good the losses. On 12 November the First Battle of Guadalcanal was fought, with the Japanese battleship *Hiei* sunk and two American cruisers badly damaged. The Second Battle of Guadalcanal, two nights later, saw the first engagement of capital ships, in which the USS *Washington* and USS *South Dakota* sank the *Hiei*'s sister *Kirishima*.

These two hard-fought actions marked the limit of Japanese success. By the end of the year the only supplies reaching the defenders were landed by submarines, and early in 1943 the Japanese High Command ordered an evacuation. While they were being evicted from the Solomons, General MacArthur's forces had cleared the ground forces from the northern coast of New Guinea, putting an end to the threat to Australia.

The next major offensive was an attack on the 'Bismarck Barrier', a chain of island bases established by the Japanese early in 1942 as a defensive perimeter. To force the Japanese to divide their forces Nimitz also formed a powerful force of carriers and battleships to drive towards the Marshall and Carolina Islands. While the Americans grew steadily stronger and refined their techniques, the Japanese were growing weaker. By November 1943 Admiral Koga at Truk had one carrier, but no organized air group on board. The cream of the navy pilots had been killed in the Solomons, and the exhaustive training course was never modified to produce sufficient replacements. The US Navy, in comparison, had established huge pilot-training facilities at Pensacola in Florida, and these schools turned out thousands of pilots. The average may have been lower than the best Japanese pilots, but they were there in numbers and the aircraft factories were now producing carrier aircraft superior in many respects to the Japanese.

Despite these ominous signs the Japanese still believed at the beginning of 1944 that their basic defence plans were still working. The original island perimeter had been breached, but they had succesfully fallen back on to a shorter defence line, stretching from the Mariana Islands, through Truk and Rabaul down to New Guinea and Timor. The Navy's commanders still hoped to bring the main Pacific Fleet to action on its terms, ideally using their giant 64,000-ton, 18in-gunned battleships *Yamato* and *Musashi*. The US Navy also hoped for a decisive surface action, but only on their terms.

The assault on the Marshall Islands in February 1944 brought the war much closer to the Home Islands. Kwajalein was taken after four days of fighting, but the garrisons of the bigger atolls were left to wither on the vine. The atoll of Majuro was immediately turned into a large anchorage for the fleet train. When Eniwetok fell the Americans were now only 700 miles from Truk, the main Japanese fortified fleet base in the Caroline Islands, and the fast carriers could now strike at it. In fact, Admiral Spruance launched the Fifth Fleet under Admiral Marc Mitscher against Truk before Eniwetok had been captured, catching the defenders by surprise and wiping out two hundred aircraft. Admiral Koga's Combined Fleet escaped by withdrawing to Palau, but Spruance's carrier aircraft destroyed 137,000 tons of shipping.

Rabaul was the strongest fortified base in the Pacific, garrisoned by forty-five thousand troops and defended by two hundred aircraft and four hundred anti-aircraft guns. The Americans avoided a frontal assault, and simply subjected it to continuous bombardment. By the end of May the fortress was impotent, and could be left isolated. Meanwhile the submarine offensive was stepped up, sinking nearly 500,000 tons of Japanese shipping in the first five months. Minelaying by aircraft and submarines increased the Japanese losses.

The Royal Navy was making strenuous efforts to assemble a force for the Far East, and by March 1944 Admiral Somerville's Eastern Fleet at Trincomalee in Ceylon (Sri Lanka) included the carrier HMS *Illustrious*, two smaller escort carriers, the battleships HMS *Queen Elizabeth* and HMS *Valiant* and the battlecruiser *Renown*. Pending the arrival of two more carriers, HMS *Formidable* and HMS *Indomitable*, the US Navy lent the large carrier USS *Saratoga* for raids on Sabang and Soerabaya in the East Indies. The smaller British submarines were also able to operate in waters denied to the big American fleet boats, further taxing the over-stretched Japanese escort forces.

In June 1944 the assault on the Marianas precipitated another great carrier battle, the Battle of the Philippine Sea. American submarines sank the carriers *Taiho* and *Shokaku*, and air strikes sank the *Hiyo*. Just under three hundred Japanese aircraft were shot down by the American carrier pilots for the loss of only thirty of their own, an action nicknamed 'The Great Marianas Turkey Shoot'.

The last all-out effort by the Japanese was an attempt to destroy the American amphibious landings in Leyte Gulf in the Philippines in October. The result was the greatest naval battle in history, or more accurately a series of battles over an enormous area. Once again the Japanese plans were over-complex, and partial success was not followed up. The giant battleship *Musashi* was sunk, along with many other ships, and the Imperial Navy never put to sea again as a fleet.

The last big naval operation of the war was the occupation of the Ryukyu Islands, only 800 miles from Japan. The preliminary assault on Iwo Jima in the nearby Bonin Islands proved costly: four thousand Americans killed and seventeen thousand wounded, and twenty-two thousand Japanese killed. The attack on Okinawa on 1 April 1945 was misleadingly easy, but five days later a mass attack by seven hundred aircraft was launched against the Allied ships. About half were *kamikazes*, handpicked volunteers who were to dive onto enemy ships. The British carriers' armoured flight deck saved them from serious damage but several US Navy carriers were severely damaged and the radar picket line of destroyers bore the brunt. The biggest *kamikaze* of all was the battleship *Yamato*, ordered to make a one-way sortie against Okinawa, but sunk by massive air attacks.

In the final phase, the remaining ships of the Imperial Japanese Navy lay in their harbours immobilized by lack of fuel. They were sunk systematically by air strikes from American and British carriers, while battleships bombarded industrial targets with impunity and submarines roamed at will in coastal waters. With hindsight it is easy to say that the two atomic bombs dropped on Hiroshima and Nagasaki were unnecessary, but that sentiment was not shared by the soldiers, marines, sailors and aircrews who would have suffered heavy casualties in an amphibious landing in Japan.

One other major naval power remains to be mentioned, the Soviet Union. Despite having a large number of submarines in the Baltic, Black Sea and Northern Fleets they made very little impression on the Germans. Sailors of the Naval Infantry fought heroically in the defence of Leningrad and Sevastopol, but the Soviet High Command saw the role of the Navy as a means of protecting land flanks, and not a truly independent force. Light forces staged raids behind enemy lines and occasionally submarines scored successes, but the contribution of the Navy to the Great Patriotic War was, by American and British standards, uninspired.

"Pirates from poorer countries rob the travelling stores of wealthier nations, for survival. In this case of maritime mugging, highspeed motorboats have replaced the galleons topped with billowing sails; the booty is no longer spices and gold but the less glamorous and more easily disposed of goods that are seized in any land-based heist — from hairdryers to dollar bills."

J. Stanley: *Bold in Her Breeches* (1995)

CHAPTER SIX

SUPPLYING THE WORLD

Alastair Couper

THERE IS AN OLD SAYING 'THE SEAWAY IS A FREEWAY'. What this means is the buoyancy provided by seawater and the vast open ocean has allowed vehicles of enormous size to be filled with cargoes and moved freely between countries many thousands of miles apart. Furthermore, long before the age of mechanical propulsion, ocean voyaging utilised wind energy that was not only free but also inexhaustible.

With the introduction of fossil fuels in the modern era, ships continued to be the cheapest form of transport, moving thousands of tons of cargo with minimal expenditure of energy and very low cost per ton/mile.

As a result of improvements in ship technology economic distances (as distinct from physical distances) in the world have been greatly reduced. Measured in transport costs a ton of iron ore, for example, can be transported for 10,000 miles by sea cheaper than it can be moved 100 miles on land. Because of these economies, ships transport over 80% of international trade. This has allowed locational specialisations throughout the world in agriculture and manufacturing that serve global markets. Indeed, in the international division of labour some of this trade is actually circulation, with items moving from one country to another by ship and each location contributing a specific processing input towards the final product.

The modern world has thus become highly integrated and dependent on shipping for food, raw materials, energy and manufactured goods – freight by sea moves these goods from origins to destinations with regularity and at minimal costs. The total annual seaborne trade of the world is nearly 5000 million tons, and the value of all the world imports in 1995 came to $4,688,673 million. Of this 6.6% was freight charges.[1]

This chapter concentrates on these developments of maritime trade in the twentieth century. We start with a snapshot of the first great shipping revolution in modern times – the move from sail to steam. This was virtually complete in the western world around 1900. Some seventy years later there was a second shipping revolution (containerisation) which, like the first, had major global impacts; the end of the millennium saw the start of a third revolution driven by electronic commerce and trade liberalisation.

By the mid-nineteenth century merchant ships had changed very little over the previous one hundred years. They were built of wood and with their bluff bows few had any need for speed. The exceptions were mail packets, and ships engaged in slave running and the opium trades.

In 1870 sailing vessels continued to carry most of the raw materials and foodstuffs from European colonial possessions. Grain, sugar, coffee, tea, tobacco, coconut oil, timber, guano, saltpetre, and much more flowed into Europe, and especially to Britain. Outwards went textiles, guns, consumer goods, machinery, anchors and cables, soldiers and settlers, and soon regular cargoes of coal. Britain generated about half of world trade, and more than half of world shipping flew the British flag, or that of a British colony. But the abolition of the British Navigation Acts in 1849 had removed protectionism from British shipping and opened her colonial trade to competition.

The Americans in particular responded to the period of free trade with streamlined wooden clipper ships, such as the *Oriental*. This vessel entered the China tea trade and was so fast compared with traditional British vessels that she commanded double freight rates for tea to London.[2] The 1850s saw the building of many such ships. They made voyages to the Californian Gold Fields and to Australia, and in this boom period made fortunes for their owners. British companies soon bought these new ships from North America.

The American Civil War from 1861 to 1865 curtailed merchant ship building on that side of the Atlantic. British shipyards began to provide even more elegant raked stemmed clippers, like the *Thermophylae* launched in Aberdeen in 1868, which ran from London to Melbourne in fifty-nine days.[3] The *Cutty Sark,* built at Dumbarton in 1870, was an equally fast, handsome tea clipper of 963 tons.

1 UNCTAD, *Review of Maritime Transport*, 1997.
2 Hope, R, *A New History of British Shipping*, 1993, page 293.
3 ibid, page 298.

⇒ SHIP BUILDING – AN ⇐
ASSEMBLY INDUSTRY

The ship has been described as the largest factory-produced product.[1] It has also become mass-produced and transformed from a labour-intensive building process starting at the keel upwards, to a system of prefabrication with modules welded together and lifted on in a building dock. This highly integrated process in modern shipbuilding was facilitated in Japan in particular by commercial linkages. An enterprise such as Mitsubishi had banking, overseas raw materials, steel mills, engineering, shipyards and ships all under its control.

The sequences at the shipyard now involve steel deliveries in appropriate sections, which are then laid out in sequence, retrieved under computer control for rust blasting, trimming, and coating, shaped, and components are then welded together as frames and plate structures, and lifted into place in the building dock by massive gantries.

The various processes in building the ship are computer aided from the design stage onwards and all construction work is generally done under cover in enormous sheds. Many tasks take place simultaneously in sub-assembly plants such as pipe bending and welding. The yards have on-site stocks of pumps, electrical switchboards, winches and many other items and spares for a standard ship by size and type.

One of the basic differences between the old and new industry is the construction of standard ships. In the Hyundai shipyard at Ulsan in South Korea, for example, as many as thirty standard VLCC, OBO and bulk carriers could be under construction at any one time, with work taking place at the same time on accommodation modules, navigational bridges and other units and lifted into place at the appropriate delivery date. In Italy and Finland specialisations are on the less standard cruise ship, but prefabrication is still paramount, except in a few niche markets such as mega-yachts.

After construction, ships are floated out to lie alongside for inside fittings and equipment that have been pre-programmed on a critical path basis to meet undocking times.

At the end of the twentieth century, many of the modern yards geared up for the highly competitive flood of orders which was expected at the start of the new millennium, as a result of the need to replace more than half of the world's commercial fleet, which was over twenty years of age. Obsolescence of other vessels also arose from requirements in structure and design that will be mandatory for ship safety and environmental protection in the near future. Already several of the major yards are into speculative construction in anticipation.

1 Stopford, M, *Maritime Economics*,1988.

These, and many others, were great ships but they appeared just as the industrial revolution reached its peak with iron and steel production and steam energy. The industrial revolution did sustain sail for a brief period for it enabled ships to overcome the limits which wood construction placed on size.

The deathblow to the sailing vessel had actually been struck in 1869 with the opening of the Suez Canal. Sailing vessels were greatly disadvantaged compared with steam ships due to their requirements for tugs in the canal and delays with variable winds. For steam ships the distance to the Far East was reduced using the canal by 3000 miles and coaling stations were established at Suez, Aden, Bombay, Colombo, Penang and Singapore.

The men who crewed ships during these last days of sail, faced a hard life. To compete with steam every economy was made and risks taken. In 1896, one in sixty seamen still lost their lives on board British ships (more deaths than coal mining) whereas on the new steam driven vessels the death rate, while still high, was reduced to one in one hundred and seventeen.[4] Many on sailing ships were killed falling from high rigging, others were lost overboard when hauling on ropes on deck in bad weather. A sailor recalls a near escape: 'When slithering about on deck . . .' a hand will catch you, and a voice, "By Christ you were near for it then weren't you?".[5] They had not only to look after themselves but also their shipmates. It was a tough but highly mutually dependant community on these ships. Some survived throughout the First World War, and Norwegian, Swedish and Greek Captain-owners continued to compete with their low cost ships into the 1920s.

It would be mistakenly Eurocentric to give the impression that commercial sail has totally disappeared from the seas. The most ancient of sailing vessels – the Chinese Junk – with its high bluff bow and batten sails, continues to trade. Some of them have had hull modifications towards a western style, and many more are motorised, but once in the open sea they are under sail. Yet others retain sails and main characteristics but have been built of pre-stressed concrete.[6]

Similarly, in the Indonesian Archipelago wooden sailing vessels are still built in the villages of South Sulawesi, and are operated as of old by Boganese seafarers. With luck one can still see the handsome Pinisi crossing between Ujung Pandung and Suribaya. In the port of Titicoran in Southern India, big wooden vessels

4 Säger, E, *Seafaring Labour, The Merchant Marine of Atlantic Canada, 1820-1914*, 1989, page130.
5 ibid, page 224.
6 Dequng, P, *Ships of China* , 1988.

entirely dependant on sail unload cargoes from Ceylon and the Maldive Islands, and, in the Dhow Harbour at Mombassa sailing vessels can be seen (again, however, all with auxiliary engines). In the Caribbean sail schooners carry out their vital trading functions between islands.[7]

Finally, we might note attempts to revive sail in the longer commercial routes. The main problem was the concern for keeping schedules and the need for employing large crews to work the rigging. The new approach was to design sail-assisted vessels rather than sailing ships. Primarily, the sails were controlled by computer that trimmed them to the angles required to get maximum benefit from the wind. These ships like the *Shin Ciitobu Maru*, a tanker of 1600dwt, were power propelled but when the wind came away the computer automatically reduced the engine output and allowed the wind to supplement and retain the speed of the ship. At least one bulk carrier was trading in this way between Japan and North America. Other ships had wind turbines, turbo sails and other wind-assisted propulsion devices.

In terms of economics there appeared only small gains from wind-assisted ships, on the other hand, they were certainly energy saving and had environmental benefits.[8]

The great advantage of steam propulsion was that it freed ships from following long wind-determined passages, delays when beating against adverse winds, and the frustration of waiting for wind under calms. The period from 1820 to 1880 was one of invention, experimentation and developments in steam. In 1865 compound engines (that used the steam twice) were introduced lowering coal consumption; and in 1881, the SS *Aberdeen* was launched with a triple expansion engine. She was able to make a passage from Plymouth to Melbourne in forty-two days, coaling on the way.[9] Fast, regular liner shipping was now well established.

Cargo liners operated advertised scheduled services to a range of ports over their routes. They were multi-decked vessels, and carried thousands of separate consignments packed in boxes, bags, bales, barrels and crates. Livestock, heavy machinery and railway engines would be carried on deck. On return voyages cargo included tea, coffee, cotton, wool, latex, vegetable oils, refrigerated meats, dairy produce, and fruit, and on deck, tropical hardwoods, according to the

7 Couper, A D, *The Problems of International Transport* , 1990.
8 Couper, A D, 'The Practicality of Commercial Sail', *Journal of Navigation*, 1997, pages 163-171.
9 Falconer, J, *Sail on Steam 1840-1935*, 1993, page13.

SHIP ARCHITECTURE

Peter Quartermaine

The very considerable stresses to which ships are regularly subject in their seagoing work, together with regularly upgraded safety regulations, mean that standards to which modern ships must be built are unparalleled except in aviation. The quality of the basic materials, the building process itself and the overall design and operation of the vessel are all subject to stringent controls at every stage. Moreover, Computer Assisted Design (CAD) now means that every aspect of a planned vessel, from stability to detailed cabin decor, can be studied in detail before any actual construction starts; this not only greatly reduces planning costs but also means that modifications can be made efficiently by calling up the original plans.

Prior to such technology, every detail of a ship's basic construction was drawn full-size (later one tenth size) in chalk by skilled draughtsmen in a mould loft at the shipyard. These intricate shapes were precisely transferred to steel plates which were cut and then joined by rivets which were inserted red-hot and their heads swiftly beaten down; as they cooled contraction held the plates tightly together. The Second World War German battlecruiser *Scharnhorst* and

trading regions. The refrigerated liner ('reefer') transformed farming in South America, Australia and New Zealand. In the 1890s, ships like the 5534 GRT *Buteshire* had full cargoes of frozen products.[10] Most liners had accommodation for twelve passengers, and would carry mail and bullion.

British liner companies such as Blue Funnel, P&O, Royal Mail, and Elder Dempsters, had distinctive ships and specific routes, as did their foreign competitors, the Hamburg America Line, the French Messageries Maritimes, and the Dutch, Italian and Japanese companies.

On several routes these companies began to agree sailing schedules, and formed Conferences that fixed freight rates and, under a closed system, limited the number of entrants to the trade. The only competition permitted between Conference members related to the quality of service offered to shippers. The closed liner Conferences – and about one hundred and thirty of them were eventually formed – were ultimately prohibited on trades to and from the United States as a violation of Anti-Trust laws. They survived to this day, albeit with

10 Marradon, J, 'Refrigerated Transport' in Couper, A D, *The Shipping Revolution,* 1992, page 15.

pocket battleship *Admiral Graf Spee* were the first large ships to be welded, a method in which molten metal rapidly joins the steel plates edge to edge, giving a smooth surface and saving weight. First widely employed in constructing emergency 'Liberty ships' during World War Two, it is universally used today in ship construction, with very large sections often being constructed offsite and brought to the shipyard, itself often covered, at an advanced stage of completion. In the modern cruise liner, for example, not only may complete cabins arrive as modules to be fitted into carefully prepared sites on board (with the possibility of re-arrangement at a later date) but, as with the 1998 *Disney Magic*, a whole bow may even be built elsewhere and towed to the main shipyard for welding to the hull.

Ships have always been the largest mobile objects created by mankind, and seem likely to remain so until the permanent space station 'cities' of science fiction become a reality. As such their design, construction, operation and maintenance all require a wide range of advanced skills, though some of these vary depending on whether the ship in question is a cargo vessel, warship or passenger vessel. A tanker or dry cargo vessel is (to overstate the case) basically a large floating container with added engine and crew quarters; but the function of both warships and passenger vessels demands highly complex and detailed fitting-out at the ➤

reduced powers.

The great passenger liners were likewise a product of this period at the turn of the century. Several companies under the same flag combined, and competed on a national basis for passengers, speed, size, and luxury in crossing the Atlantic, and on voyages to the Far East.

The opening of the Panama Canal in 1914, was of great value to the United States in their growing inter-coastal trade, and to Japan in penetrating American and European trading areas. It offered new routes to West Coast South America and to New Zealand. The dimensional limits of the Canal did, however, curtail the size of ship on these inter-oceanic passages until recent times.

While many cargo liners were splendid looking ships and were associated with trade in high valued goods, the workhorse of the sea was the tramp steamer. These carried full loads of lower valued cargoes such as grains, coals, ores, fertilisers, sugar, copra, timber, and scrap. Tramp ships made many voyages under ballast to pick up their next cargo. The availability of ships and cargo was facilitated by the use of the new submarine telegraph communications.

The method of charging for the carriage of bulk cargoes was different from that

➤ construction stage, as well as skilled service and maintenance, to remain at a high state of readiness throughout their working lives. The 'working life' of any ship in fact varies greatly, depending not only on its build quality but also on the cargo carried (bulk-loaded heavy iron ore produces punishing hull stresses) and on other unpredictable factors (warships are very susceptible to political, as well as technological, developments which can render them obsolete).

Quite apart from the highly complex technical calculations which determine the safety and operational efficiency of any vessel, ship architecture can also claim to be architecture in the true sense: ships are multifunctional working environments for their crews and, in the case of modern cruise liners, floating entertainment environments for some three thousand five hundred passengers, plus a crew of around one thousand five hundred. With cruise vessels that need to sell themselves in a highly competitive market, the appearance of the ship (initially in a colour brochure, later in reality as the passenger approaches and

of the administered Conference rates in the liner trades. Tramp ships were hired to carry full shiploads either for single voyages between two countries (a voyage charter) or for a number of voyages over a specified time (time charter). Alternatively, a charterer could take over a ship for a protracted period and virtually become the owner including supplying the crew (bareboat charter).

The centre for fixing charters between cargo interests and shipowners was, and still is principally, the Baltic Exchange. Here, on the basis of availability of ships and the requirements for cargoes in different parts of the world, freight rates were determined by supply and demand. Consequently tramp rates are far more volatile than the rates for liner cargoes.

The British, Norwegian and Greek were very active in tramp shipping in the early part of the century. In 1906, for example, Captain Syrmos from the Island of Andros in Greece came to Sunderland to join the newly built tramp steamer *Andriana* of 1867 NRT. He had with him his son Theodores as second mate. This was very typical of Greek shipping, with the owner, Captain and crew coming from the same island. Similarly in Norway there were strong kinship ties amongst a crew, and certainly in Britain tramp companies based in Glasgow, Cardiff, Liverpool and Tyneside would sign on local crews.

The voyages of the *Andriana* were typical of Greek tramps at the time. From July 1906 until January 1907 the pattern of trading (with ballast-legs) was: Newcastle to Marseilles (coal); Achtory to Bremerhaven (grain); Cardiff to Naples (coal); and Brucla to Antwerp (grain). The ship, which had a cost of £27,600 in boards) is crucial. Modern vessels increasingly often adopt upperworks styling which might be thought more appropriate to fast cars – and which certainly is required not by their modest speeds, and mostly boxy hull, but rather by passengers' expectations. More widely, naval architects have always sought to give their vessels character and proportion, and in this respect cargo vessels can certainly be as attractive as other ships. The modern container ship is as different from the traditional cargo ships as the modern cruise ship is from earlier liners; one characteristic they have in common as examples of ship architecture is that, no matter how much we may delight in their appearance, we rarely know who designed them. The design of ships is typically the work of committed experts whose technical knowledge is matched by a love of their work and an alertness to maritime tradition and innovation alike. Ship architecture is an unjustly neglected example of human creativity – and of our enduring wish to make functional things as beautiful as we can.

Sunderland, was paid for within four years. However, when Captain Syrmos requested a holiday 'to have a little rest' after ten years continuous work, he was refused but told he could resign. He replied, "I will not leave my position until the time comes to be replaced by my son".[11]

The crew of a Greek ship of the size of Captain Syrmos' in 1906 was about twenty-eight. By 1912 a cargo steamer of 7770 tons could have forty-three men on deck and thirty-four in the engine room. A ship's company had now changed radically from the days of sail, with the addition of Engineers, Donkeymen, Greasers, Firemen and Trimmers.[12] There were reductions in engine room labour when the diesel engine was adopted after 1910.

At the turn of the century specially designed tankers appeared for the carriage of oil. The first bulk oil carrier was the *Gluckauf* in 1886.[13] After that, and especially with the advances in the internal combustion engine, oil became vital. Tanker fleets grew fast and were owned by the major oil companies, which chartered in additional tonnage from independent owners when required. The oil refineries were established at ports close to the oil fields, and the tankers carried products to terminals near market areas. These were vessels of around 3000 tons with subdivided tanks, and by the 1920s had the engine room aft. The basic design of tankers remained much the same until the giants of the 1960s when the

11 Horlaftis, G, *A History of Greek Owned Shipping*, 1996, page 157.
12 Hope, R, 1990, page 342.
13 King, G A B, *Tanker Practice*.

PIRACY AND
POLICING THE OCEANS

Pirates have seldom, if ever, been the romantic figures of fiction. Some were privateers authorised by states to take merchant ships of unfriendly countries. Others were buccaneers operating from island bases in the Caribbean and elsewhere against any ship presenting opportunities for pillage. Elsewhere, as off the Barbary Coast of North Africa, immunity could be purchased against pirate attacks by payments to state rulers.

Some modern pirates also appear to have the sanctions of local officials and security forces in their marauding. Many work with military precision and have sophisticated communication back up. They are linked to informants who can provide computerised data derived from shipping agents on the time a ship will sail, its cargo, stowage plan, speed, crew nationality, destination and route. The ship will then be intercepted by high speed craft and boarded, robbed, or hijacked.[1]

Pirate attacks on merchant shipping are on the increase. This has been attributed to the decline in naval forces since the end of the Cold War, civil upheaval in many countries, and lack of the will and finance to combat pirates.[2] Table A indicates the sea areas where pirate activities have been most prevalent, and Table B indicates the nature of the attacks.[3]

Sometimes considerable violence is used and seafarers have met ugly deaths. In 1997 there were also reports of four hundred and twelve seafarers being held as hostages by pirates.[4] In the case of hijacking there is a similar disregard for the crew. The cargo ship *Anna Sierra* (13,000dwt) was boarded in the Gulf of Thailand in September 1995 by '30 pirates armed with machine guns, pistols, and knives'. They set the crew adrift in a small boat and raft, renamed the ship *Arctic Sea*, and sold the cargo of sugar in the South China port of Beiha.

Pirates are outlawed by the Law of the Sea; and, as with slave traders and drug smugglers their ships can be arrested on the high seas by the naval forces of any country. Unfortunately, they seldom are, and the distress signal 'Piracy Attack' which has been introduced through the marine satellite system Inmarsat C has been ignored.

The International Maritime Bureau (IMB) which is London-based investigates pirate attacks, but does not always receive co-operation from

bridge and accommodation were also constructed aft.

By the outbreak of the First World War in 1914, coal- and oil-powered ships had tied the world into a massive trading system with far-flung interdependencies. During the war neutral shipping expanded in both tramp and governments. The IMB has issued guidelines for ships in pirate-prone waters. Other policing activities at sea relate to illegal fishing. This is normally undertaken within the 200 nautical miles Exclusive Economic Zones of countries by the Coastguards and the Fishery Protection Services. There are also some attempts to enforce prohibitions on drift net fishing, whaling moratoriums, and access to certain Antarctic fish stocks through international co-operation.

There are a vast number of international conventions, including those on safety of life at sea and protection of the marine environment, and the very comprehensive 1982 Law of the Sea Convention, which govern activities in all zones of the ocean. However, the implementation of law and policing depends not only on actions at sea but to a very considerable extent on the enforcement by the state whose flag a ship is flying (Flag State), and on the actions of states into whose ports offenders enter (Port State Control).

1 'Records of ship movement transmitted to pirates', *Trade Winds*, Feb 1993, page 18.
2 Ellen, E, 'Piracy: A myriad of reasons, but a simple solution', *BIMCO Bulletin*, Vol 92, No. 1.
3 *Lloyds List 27*, Nov 1995 and *Lloyds List 16*, Oct 1996.
4 *Telegraph*, NUMAST, Vol 31, No 2, Feb 1998, page 1.

Table A Piracy Incidents – 1995

Area	No. of Violent Incidents
Indonesia	34
China	29
Brazil	17
Somalia	14
Hong Kong	12

Other incidents reported in:
Iran, West Africa,
East Africa,
Arabian Peninsula

Source: International Maritime Bureau, London

Table B 1995 Main Types Reported

Boarding	37
Attempted Boarding	15
Hijack	12
Fired on	9
Detained	8
In-Port Attacks	5

Source: International Maritime Bureau, London

liner markets, with the increased demand for cargoes and the withdrawal of British vessels from traditional routes both contributing to this. The latter became concentrated on carrying supplies to the home country and for the war effort. The United States experienced a scarcity of shipping and likewise expanded their merchant navy and building programmes. This was stimulated further by the entry of America into the war.

The British lost nearly half of their merchant ships due to enemy action, along with about twenty-one thousand merchant seamen from actions, accidents, and disease.[14] Merchant shipping was recognised as playing a vital role in war. The enemy realised that to win the war merchant ships had to be stopped, particularly oil tankers, the cargoes of which had become indispensable.

The importance of food, ammunition and oil by merchant ships was identified even more closely at the outbreak of the Second World War. Indeed, only hours after the war broke out a British merchant ship was attacked and sunk. The Atlantic was clearly the lifeline and vessels were subject to attacks by submarines, surface raiders, and aircraft, and exposed to mines. During 1940 over three million GRT of British and Allied merchant ships were sunk. But even neutral vessels were regularly attacked. Passenger ships were converted to troop ships and the movements of a large part of the world's merchant fleets were determined by the war.

Winning the war meant winning the Battle of the Atlantic. This was a struggle to maintain lines of communication by sea. It depended on providing protection for merchant ships under convoy, sinking U-boats and replacing vessels and seamen lost. New technology in finding and sinking U-boats was introduced, and by 1943 shipyards reached an output of ships exceeding those being lost. In America the Liberty ship, an oil-burning, all-welded tramp vessel capable of about 10 knots, was being built, each taking forty-two days to complete. Between 1941 and 1945, two thousand seven hundred and ten of these came into operation. Another vital component was the 16,400dwt T2 Tanker also built in North America.

In the course of the war, British merchant seafarer casualties reached fifty thousand five hundred and twenty-five individuals.[15] As a percentage of forces involved, the merchant navy had the highest rate of casualties.

After the Second World War merchant shipping entered an era of relative prosperity for shipowners and seafarers in most countries. But not right away:

> I always remember being on an old tramp ship when the war finished and the mate said 'okay you all now had a bloody good time, get the chipping hammers out and start hammering off

14 Hope, R, 1990, pages 349-356.
15 ibid, page 382

the grey paint. The Ministry of Transport have been paying you all that time, now get cracking and start earning your cash'." [16]

The ships were repainted back to company colours. Then the United States had the largest merchant navy. They formed over two thousand into a reserve fleet, anticipating other wars. There were still many liberty ships beyond US requirements; these they sold at bargain prices. The biggest buyers were Greek shipowners and they operated these ships into the 1960s. However, Greece at the end of the war was politically unstable, and sales were made with the understanding that registration would be under the flag of Panama, as a precaution against the ships falling into the hands of a government unfriendly to western powers. So started the first use of flag of convenience in the modern era, a procedure which, for other reasons, was to escalate in subsequent years.

Shipping went through a period of prosperity until 1956, and a veritable boom in that year with the closure of the Suez Canal during the conflict involving Britain, Egypt, France and Israel. Freight rates soared as tankers, and many dry cargo vessels, were diverted to the longer route around the Cape. This precipitated a surge in orders for bigger ships. When the Canal re-opened in 1957 there was surplus shipping and building capacity, and a fall in freight rates. This continued until the Canal was closed in 1967 and remained so until 1974, once again leading to vast earnings.

A revolution in the size and design of ships was now underway. Bulk carriers of 150,000dwt and above were in service, and in 1973 the tanker *Globtik Tokyo* of 493,664dwt was launched. Ships were being built for specialised cargoes and the first container vessel in international trade was already in service by 1969 displacing break bulk liners. The emphasis was now on economies of scale with ships designed for long hauls by-passing Suez. This, however, did not anticipate the actions by OPEC in 1973 to raise the price of oil and cut back production that resulted in a world economic crisis. The huge surplus of shipping became more evident with the re-opening of the Suez Canal in 1974.

The concept of packing general cargo into a container and loading the container onto the vessel was introduced on the United States Coast by Malcolm McLean in 1956. It was further developed by the Matson Line in their trade to Hawaii. This unit load system was introduced to international trade with enormous impact. The container became standardised in units of 10ft, 20ft, 30ft,

16 Pack, J, recorded for Couper, A D, *The British Seafarer*, BBC, 1980.

and 40ft x 8ft x 8.5ft. The carrying capacity of a container ship is therefore expressed in 20ft equivalent units (TEUs).

The cellular container vessels with their cell guidance systems in holds and ultimately a height of five containers on deck appeared in the late 1960s on the Atlantic and Pacific routes, in 1969 on Europe-Australia, and the 1970s on Europe-Far East routes. Vessels grew in size from 1000 to 5000 TEUs and in tonnage to almost 60,000 GRT.[17] A constraining factor in the size of ship was the Panama Canal with limits to less than 39m breadth in the locks. Several ships now exceed this (Post Panamax) and they trade primarily on US West Coast to the Far East, and Europe to the Far East.

The roll on-roll off (ro-ro) vessels were also revolutionary in carrying wheeled vehicles with containers on coastal and short sea routes. Deep-sea ro-ro came into operation in the 1970s and quite large vessels like the *Atlantic Conveyor* carry near 3000 TEUs.

The barge carrying vessels (BCV) were also a unitised development. Barges could be lifted (LASH ships) or floated (Seabee) fully laden into the BCV and carried overseas to enter inland waterways on discharge. These were however only of limited success in particular regions.

Enormous investment was made in the container ship system, and new companies such as Evergreen, which developed over fifty container vessels, rose in Taiwan. The container ship has grown to the giant *Regina Maersk* with six thousand containers, and the 1999 mega-carriers of 7700 TEU, nearly a quarter of a mile long. These superships operate to a few hub ports to connect with smaller feeder container ships for onward movement.

The oil trade is conducted by so-called clean and dirty tankers. The former are the product carriers. These operate from refineries and are of sizes up to about 70,000dwt. They range around many ports carrying fuel oil, diesel, kerosene, petrol and other lighter distillates. The latter ships are crude oil carriers hauling cargoes from pipeline terminals in the Middle East, West Africa and the Caribbean, as well as in more recent years from North Sea loading points and the Valdez terminal of the Alaska pipeline.

The triggers in the tanker size revolution were: the shift of refineries from resource to market oriented locations; the geopolitics of the Middle East and closures of the Suez Canal; and the economies of scale evident in the haulage of homogenous crude oil from limited areas of supply to areas of enormous demand.

17 Gilman, S, 'Container Shipping' in Couper, A D, *The Shipping Revolution*, 1992, pages 42-69.

1. HMS *Dreadnought*. Launched on 10 February 1906, *Dreadnought* was a revolutionary ship and she set the standard for other battleship designs to match early in the twentieth century.

2. A *U-151* class U-boat. The *U-151* class served the German Navy in the First World War. Early submarine tactics included surfacing and using the deck guns (clearly shown in this photograph) against targets, until the anti-U-boat war made this a dangerous method of assault.

3. An impressive aerial view of the West Side docks, New York (photographed in 1960). Ocean-going passenger liners berthed in New York at Manhattan's West Side docks; on the right of the photo is the liner *United States*.

4. The Blue Riband trophy. This trophy was awarded to the ship that made the fastest Atlantic crossing, and was unofficially – yet very enthusiastically – competed for by liners from 1840 to 1952.

5. The US icebreaker *Atka*, dwarfed by a giant iceberg drifting in McMurdo Sound, Antarctica. Taken in the 1960s, the iceberg shown in the photograph is 'Moby Dick" – weighing one and a half million tons, estimated to be 500ft long, 200ft wide and 100ft high.

6. The Soviet nuclear submarine *Leninsky Komsomol*. In this photograph, the submarine is shown surfacing through ice near the North Pole in 1963.

7. A destroyer crew in 1941. In the war at sea, enemy ships were not the only danger to a ship's crew – the age-old battle between the mariner and the elements also continued. Note that some of this photograph's detail did not escape the wartime censor's eye, and was deleted (on the horizon and on the left side of the photograph).

8. HMS *Hood*, photographed in 1937. The ageing battlecruiser *Hood* was the pride of the Royal Navy, but was sunk in May 1941 by the German *Bismarck* and *Prinz Eugen*.

9. *U-69* photographed on 19 September 1940. This unusual photograph shows the whole of a German U-boat submarine above water in a wartime dockyard.

10. The inter-war American battlefleet in formation for concerted action off San Pedro, California.

11. The Italian battleship *Roma*, photographed in 1942. A German radio-controlled bomb sank *Roma* on 9 September 1943, as retribution for Italy's attempt to sue for peace with the Allies.

12. Swedish fishing ketches photographed alongside their wharf. Although less glamorous than their liner and battleship sisters, fishing ships are amongst the most numerous vessels to put to sea.

13. Fishermen at work. These fishermen, from Kamchatka in Russia, are clearly working in better sea conditions than the destroyer crew in plate 7; the catch being emptied comprises of calico and salmon, and is part of the two million fish that Kamchatka fishermen expected to trawl each spring and summer.

14. *Shamrock V.* Sir Thomas Lipton's last challenger for the America's Cup was built in 1930 as a J class vessel.

15. *Carina II.* A typical ocean racer of the mid-twentieth century, *Carina II* won the Fastnet Race twice when owned by the American yachtsman Dick Nye. She was one of the first ocean racers to have synthetic sails.

16. The launching of the *Regent Liverpool*. On 5 April 1962, *Regent Liverpool* was launched at the Harland and Wolff shipyard in Belfast. At 47,600dwt and an overall length of 746ft, she was the largest tanker built in Belfast up to that time.

17. The *Queen Elizabeth*. Photographed leaving Southampton in 1954, after an annual overhaul. The dwarfed tugs and buildings around her put the size of the *Queen Elizabeth* into context.

18. *Costa Victoria*, the largest cruise ship ever built in Germany. Photographed in 1997, *Costa Victoria* is shown to be an imposing ship of massive proportions.

19. USS *Independence* after atomic tests. The first atom bomb tests were carried out on 1 July 1946. In this photograph, the aircraft carrier *Independence* bears little resemblance to the ship that entered Bikini Atoll a few days earlier, and stands as a stark reminder of the power of atomic and nuclear weapons.

20. HMS *Victorious* photographed in the Mediterranean in 1967. In this photograph the Royal Navy aircraft carrier is being refuelled and its stores replenished by RFA *Wave Baron* and RFA *Lyness*.

21. USS *Ticonderoga* photographed in the Suez Canal, 1990. *Ticonderoga* typifies modern warships – her main armament is her missiles, with the prominent bow-mounted cannon a secondary weapon.

22. Exploration beneath the waves. A skin diver illuminates an undersea exploration vehicle designed and built by Jacques-Yves Cousteau. The vehicle was capable of operating at depths of up to 1000ft and had a submerged speed of 1.5 knots.

23. The *Torrey Canyon* disaster, 1967. Waves break over the hulk of the tanker as she lays in two, stuck fast off the Isles of Scilly. Later in the day, she was bombed from the air to fire the crude oil gushing from the vessel.

24. An aerial view of the fire aboard the *Johannishus* in 1955. The Swedish tanker collided with the Panamanian freighter *Buccaneer* in the English Channel; flames from the blazing oil cargo can be seen in the water, whilst smoke billows into the air.

The sizes of crude oil tankers moved rapidly from the wartime T2 of 16,400dwt, to ships of 35,000dwt in the late 1950s and the very large crude carriers (VLCC) of 250,000dwt in the 1970s. These were followed by ultra large crude carriers (ULCC) like the seaways giant of 564,000dwt in the 1980s.

The giant ships reduced the cost per ton of oil carried, but when the Suez Canal re-opened in 1973, and OPEC increased the price of oil and restricted supply, there was a major recession. Surplus ships were a feature of the world market from then on, this was accompanied by low freight rates, low rates of return, and a search for further economies in design, building, propulsion and crewing.

The concern over pollution of the sea from tanker operations and accidents also resulted in new ship structural and procedural regulations. These were made mandatory by governments under the International Maritime Organisation Conventions. A major development in this respect followed the grounding of the *Exxon Valdez* in Alaska, which resulted in the requirement that tankers were built with double hulls.

Other types of tankers were designed for the carriage of chemicals. The chemical industry throughout the world moves a great variety of liquid substances, many highly dangerous, and the tankers that carry them are built in classes according to the degrees of risk from the cargoes. Some carry a number of separate parcels of chemicals, others are designed for single products such as phosphoric acid. The liquefied gas carriers are the most complex and expensive of these specialised tankers. Natural gas can be reduced in volume by a factor of six hundred by liquefaction. It is then transported on ocean voyages by ships of around 70,000dwt in which the liquid is maintained at -162°C.

There are still some small tramps in the bulk cargo market, and remnants of the liberty successors such as the British SD14 and the Japanese Freedom class of ship. Now the multi-purpose tramp is the 'handy size' bulker of 20,000-40,000dwt. These may act as feeders from large port stock piles for onward shipment. They also move around the world transporting many of the minor bulk cargoes including sugar, cement, salt, sulphur, scrap, where and when required.

The major bulk trades are in iron ore, coal, and grain. These tend to move in very large specialised ships. The ships fall into three categories by trading routes: roughly Panamax 60,000dwt, Suezmax 120,000dwt and Capesize above 120,000dwt. The biggest bulk carriers reached 350,000dwt in the 1980s. In terms of cargoes there are single-purpose vessels such as iron ore carriers, but also multi-purpose. The latter comprise Ore-Oil (OO) and Ore-Bulk-Oil (OBO).

Table 1: Top Twelve Maritime Countries – 1996

Country or territory of controlling interest	No. of Vessels		
	National flag	Foreign flag	Total
Greece	912	2003	2915
Japan	922	1829	2751
United States	482	732	1214
Norway	836	568	1404
China	1594	38	1972
Hong Kong	104	503	607
Republic of Korea	501	303	804
United Kingdom	388	510	898
Germany	478	984	1462
Russian Federation	2595	239	2834
Taiwan Province of China	179	254	2834

Source: Lloyd's Maritime Information Services Ltd (London)

These are designed to move between markets and also minimise ballast voyages.

The bulk carriers are generally on charter, the big end user companies have mainly disposed of their own fleets so as to hire ships of independent owners at low freight rates. There are also small bulkers engaged in coastal trades, and the River Sea ships of 1500-1700dwt capable of making long ingresses into inland areas with bulk cargoes, and also containers. In addition there are many specialised ships designed for the carriage of radioactive waste, livestock, cars, forest products, wine, fruit juice, molasses, sulphur, phosphoric acid, asphalt, and cement. There are also (for containers and bulk) pusher tug and barge systems with capacities of 40,000 tons.

The second shipping revolution saw a transformation in shipowning and seafaring. To reduce costs there was a transfer of ship registrations to Flags of Convenience thereby avoiding taxes and enabling crew recruitment globally. In addition there was a rise of new shipping companies in the Far East. Table 1 shows the top twelve maritime countries by numbers of ships and the ship distribution between national and foreign flags, out of a world cargo fleet of 28,754 vessels (above 1000 GRT/1996). In terms of tonnage over half of the

Table 2: Top Twelve Seafarer Supplying Countries 1995

1.	Philippines	224782
2.	Indonesia	83500
3.	Turkey	80000
4.	China	76482
5.	India	53000
6.	Russia	47688
7.	Japan	42537
8.	Greece	40000
9.	Ukraine	38000
10.	Italy	32000
11.	USA – Lakes	30871
12.	United Kingdom	23500

Source: BIMCO/ISF 1995

world fleet now sails under FOC – primarily Liberia, Panama, Cyprus and Bahamas.

Crew sizes have been reduced steadily, from forty-five to twenty on tankers and dry bulk, and to twelve on some reefers. Engine rooms are now frequently unmanned and crews are multi-skilled. There are about one and a quarter million merchant seafarers in the world. Table 2 shows the top twelve countries (out of forty) from which they are drawn. As a result of globalisation in recruitment most merchant ships have multi-national crewing.

An even more dramatic locational change has taken place in shipbuilding. The move has once again been predominantly from Europe to Asia, and there has been a transformation of the industry from that of labour-intensive construction, to computer-assisted and assembly processes. At the turn of the century, three-quarters of all merchant ships launched in the world were from British yards. This supremacy was gradually eroded and, after the Second World War, completely overwhelmed by new centres of shipbuilding.

Japan by the 1950s was on the ascendancy, followed by South Korea and subsequently Taiwan, Brazil and eventually China. The boom period from 1950 until 1974 saw a massive increase in building capacity, and methods of building. This was followed by a world recession and a vast surplus of ships.

Table 3: New Completions (1000 GRT) Top Ten Countries – 1996

Japan	10182
South Korea	7374
Germany	1202
China	1148
Poland	629
Spain	616
Denmark	492
Taiwan	454
Russia	299

Source: BIMCO/ISF 1996

Shipyards in the Far East continued to build, often speculatively, and were aided by government support and generous credit terms to world shipowners. In 1996 surplus tanker tonnage was 10% and bulk carriers 17%. The new completions in that year for the top ten producer countries are shown in Table 3. Britain in 1996 launched only 187,000 GRT and the US 25,000 GRT, which are well down the building league.

The impact of the revolution in shipping on the seaports of the world has been totally pervasive. Ports have been moved out of the urban locations in which they originally developed, downstream to deep-water sites. They have become more specialised to receive specific types of ships and cargoes, and to fit road, rail and waterway infrastructure for uninterrupted onward movement. There has been enormous investment in massive port equipment for container handling and bulk loading and unloading. Consequently there are high levels of mechanisation and automation and there have been major reductions in the number of people employed. Most ports, like most modern ships, are now high-tech and highly competitive enterprises.

It is usually only at small ports that ships and the flow of cargoes can still be seen, as the big container and industrial ports are not generally accessible to people. Even less visible is the continuous movement over the world ocean of the thousands of ships engaged in carrying fuel, raw materials, food and manufactured products which keep industry going and fill the showrooms and shops. The great tankers and bulkers are like an interrupted pipeline linking world resources to processing plants. Container ships have cargoes geared to just-in-time programmes between manufacturers and consumers, and reefers even out imbalances in the seasonal supply and demand for fruit and vegetables globally.

These vital and largely unobserved movements over the world ocean depend on freedom of the high seas, seaworthiness of ships, the skills of seafarers and port efficiency. There are storms and many other dangers to face – including a revival of piracy – but for all that, and despite some well-publicised accidents, sea transport is still the safest, cheapest and most environmentally-friendly method of carrying goodsacross the world.

At about three in the morning I awoke again to the sound of a rushing squall, and hurried aft to find Beryl with the mizzen already down . . . I could see her momentarily leaning over the boom as she tied the sail, one foot on the tiller to prevent Tzu Hang *coming up into the wind.*

Miles Smeeton: *Because the Horn Is There* (1970)

CHAPTER SEVEN

LEISURE SAILING IN THE TWENTIETH CENTURY

Ian Dear

B Y 1900 SAILING WAS ALREADY a well-established, worldwide pastime for the moneyed classes. But at first the development of it lay in the hands of Britain and the United States, for together they then owned five times more sailing yachts than all other countries combined. Yacht clubs were already in place around their coastlines, catering for those who wished to race their small keel dayboats as well as those who cruised or raced in larger yachts. The exception was the elite Royal Yacht Squadron whose attitude was summed up by the couplet:

> Nothing less than 40T [tons]
> May ever race with our burgee.

By the end of the first decade, British organizations such as the Cruising Club and the Cruising Association had already been founded, though the former's American equivalent, the Cruising Club of America, was not started until 1922. In 1910 a knowledgeable proponent of cruising in open waters, Claud Worth, wrote a book called *Yacht Cruising* which defined exactly what this meant to a yachtsman of his era:

> It could be either a pastime or a sport.
> To sail from port to port by easy stages in picked

weather is a most pleasant *pastime*. To make an open
sea cruise in a seaworthy little yacht, neither
courting unnecessary risks nor being unduly anxious
as to weather, and having confidence in one's
knowledge and skill to overcome such difficulties as
may arise, is, to one who loves the sea, the most
perfectly satisfying of all forms of sport.

The difference is worth bearing in mind when considering the exploits of some
sailors during the latter half of the century. More explorers than yachtsmen, they
answered an inner challenge by setting astonishing new standards for cruising as
a *sport*; while the idyllic wanderings of most nautical globetrotters would fall into
the category of *pastime*, as neither the goals of time nor place ranked with them
beside the sheer pleasure of cruising for its own sake.

However, during the first quarter of the century the inner challenge was largely
unexpressed, for publicly taking risks at sea in order to achieve any sort of goal
would have been condemned as unseamanlike; Claud Worth was among those
who opposed ocean racing when it was first proposed in British waters in 1925.

Before this date ocean racing, with amateurs (or 'Corinthians' as they were
called) at the helm, was unheard of in Europe where professional paid hands were
hired to do the sailing. But in America it flowered briefly when, in 1904, the
editor of *Rudder*, Thomas Fleming Day, suggested a 300-mile race between New
York and Marblehead. He was roundly criticized for doing so – just as were those
pioneers who organized the first Ocean Race in British waters. But while their
robust defence of the new sport was clothed in gentlemanly terms, Day's was
vitriolic:

What do these miserable old hulks, who spend
their days swigging booze on the front stoop of
a clubhouse, know about the dangers of the deep?
If they ever make a voyage from Larchmont to Cow
Bay in a ten-knot breeze it is the event of their
lives, an experience they never forget and never
want to repeat. What does the average yachtsman
know about sea sailing? Absolutely nothing! Then
let him hold his tongue.

The Marblehead Race was followed by others along the eastern coastline. In

1906, Day organized the first 600-mile Bermuda Race, and the inaugural 2250-mile Transpac Race from Los Angeles to Honolulu was also held. Both events attracted only a handful of amateur yachtsmen, and by 1912 both races were defunct. But the amateurs who skippered yachts in them were the real pioneers of modern ocean racing; while the rich gentlemen who entered the 1905 Transatlantic Race – in yachts of large tonnage, even square-rigged ones, manned by professional paid hands – were definitely not.

Though ocean racing was still in its infancy before the First World War, inshore racing for small keel yachts and their larger brethren had been well established for decades. But the method of handicapping was crude and the development of sails, rigging and hull, with speed solely in mind, was still at an elementary stage. Keel yachts, whatever their size, were usually gaff rigged, for it took time for designers to grasp, and for aerodynamics to demonstrate, that the Bermudan sail, with its high aspect ratio, was infinitely more efficient. It took time, too, to develop the masts and rigging for the Bermudan sail, and the bigger the yacht the greater the problem. As it was, the gaff rig, with its ludicrously heavy wooden spars, huge mainsails and disproportionately small headsails, was too inefficient to drive to windward the heavy, narrow, deep-hulled, long keel designs that the traditionally-minded British relished.

In America the great designer, Nat Herreshoff, exploited the existing rating and measurement rule by producing the skimming dish, wide-beamed, shallow-drafted craft with fin keels and huge overhangs. Suited to the sheltered conditions that Americans often raced in, they were derided by the British who considered them unseaworthy. This was a vital difference when the two countries competed for what is still the holy grail in yachting, the America's Cup, as in those days the British challenger always had to cross the Atlantic on her own bottom. Herreshoff designs defeated Thomas Lipton's first three efforts to win the Cup between 1899 and 1903, and though *Shamrock IV* gave the Americans a fright in 1920, Herreshoff's *Resolute* kept the ornate silver ewer bolted to its plinth in the New York Yacht Club.

The America's Cup remains an esoteric corner of sailing reserved for the super-rich. But it was, and still is, at the sharp end of yacht development and its influence on the sport during the twentieth century must not be underestimated. What is hi-tech today, the world uses tomorrow.

The most common form of racing was 'round the buoys' in sheltered waters, as it is today, but the yachts themselves were very different. The skimming dish might not have been considered seaworthy by the British but this did not stop their rating and measurement rule being exploited by designers, as was the American rule, to produce extreme designs along the same principle for the smaller keel classes.

Constant changes to try and plug the rules' loopholes during the last decade of the nineteenth century alienated racing yachtsmen so that by 1900 'Big class' racing, which had included the Prince of Wales's *Britannia*, had died out, while those racing in the smaller keel classes had turned to a new concept already established by the Water Wag dinghies in Ireland. This was the one-design, where the hulls and sails were identical, so that winning depended almost solely on the crew's skill, not on the latest exploitation of the rule.

General disillusionment with the measurement and rating rules on both sides of the Atlantic led to the New York Yacht Club adopting Herreshoff's Universal Rule in 1903 and to a number of European nations holding two conferences in 1906-7. The first conference agreed the new International Rule; the second drew up the racing rules and formed the International Yacht Racing Union (IYRU), now the International Sailing Federation, from the members of the national authorities of each country.

The sizes of the new International classes were expressed in metres and they ranged from 5-metres up to 23-metres with the 6-metres becoming the most popular. This was an Olympic Class for many years and is still raced as a classic yacht by the cognoscenti today. An even more enduring competitor in the Olympic Games, which initially accepted yachting as a sport in 1900, has been the American Star class, a 22ft 9in open keelboat. This first raced in Long Island Sound in 1911, became an Olympic Class in 1932, and except for 1976 has remained one ever since.

The roots of the modern dinghy classes – the word dinghy derives from the Hindi for a small, open riverboat – were already firmly planted in the late nineteenth and early twentieth centuries. But they took time to grow and it was not until after the Second World War that they multiplied to satisfy a public which, for the first time, had the money and available leisure hours to enjoy a sport previously confined to the prosperous few.

In Ireland the Dublin Water Wags had used the standing lug rig before changing to the more efficient gunter in 1900, and these two types were the most common ones used by European dinghies in the early part of the century. In America, where the winner of a British-American small boat challenge had

⸺ A REVOLUTIONARY OCEAN RACER ⸺

In the summer of 1931 the Americans repeated their 1851 America's Cup triumph when they again beat the British by putting 'a hawk among the pigeons'. This time the 'hawk' was a slim, white-hulled yacht called *Dorade* that was to alter the face of ocean racing. Launched in 1929, she was only the seventh design of twenty-one-year-old Olin Stephens, who worked with intuitive genius to produce the lines of his 52ft Bermudan-rigged yawl. With the easy narrow proportions of the 6-metre class, she had a moderate keel, and a fine entry that enabled her to slice through a sea.

Dorade's most remarkable feature was her practicality. Everything unnecessary had been eliminated. Wherever experience had shown a cleat, a snatchblock, a fairlead, or a handhold to be useful, there one was. Every cleat was turned at the proper angle, every block and lead was exactly in place. Though

designed by Olin – who skippered and navigated her in 1931 – she was the product of a joint family enterprise. Olin's father, Roderick Snr, had provided the finance, while Olin's younger brother Rod had supervised her construction at the Minneford Yacht Yard on City Island, New York, and had designed her sail plan, rigging and deck layout.

Dorade's first big event was the 1930 Bermuda Race. Though overrigged, she still managed to finish second in her class. But it was in the 1931 Transatlantic race that she showed just how good she was, winning by the extraordinary margin of four days on corrected time. She then went on to win the prestigious Fastnet Race with equal ease – a victory she was to repeat in 1933 – and on their return to New York, the crew received a Broadway tickertape reception, a unique tribute never before given to any yachtsman.

employed a Bermudan sail as far back as 1895, the catboat rig was also widely used. By the 1920s, the gaff rig, still *de rigeur* in cruising circles, had been replaced in all but the largest racing yachts by the Bermudan. Adopted first by the smaller metre classes and their Universal Rule equivalents – where letters not numbers often indicated their class size – by 1931 even the largest cutters in the resuscitated 'Big class' were rigged in this way, *Britannia*, now owned by King George V, being one of the last to have it.

In 1930 Lipton made his fifth and final attempt to lift 'the auld mug', as he called the America's Cup. The New York Yacht Club defended with a J-class yacht built to the Universal Rule. Called *Enterprise* she had one of the most remarkable yachtsmen of the era, Harold Vanderbilt, at her helm. Dubbed 'the mechanical ship' she made full use of all the latest techniques and equipment that a modern industrialized society could provide, and she beat an already dated *Shamrock V* with ease.

By then ocean racing in America had been re-established for seven years, as in 1923 both the Bermuda Race and the Transpac Race were revived. An Englishman, Weston Martyr, who crewed in the 1924 Bermuda Race (which became biennial thereafter), was so taken by what he called 'the King of Sports' that he urged British yachtsmen to organize a similar event. He enthused George Martin, an influential and experienced yachtsman, who in 1925 arranged a race from Cowes, around the Fastnet Rock off south-west Ireland, to the finish at Plymouth, a distance of 615 miles. Martin won in his French pilot cutter, *Jolie Brise*, and at a dinner after the race the Ocean Racing Club was formed with Martin as its first commodore. The fixture became one of the classic events in the ocean-racing calendar and is now raced in odd numbered years, attracting up to three hundred starters.

The new sport evolved slowly but in 1931 the Ocean Racing Club received its royal warrant and by the mid-1930s its programme included races to France, across the North Sea, and across the Atlantic. For years, however, yachting magazines continued to report its activities in their cruising columns; and it was not until 1935 that the first yacht, *Trenchemer*, was specifically built to the Royal Ocean Racing Club Rule drawn up to handicap the diverse cruising yachts entering the club's races.

Ironically, *Trenchemer*'s designer was not British – among whom there remained a lingering doubt about the sportsmanship of building to the rule to obtain the best rating possible – but a young American, Olin Stephens. His designs won all the Fastnets between 1931-37, and it not until 1939 that a British designer, Charles E Nicholson, who had designed Lipton's last two challengers, produced the winning yacht. Called *Bloodhound*, she became, by virtue of her purchase by the Royal family in 1962, the best-known ocean racer of the postwar era. Even then the victory was somewhat muted for at the time she was owned by an American based in Britain.

Lipton died in 1931 and his mantle was assumed by the aircraft millionaire Tommy Sopwith who challenged twice, in 1934 and 1937. His first challenger, the J-class, Nicholson-designed *Endeavour*, was 'state of the art' as Sopwith, aided by an outstanding aviation engineer, Frank Murdoch, poured all his aeronautical expertise into the yacht's rigging and equipment which included tension meters, speedometers, wind gauges and range finders. Metal rod shrouds, instead of wire ones, were also added after the Americans put them on their defender, enabling the mast to carry more efficiently the powerful double headsails then being developed to replace the traditional triple-headed rig.

Endeavour was faster than Vanderbilt's *Rainbow*. But a yacht's speed is only one factor in the equation of winning and when nearly all Sopwith's professional crew struck for higher wages he replaced them with amateurs. This and other factors militated against the challenger, and she lost the series after winning the first two races. By the time Sopwith returned with *Endeavour II* American yacht design had again moved ahead of the British with technological advances such as tank testing; so much that the Vanderbilt Super-J, *Ranger*, designed by Burgess with the assistance of Olin Stephens, won every race.

In 1920 the 'Big class' in Britain had been resurrected when King George V decided to race the aging but remarkable *Britannia*. Where the King led others followed and during the next decade and a half the 'Big class', which included 23-metres amongst others, raced in the regatta circuit around the British coast, thrilling spectators with many closely fought encounters. But in January 1936 the King died and *Britannia* was scuttled. This, and rising costs, finished the 'Big class', and their owners took to racing 12-metres, the largest sized boat class to survive into the 1930s.

The Second World War was responsible for even greater technological advances in yachting than had the first, particularly in the area of synthetic fibres and resins, high-tensile materials, and navigational aids. Rayon and nylon had been used experimentally for light-weather sails in America before it had entered the war, and by the mid-1950s lighter and stronger synthetic fibres began to supersede their natural equivalents. A yacht's sheets and running rigging, made of natural fibres like manila, were replaced by much stronger and lighter synthetic rope that chafed and jammed less, and did not rot. At the same time sail cloth known as Dacron (Terylene) – which stretched less, was not absorbent, and did not rot – started to replace the traditional cotton sails universally used by every yacht. Nowadays, 'state of the art' racing boats have their sails made from polyester film (Mylar) or Kevlar, which stretches even less than Dacron.

New techniques also produced lighter, stronger hulls. Large yachts, like those competing in the America's Cup, had been commonly made of steel or had been composite built (that is constructed with steel frames and wooden planking), while the smaller ones had been wooden built in the traditional way. However, after the Second World War, the moulded wooden hull – formed by gluing thin strips of wood layer upon layer – came into its own. It was not new, but improved methods and materials, and better glues, now made it suitable for the explosion in dinghy classes which occurred from the late 1940s onwards.

In the vanguard of this dinghy revolution was the British designer Uffa Fox. Fox's service in seaplanes during the First World War had made him realize that by making the hull of a dinghy v-shaped it would ride over its own bow wave and therefore increase its speed by planing. He employed this principle in 1928 in *Avenger*, a 14ft design that revolutionized the dinghy world; and after the Second World War he designed a whole string of successful dinghies and small keel boats such as the 12ft *Firefly* (1946), the *Flying Fifteen* (1946) and the *Albacore* (1954) to answer the demand for exciting sailing at a comparatively modest price.

But perhaps the most prolific and successful British dinghy designer of the era was Jack Holt whose dinghies – the *Cadet* (1947), the *Hornet* (1952), the *Enterprise* (1956) and *Mirror* (1963) to name but a few – introduced tens of thousands of people to the world of dinghy racing or to the pleasures of just pottering about wherever there was enough water to accommodate them. By the late 1980s, when trapezing had become a necessary skill to race in many racing classes, there were, for example, sixty thousand Mirror dinghies in one hundred countries. As in other types of yacht racing, the dinghy classes have absorbed the latest technological advances, and new classes like the 49er, used in the Sydney Olympics in 2000, are constantly being evolved.

Dinghy numbers were also boosted when the advances in marine plywood made during the Second World War enabled the home builder to construct his own craft from a kit. But the biggest advance of the twentieth century for yacht building came in the 1950s when hulls of all sizes began to be made of another wartime development, glass-reinforced plastic (GRP), where a boat's hull was produced from a mould, and could therefore be turned out in large quantities. Other materials, such as light alloys and even ferro-cement, have also been used in yachts' hulls since the war, but the hulls and spars of today's hi-tech, immensely strong, but light, racing yachts contain such exotic materials as Kevlar, titanium, epoxy resins, and carbon, materials which owe more to the space age than the war.

Another type of sailing boat which experienced a huge surge in popularity was the multihull – the catamaran (twin hulls) and the trimaran (single hull, twin floats). Herreshoff had produced the first catamaran yacht in 1876, and there had been limited racing in them, but even by the late 1950s they were, as one expert commented, 'very rare, quite unsophisticated, often badly sailed, and openly condemned by sailors of conventional boats.'

But in the right conditions multihulls go like greased lightning. As sheer speed has always attracted sailors – which is why motor racing terms like 'Grand Prix' and 'Formula 40' have entered nautical phraseology. They evolved so rapidly that within a short time yachtsmen accomplished circumnavigations – David Lewis being the first in 1964-7 – and cruised extensively in them. Inshore catamarans are mostly used as out-and-out racing machines and, represented by the 20ft *Tornado*, they have taken part in every Olympic Games since 1976. Some use vertical foils instead of sails to maximize their speed.

Offshore, both catamarans and trimarans are used in trans-ocean events like the French-organized single-handed Route du Rhum (St Malo-Guadeloupe) and double-handed Transat en Double (Lorient-Bermuda-Lorient), and in the British-organized double-handed Round Britain Race. These long-distance events were inspired by the Observer Singlehanded Transatlantic Race (OSTAR). The first-ever regularly held trans-ocean solo event, it was invented by 'Blondie' Hasler who, with four others, raced east to west across the Atlantic in 1960. Now run quadriennially under the name of different sponsors, both monohulls and multihulls compete in it in separate classes.

The latest breed of multihulls are truly the 'Formula One' racing cars of the high seas. They are built to make and break records, and compete for such prizes as the Jules Verne Trophy, awarded for the fastest circumnavigation.

In 1930 the Americans and British had agreed to use the Universal Rule for yachts over 12-metres and the International Rule for the rest. But by 1945 the former was dead and the classes of the latter dying. The 5.5-metre, introduced in 1949, flourished briefly and today a 1961 version of it still races as the 33ft *Daring*, a tiny elite fleet based at that mecca of yachting, Cowes. Otherwise only the 12-metre, courtesy of the America's Cup, and the 6-metre continued to be raced in international events.

Unlike metre boat racing, the ocean variety thrived after the Second World War, though in a cash-starved Britain it took time to do so. Where competitors always raced on handicap, until level-rating racing made its mark from the mid-1960s onwards, offshore racing was vulnerable to the exploitation of the various rules that governed it. John Illingworth was particularly adept at building boats that exploited the RORC rule. When his 38ft *Myth of Malham* appeared in 1947 she not only drove a horse and coaches through it, but, with her chopped off stern

AROUND ALONE

When the American captain Joshua Slocum made the first solo circumnavigation in his 35ft sloop *Spray* at the end of the nineteenth century, little did he know he would be the inspiration for the most adventurous and daring of today's yachtsmen and yachtswomen. An American farmer called Harry Pidgeon made the next successful solo circumnavigation, between 1921 and 1925 in his 34ft yawl *Islander*, and sixteen years later he repeated the feat in the same boat 'in order to look up old friends'.

Between these two voyages a Frenchman, Alain Gerbault, sailed alone around the world in the 39ft cutter *Firecrest*. When he returned to Le Havre in 1929 he received a hero's welcome and a decoration from an admiring nation, which is more than either Slocum or Pidgeon ever did. The Argentinian, Vito Dumas, went via the Panama Canal, as had Pidgeon, when he departed from Buenos Aires 'without wireless, without funds or a spare oilskin'. He received no publicity either, which was not surprising as he completed his voyage during the Second World War. He sailed as far as possible in the high southern latitudes – the 'Roaring Forties' – to avoid encountering the war zones and it was he who first called them 'the impossible route'.

Leslie Powles was another yachtsman who preferred anonymity, and his double circumnavigation, between 1975-78 and again between 1980-81, caused little comment. However, by then round-the-world yachtsmen more commonly created huge media interest and obtained commercial sponsorship on the back of it. With Francis Chichester it paid off and he was feted, and knighted, when he docked at Plymouth in May 1967, after becoming the first yachtsman to make a solo circumnavigation with only one stop – at Sydney, Australia. He failed in his objective to beat the hundred days taken by the clipper ships; but to take only a week longer in his 53ft ketch, *Gipsy Moth IV*, was a remarkable achievement for someone who reached pensionable age during the voyage. Chichester's feat was quickly followed by Alec Rose who, without any time in mind, sailed solo to Australia in his 36ft *Lively Lady* and then returned, as Chichester had done, via Cape Horn. He too was knighted.

These voyages inspired a Sunday newspaper to offer a Golden Globe Award and five thousand pounds for the first yachtsman to make a solo non-stop circumnavigation. Nine accepted the challenge but only Robin Knox-Johnston succeeded. On 22 April 1969 he finished, as the rules stipulated, at his starting place, completing the 30,123 mile course in his 32ft ketch *Suhaili* in three hundred and thirteen days. Another competitor, Bernard Moitessier, actually finished a circumnavigation first, but instead of returning to his starting place decided to go round again.

Knox-Johnston's voyage inspired all sorts of trans-ocean races as well as individuals racing against records set by others, but the next immediate peak to conquer was sailing non-stop around the world 'the wrong way', that is east to west against the prevailing winds. For this extraordinary feat of seamanship and endurance Chay Blyth built the 59ft ketch *British Steel*, and after two hundred and ninety-three days at sea he returned to his starting point in August 1971. The current record holder for this gruelling course is Mike Golding who, in May 1994, completed it alone in an astonishing one hundred and sixty-one days in his 67ft steel yacht, *Group 4*.

By then modern technology – light hi-tech materials, satellite navigation, and so on – had opened the floodgates for those determined to break new records. In 1977 three women tried to become the first to make a solo circumnavigation: Krystyna Chojnowska-Liskjiewicz from Poland who used the Panama Canal; Brigitte Oudry from France; and twenty-eight year-old New Zealander Naomi James. All succeeded but James, sailing the 53ft *Express Crusader*, was the first to circle the world via Cape Horn. Then in June 1988 the Australian Kay Cottee completed the first female solo non-stop circumnavigation, when she arrived in Sydney in her 38ft *Blackmore's First Lady* after sailing 25,000 miles in one hundred and eighty-nine days. This feat was repeated by Lis Clayton in 1995 and then by Samantha Brewster two years

later who did it against the prevailing winds.

Teenagers, too, have set their own solo records. American Robin Lee Graham was only aged sixteen when he began his circumnavigation in *Dove* in July 1965; Australian David Dicks was just eighteen when he sailed into the records in November 1996, the youngest-ever sailor to complete a solo non-stop voyage.

Perhaps the most remarkable record of all – yet to be beaten – was established by an Australian, Jonathan Sanders, when he started a double non-stop circumnavigation from Fremantle in September 1981 in his 34ft sloop *Perie Banou*. He sailed eastwards round Cape Horn and thence to Plymouth where, without stopping, he picked up mail and supplies. He then sailed twice round Cape of Good Hope and once round Cape Horn before arriving in Fremantle in October 1982. Not satisfied with this he then completed a triple circumnavigation between May 1986 and March 1988 in the 46ft sloop *Parry Endeavour*.

For those who like to compete against others as well as against themselves, there are currently two solo round-the-world races organised on a regular basis: the BOC Challenge, now renamed Around Alone, which has stops, and the ultimate event of all, the non-stop Vendée Globe. This Everest among races hit the headlines in 1997 when two competitors were involved in dramatic rescues after their yachts had capsized in the Southern Ocean.

and bow, powerful foresails and tiny mainsail, showed how the understanding of what made a yacht go faster in 1900 had by then been stood entirely on its head.

Altered in 1949 and extensively revised in 1957 the RORC Rule, which had been adopted by many countries, remained in force until 1970 when it was replaced by the International Offshore Rule (IOR). But by the early 1990s this had fallen from favour and the state of offshore racing at the end of the century, so far as the rating rules were concerned, was not unlike the situation in 1900.

The first two post-war America's Cup challenges mounted by the British (1958 and 1964) were disasters and if the Australians had not intervened in 1962 the event might well have died out. It took them over twenty years of trying before they succeeded in lifting 'the auld mug', during which time the series evolved into the international jamboree we know today with elimination trials being introduced in 1970 for both potential defenders and challengers.

Eventually, in 1983, Alan Bond's wing-keeled *Australia II* beat *Liberty*, skippered by Dennis Conner, by four races to three. Conner won the trophy back in 1987, when the races were held off Fremantle, Australia. The New Zealanders then stepped in and challenged, not with a 12-metre but with a yacht built to the maximum size allowed under the original deed of gift, 90ft on the waterline. Conner responded by building a hi-tech 60ft catamaran *Stars and Stripes*, well suited to the light airs off San Diego where the races were held.

Conner won two-nil and the courts subsequently upheld his right to use a multihull. From this legal dispute there emerged an entirely new type of 75ft monohull, the International America's Cup Class, which is 30% lighter than a 12-metre and has nearly double the sail area. It was in this class of yacht that a New Zealand syndicate won the cup in 1995 and kept it in 2000.

It was not only in the America's Cup that the Australians and New Zealanders began to excel after the war, for they are now firmly among the top offshore racing nations of the world. Ocean races had taken place in the Tasman Sea between the wars but it was not until the Sydney-Hobart 600-mile classic was founded in 1945 – by John Illingworth – that the Australians began to take the sport really seriously. Though Illingworth had tried to revive the dormant America's Cup with ocean racers, there was no real international competition for them until the Admiral's Cup was started in 1957.

Myles Wyatt, the RORC's Admiral at the time, wanted to encourage American yachtsmen to race in British waters and a team of three American yachts accepted his private challenge to compete for an old racehorse trophy he and his friends had bought. The British team scored the most points in the four races, which included the Fastnet, and the RORC organized the next series in 1959 when it was opened to all countries. The Admiral's Cup format was soon copied in the Mediterranean (Sardinia Cup), the Western Atlantic (Onion Patch), the Tasman Sea (Southern Cross), and even off Hawaii (Kenwood Cup).

International team racing was not new in yachting – the British-American Cup was a team event first raced in 6-metres in 1920 – but it was entirely so for those who raced offshore. Its popularity eventually attracted sponsorship and advertising, not allowed at first, and now involves big money. For some this ruined what was essentially an amateur sport; for others it provided a living, and a whole new breed of professional sailor has now appeared – shades of days gone by. During the 1970s as many as nineteen teams took part, but by the 1990s, with time and money in short supply, the numbers dropped, and to revitalize the series the RORC has abbreviated it in 1999 by substituting the Fastnet Race with a much shorter one around the Wolf Rock.

Far removed from 'Grand Prix' racing are the regattas held for classic yachts, yet another modern way for anyone interested in sailing to spend his money. When it comes to rehabilitating the early metre classes, or the J-boats, plenty is needed; but restoring any wooden boat to pristine condition is an art and an aesthetic pleasure for those who have the skills, and many an unrecognizable hulk has become someone's pride and joy.

The highly competitive nature of contemporary offshore racing – where crews dangle their legs over the side day and night to maximize the speed of their 'Grand Prix' machines – could hardly be termed pleasurable, but for every keen racing 'yachtie' there must be dozens who sail at a more leisurely pace.

Nevertheless, the racing mentality has gradually percolated into the cruising world so that today a popular event for those who don't normally race is the Atlantic Rally for Cruisers (ARC), which held its inaugural meet in 1986. This attracts cruising yachts to compete between specified destinations in order for their crews to get together at the end of a leg to enjoy each other's company. There are several divisions for different types of yachts and the prizes, which include ones for the youngest and oldest crew member, reflect the relaxed nature of the contest.

Hilaire Belloc's dictum that 'cruising is not racing', though true when he wrote it in 1925, is therefore no longer valid. This is especially so when considering the feats of sailors like Tristan Jones and Bill Tilman – and Francis Chichester for that matter – for they were cruising men only in the sense that they were not racing against anyone else. Their competition was within themselves, the same desire that drives mountaineers to climb 'because it is there'.

It was actually a mountaineer, Bill Tilman, who set the pace when, in the 1950s, he began exploring both the Arctic and Antarctic in a pilot cutter manned by a small crew. When he reached his destination he would leave his boat and climb the nearest mountain, and it was he who devised the Three Peaks Race in 1977, perhaps the most unusual yachting event ever created, involving as it does members of the crews of the competing yachts climbing peaks in Wales, the Lake District, and Scotland. So unique were Tilman's explorations that his pilot cutter *Mischief* is possibly the only yacht to have given its name to official geographical places, Mt Mischief on Baffin Island being named in the yacht's honour.

Equally singular was Tristan Jones who made a succession of outlandish voyages. During the 1970s he established the unusual record of sailing in the lowest navigable waters of the world (the Dead Sea) and then the highest (Lake Titicaca), an achievement which included a diversion up the Amazon further than anyone had sailed before. In a second voyage he sailed closer to the North Pole than any previous yachtsman and, for his efforts, was nearly eaten by a polar bear.

Quite unlike Tilman or Jones were Eric and Susan Hiscock who, in their yachts aptly called *Wanderer*, sailed round the world several times after the war writing extensively about their leisurely adventures, particularly in the exotic Pacific Islands. Some of their books became best sellers and were the inspiration for those who travelled in their wake. From the 1960s onwards these became legion and nowadays a circumnavigation, even a solo one, passes almost unnoticed unless it breaks a record.

Inevitably, such voyages led the globe to become the course for ocean racing. In 1973 the first regular round-the-world race, sponsored by Whitbread, was staged for crewed yachts. Held quadriennnially, it is currently sponsored by Volvo. Hot on its heels came other, similar, inter-ocean events, some crewed, some solo, and the future of this branch of racing seems assured, as does long-distance sailing generally. The trend for shorter, more complex courses in offshore racing for those too busy to leave their offices for long also appears likely to continue, while the popularity of dinghies and small keel yachts shows no sign of abating.

No doubt new forms of racing, rigging and sail plans will continue to be introduced, but it is interesting to note that despite the huge increase in leisure sailing during the twentieth century only one entirely new concept, windsurfing, made its mark. Boardsailing or sailboarding, as it is also called, was first developed off the Californian coast in the late 1960s by surfers wanting to manoeuvre their boards beyond the breakers without paddling. The idea took off and today windsurfing is part of Olympic yachting, and millions practice the delicate, exhilarating art anywhere where there is wind and water and space to take them. Will another such inventive form of popular sailing appear in the twenty-first century? Almost certainly it will.

It raced to meet the ship, and, with a pause, as of girding the loins, the Nan-Shan *lifted her bows and leaped. The flames in all the lamps sank, darkening the engine room. One went out. With a teasing crash and a swirling, raving tumult, tons of water fell upon the deck, as though the ship had darted under the foot of a cataract.*

Joseph Conrad: *Typhoon* (1903)

CHAPTER EIGHT

PASSENGERS AT SEA

Peter Quartermaine

TO FIND OURSELVES 'ALL AT SEA' still expresses a sense of loss, literally of bearings but also of what is familiar and valued in our everyday world; an unsettling, even overwhelming, experience. At the same time, our romantic instincts still envision the sea as an empty yet empowering space offering freedom and adventure – and always with just that tinge of unpredictable excitement. Passenger travel by sea during the last century always operated somewhere between these two extremes, offering travel and recreation – or simply escape – on vessels which reassured the passenger by relatively familiar interior design features, while at the same time stressed the 'sea breeze' aspects of ocean travel. Today, as ever, companies boast about the technical features of the ship itself, from (once upon a time) the number of funnels to (nowadays) the height of the atrium or the size of the golf course. This brief look at changes affecting passengers at sea over the past century charts some of the more important ways in which these enduring, but seemingly contradictory, aspects of ocean travel shaped those vessels which have transported people across oceans large and small. It closes with a look at how very recent developments in both technology and cultural attitudes offer not so much travel by sea as residence at sea.

Passengers have found themselves at sea for a variety of reasons, from forced emigration to sheer pleasure, and the term 'passenger' is itself problematic – do the most desperate and impoverished sea travellers of our own times, from Vietnamese boat people to those illegal immigrants from Albania, Turkey and North Africa who land by night in southern Italy, count as passengers here? Certainly the reasons they travel by sea are the time-honoured ones of relative cheapness and the ability (they hope) to evade the authorities on a deserted beach;

it is worth remembering that in times of crisis the ship is still an important means of escape for many. This chapter centres, though, on changes in scheduled passenger travel and on the growth of the modern cruise vessel in contrast to those patterns that had held since the fine North German Lloyd liner *Kaiser Wilhelm der Grosse* set new standards on the Atlantic in 1897. Its overall focus is therefore on ways in which our land-bound culture defines its shifting relationship with the sea.

For today's cruise passenger, going to sea is a deliberate choice – in effect the choice of one holiday rather than another – not the necessary evil of a shipbound crossing between the port of departure and a distant destination. In this sense the expectations and experience of passengers at sea is to be understood partly in the context of wider social and cultural shifts in attitudes to the sea, and to 'the seaside'; indeed, we take for granted the pleasures of fresh air and sunshine, bathing, and informal recreation in ways that even the socially privileged would mostly have found extraordinary one hundred and fifty years or so ago. Another important difference is that whereas most liner travel until the 1960s was a very different experience in first class, second class, and in third class (or steerage), the modern cruise vessel must offer that high standard class of accommodation and service that all passengers now expect. Cruise companies still cater for a range of potential passengers, but do so by offering a choice of cruises on completely different types of vessel (from 'private yacht', sailing clipper and 'traditional' liner through to all-action 'fun ships' and vessels which operate as an integral part of a larger entertainment concept, such as the Disney liners of the late 1990s), rather than by dividing one vessel's accommodation vertically in ways which reflected social hierarchies, with the better accommodation on the airy upper decks and cheap (often communal) berths deep in the hull.

Our modern period is one which regards the sea and its shores as areas to be touristically explored and exploited (sometimes with counterproductive results), but which has lost a once-familiar broader contact with the seafaring world. The great urban commercial and passenger ports of the pre-war period have largely died, to be replaced with remote and ring-fenced container ports or highly specialised cruise terminals; above all, any direct everyday experience of a working quayside, fronting the water on one side and the city on the other, is now rare. With this loss has come a gap in general understanding of the role that ships have played in the day-to-day lives of many groups in society during decades of intense change as the result of international forces and conflicts; this chapter suggests some of these through identifying the types of ships that made them possible.

Any account of passengers at sea in the twentieth century must recognise the key role that sea travel has played in the mass population shifts of our time, in periods of peace and during the two World Wars which fall within the scope of this book. Such periods are also linked, as the years prior to the outbreak of war and those of war's aftermath often involved specific patterns (and programmes) of refugee movement, repatriation and resettlement. Foremost among peacetime movements was that of emigrants from Europe to the United States in the first two decades of the twentieth century (until the imposition of strict quotas by the US government in 1924), and that other great movement of peoples world-wide in pursuit of better lives after the Second World War, especially from Africa and India to Europe and the States, and from European countries to Canada, South America, the States and Australasia; other emigrants moved from Italy and from Japan to South America. Criss-crossing the wake of vessels in these post-war passenger trades were those of shipping serving other and older aspirations, for throughout most of this period passenger vessels of the former European colonial powers (especially Belgium, Britain, France, Holland and Portugal) operated widespread regular services between their home ports (such as Amsterdam, Antwerp, Liverpool, London, Lisbon and Marseilles) and their scattered colonies in Africa, Australasia, the Caribbean, the Far East, and South Asia; in addition, other European countries maintained services with lands linked to them by long-established patterns of trade or emigration (such as those between Italy and South America). For often poor emigrants, the sight of grand ships from their 'home' nation was an occasion not only of personal and family emotion but also of powerful pride in the country from which they had emigrated and to which they might occasionally (or eventually) return; such emotions were explicitly recognised by some shipping companies, and fostered in their publicity.

Both World Wars resulted in a massive loss of shipping (of three hundred and sixty-eight passenger vessels over 10,000 tons gross at the start of the Second World War, only one hundred and ninety-six survived in some shape or form), but equally both wars were followed by an intense need for tonnage as economies prospered; this both stimulated new-building and meant that meantime elderly vessels were pressed back into service rather than being scrapped. The Second World War, especially, was followed by an extended period in which very large numbers of people were moved by sea as part of various government and international programmes to cope with disruptions caused by that global conflict, from thousands of war brides who found themselves on the wrong side of an ocean and families taking advantage of subsidised fares to Australia (as after the First World War) to escape bad weather and worse food in Britain, to members of the Jewish Diaspora setting sail at last for the long-promised land of Israel. These were passengers embarking for very specific purposes, a pattern of movement very different from that served by either traditional liners or our present-day cruise ships, but passengers nevertheless whose hopes, labours and fortunes have helped shape our present world.

Passenger trades in the mass movement of peoples in some cases resulted in the development of specialised vessels or – if the need was urgent (and profits to be had) – the rapid adaptation of existing ones. Some post-war passenger-cargo liners, such as the Holland-America Line's 1946 transatlantic *Westerdam* carried first class travellers only (a market which has seen a revival in recent years, for holidaymakers who can afford something very different from the standard cruise package) but other ships were more basic. Canadian Pacific converted its 1938 freighter *Beaverbrae* to run westbound across the Atlantic with almost eight hundred emigrants and to return with cargo only, which she did successfully from 1948 until 1954. On the emigration run from Europe to Australia and New Zealand a whole fleet of vessels, initially mostly British but with Italian and Greek companies soon close behind, became well-known regulars in Antipodean ports after the Second World War. One of the best-loved later vessels built for this passenger trade was P&O's 1961 *Canberra*. She went to the breakers only in late 1997 after spending her later years happily cruising, but still with the communal ironing rooms and many four-berth cabins without private facilities that dated from her more modest original role. Some P&O passenger ships on the Australia and New Zealand route began their lives as traditional two-class vessels but were converted to one-class emigrant carriers in the 1950s and 1960s as air travel reduced the market for traditional liners and international competition on the emigrant routes became more intense; both the 1931 *Strathnaver* and the 1949 *Himalaya* underwent such changes (in 1954 and 1963 respectively). Other emigrant vessels were converted, to a greater or lesser degree, from former troopships or other standard wartime vessels (even including one Australian seaplane-carrier), and several proved both extremely successful and long-lived. The Australia-based *Fairstar*, which started life as the 1957 British troopship *Oxfordshire*, was scrapped only in late 1997. At the other end of the scale, the former transatlantic liner *America* became the Chandris emigrant liner *Australis*, running from Europe to Australia between the mid-1960s and 1977. Built in 1940, the *America* had only entered service in 1946, after wartime service as the troopship *West Point* with as many as five thousand troops aboard instead of her passenger complement of just over one thousand; in her new role she carried some two thousand three hundred passengers in one class. She was wrecked in the Canary Islands in 1994 while being towed from Greece to Thailand for use as a floating hotel. The Italian Flotta Lauro also acquired and converted two liners from Dutch companies (whose own traditional trade to former colonies in the Dutch East Indies was now much reduced) and these entered service as *Angelina Lauro* (formerly *Oranje*, 1939) and *Achille Lauro* (formerly *Willem Ruys*, 1947); both ships were to be destroyed by fire during their later cruising careers.

In the political and economic change of the immediate post-war period passenger vessels running between Europe and what were, increasingly, ex-colonies played a central role in the process of what has been termed 'colonisation in reverse', that is the inward movement of peoples from Africa, the Caribbean, India and elsewhere to Europe. For example, those who came to Britain from the Caribbean did so largely in reponse to advertisements by London Transport and others; they came to help rebuild what many of them saw (mistakenly in the eyes of those racists whose hostility they were often to endure) as their 'home' country; many had fought in the recent war for the country to which they were now emigrating. The former British troopship *Empire Windrush* was to enter British national mythology when, on 22 June 1948, she disembarked five hundred immigrants from the West Indies – the first of many such arrivals – at London's Tilbury passenger terminal on the Thames. The 'Windrush generation' was to change for ever the look and culture – cooking, music, politics, literature – of the former British imperial power, and the fiftieth anniversary of her arrival was duly celebrated in 1998, not least by a series of national television programmes and an accompanying book.

Ships and their passengers have over the years contributed formative elements to societies across the globe, a role now easily forgotten in an era of budget air travel and too easily softened by a selective nostalgia. Enthusiasts hanker for 'classic steam' but pay scant attention to the terrible conditions endured by stokers in the engine room, or by the native coaling teams around the world who replenished bunkers on the white liners through coaling hatches out of sight of the passengers strolling the immaculate teak decks above. Some such distinctions still exist today, in shipping as elsewhere, and an increasing number of posts below officer level are now filled by crew members from the Philippines, the Far East, Africa or Eastern Europe; on the other hand, P&O takes pride in the long tradition of South Asian crews on its vessels, and such crew members of the new *Oriana* themselves posed proudly for a group photograph when the liner entered service in early 1995. Passenger vessels are floating worlds, both for passengers and crew, and the complex human links that form on board elude adequate description in purely economic terms.

Among the migrants that ships moved in the post-war period were many who would also have sailed in such ships as troops. The Second World War was one that depended tactically upon the rapid movement of large numbers of troops and equipment by sea, often over great distances. Both the Cunard 'Queens' served as troopships, sailing alone and relying solely on their speed to evade hostile submarines. After the war their great popularity with American passengers owed something to these heroic wartime roles; with their royal names and proudly traditional style, they were seen affectionately as embodying typically British virtues. During the Cold War, the West faced the communist block countries with varying degrees of tension (which reached its height during the Cuban missile crisis of 1962) and it was in this period that the United States built the world's fastest liner, the *United States* (1952). She was designed with an eye not only to the prestige of the Blue Riband – which she easily captured on her maiden voyage – but also to the need for a fast troop carrier in any future global conflict (her engines and underwater hull shape were military classified throughout her career). In 1999 she was laid up in Philadelphia. Britain found the urgent need to call on the passenger liners *Canberra* and *Queen Elizabeth 2*, together with many other vessels, during the 1982 Falklands War, an unforeseen conflict whose distant location made the sea transport of troops and equipment from Britain essential; once again, liners found themselves with troops as passengers.

The pace of technological change in the twentieth century was unparalleled in all aspects of shipping, and market pressures ensure that it continues. Such pressure produces radical as well as minor change: new-concept cruise vessels building in Finland for the Carnival Corporation to general plans by the Company's distinctive designer Joe Farcus are intended to set new standards in cruising – something all rival companies also claim. In the early years of this century technological innovation was largely that of propulsive and related engineering and was exploited for luxurious and high-speed developments by fiercely competitive passenger liner companies, especially on the North Atlantic. The massive shift to cruising since the 1960s has made more recent priorities the efficiency of vessel operation, provision of ever-higher standards of accommodation and service for a much broader class of passengers, and above all safety at sea. If cargo vessels of all sizes have so changed in appearance as to be almost unrecognisable compared with those of the 1950s, so the great modern passenger vessels are not liners (literally ships, whether passenger or cargo, which run on scheduled international routes) but cruise vessels quite different in appearance and function, which form an important dimension of the rapidly-growing global leisure and tourist industry. People today not only travel mostly by air on medium to long hauls, but to reach the departure port of their chosen cruise, and to return home afterwards. It is therefore logical that the world leader in cruising, The Carnival Corporation of Miami, should also have substantial interests in a holiday airline company, and through this company should also own high street travel agents. With a carefully-tailored fleet of vessels plying seas from the North Atlantic and Scandinavian waters to the Mediterranean, the Caribbean, the Bahamas, and the Pacific), and with extensive interests also in hotels and casinos, Carnival represents the new fully-diversified and international character of passenger leisure shipping.

The decisive challenge to traditional passenger travel came in the late 1950s, not from within the industry itself but from the air, rather as the most significant change in cargo shipping was triggered in the 1950s by the standard cargo containers introduced by the American truck operator Malcolm McLean. Throughout the twentieth century, though, innovations in the basic nature of shipping came from non-maritime fields; it was sometimes a question of seeing new applications for what already worked in another field, but such developments were no more than a practical recognition of the key role that shipping played in all aspects of the global transport industry. One side effect was the diversification of both passenger and cargo shipping companies into land storage and road distribution, as well as into hotels and related real estate; today passengers at sea are but one element in a globally integrated market that demands ever-wider provision from the successful operator.

Cruising, which is essentially the concept of going to sea for its own sake, is nothing new in passenger shipping, though the scale and continuing rapid growth of the present market is. As early as 1844 the Peninsular and Oriental Steamship Company (now P&O) ran some cruises to the Mediterranean from

---

⇒ FOR THOSE IN PERIL ⇐
THE DEVELOPMENT OF AIR-SEA RESCUE AND
LIFEBOAT SERVICES ACROSS THE WORLD

Practical provision for the saving of life at sea is under the administration of national governments, or in the case of Britain that of the Royal National Lifeboat Institution, a registered charity which has saved thousands of lives since its inception in 1824, on the initiative of Sir William Hillary. Today it serves as the Secretariat for all countries operating maritime lifesaving provision. In the United States government rescue provision dates from 1848, and is now operated by the US Coastguard service. The adoption in 1985 of the International Convention on Search and Rescue (SAR) required all signatories to make efficient provision for SAR, and to enter into agreements with neighbouring states that would ensure efficient liaison in emergencies. Ships are also required to report their positions to shore radio stations, and this facilitates the co-ordination of prompt assistance as required. The much-reported rescue by the Royal Australian Navy of two solo round-the-world yachtsmen from the Southern Atlantic Ocean in 1997 highlighted the impressive precision rescue operations can achieve through integrated work by shore, air and sea services guided (in these particular cases) by automatic rescue beacons activated on board the yachts; these beacons also identify the specific vessel concerned. The most important advances in both navigation and distress signalling have

---

Britain, and in 1889 and 1891 respectively offered cruises to the fjords of Norway and to the Mediterranean (both of which are still popular cruise destinations for many companies today). In the early 1890s other companies ventured cruises to the Mediterranean, and to other sunny destinations from the West Indies to the Azores. The Hamburg-Amerika Line, pleased with the experiment of sending its transatlantic vessel *Augusta Victoria* (1889) to the Mediterranean during the winter months of 1891, a pattern that would be followed by many companies over half a century later, is credited with building the world's first true cruise liner in 1900 with the *Prinzessin Victoria Luise*. She was wrecked in Jamaica only seven years later, but her success had been proved, and she was replaced. Cunard's 1907 *Mauretania*, built originally with a subsidy of £2.6 million, plus an annual mail subsidy for her North Atlantic runs, was converted to oil propulsion in 1921 and also to accommodate almost six hundred passengers less than her original two thousand three hundred and thirty-five – and, significantly, with a more equal

been made possible by technology increasingly familiar to many families, the computer and the satellite, and today even a small yacht can carry simple equipment which will display its precise position at the touch of a button through the Global Maritime Distress and Safety System (GMDSS). The International Maritime Organisation (IMO) held a three-session conference on the use of maritime satellites in 1975-76 which led to the adoption in 1976 of the international Convention on the Establishment of the International Maritime Satellite Organisation (INMARSAT).

The skies have played an increasing part in maritime rescue – during the Second World War, Great Britain's Royal Air Force established the Air Sea Rescue Service to rescue the crews of aircraft which had to 'ditch' at sea on their return from action over continental Europe; fast launches were guided to inflatable survival dinghies by radio beacons. The greater range of post-war aircraft enabled them to operate for extended periods over the oceans, while the operational flexibility of helicopters – especially their ability to hover above vessels in distress and to winch survivors on board – provided the ideal complement to specially-equipped search aircraft whose radar and other equipment enabled them to locate vessels remote from land. Today's international communications render efficient lifesaving co-operation between international air and sea services ever more feasible, but at the same time the great increase in shipping movements – and not least the ever-increasing popularity of leisure craft – have made their task one in which advancing technology barely enables them to keep pace with demands on their vital skills.

distribution of first, second and third class. From 1923 she undertook winter cruises to the Mediterranean, and by 1932 was cruising the year round in a festive all-white livery. The *Mauretania* herself was scrapped in 1935, but when Cunard's *Caronia* entered service in 1949 she was the largest liner in existence designed specifically for cruising, and she also boasted all-outside cabins, a novelty now characteristic of many cruise ships. Cruising to attractive and temperate climes became increasingly popular with those that could afford it, and the 1927 Blue Star liner *Arandora Star* was converted for cruising after two years, and until the outbreak of war in 1939 proved convincingly the market for such operations; her Norwegian and Mediterranean cruises were especially popular.

In 1958 the Boeing 707 jet entered service on the North Atlantic route, with the result that more travellers crossed by 'airliner' than by ship. In the previous year traditional liners had carried a record number of just over one million passengers, but by 1959 airlines already had 63% of the passenger trade, and in

1960 alone there were seventy thousand Atlantic crossings by air. Within ten years aircraft had virtually taken over the passenger market. In their last years the large crews needed on transatlantic liners sometimes outnumbered the passengers, and the days of such vessels were clearly coming to an end. The magnificent luxury liner *France*, which entered service in 1962 on the North Atlantic, represented the finest development of such ships – fast, and elegant in both design and lifestyle. But she was to prove a costly monument to that blend of national pride and (more important) government subsidies which had long underwritten the building and operating costs of competition between European and United States shipping companies for the Blue Riband awarded to the fastest vessel. Her namesake of 1912 had been sent cruising from 1928, before being laid up in 1932, and after only twelve years in service the new *France* – despite protests from her crew and others – was herself laid up. She was to live again from June 1980 as the Norwegian cruise liner *Norway*, but with only one engine-room instead of two, a reduced crew and increased passenger accommodation. When Cunard finally unveiled plans for their long-delayed new liner to replace the two 'Queens' in 1965 (launched in 1967 as the *Queen Elizabeth 2*), she was a very different kind of vessel; designed for a more popular market, more fuel-economical – and also able to cruise in warmer and increasingly-profitable climes during the long Atlantic winter months, a pattern that Holland-America had adopted with their own innovative and successful 1959 liner *Rotterdam*. Cunard is now part of the Carnival Corporation, and in 1999 *QE2* underwent a £19m refit after carrying more than two million passengers on over one thousand one hundred and sixty voyages; a total of over four million six hundred thousand nautical miles. A new transatlantic liner for Cunard is also planned.

The unqualified ascendancy of mass air travel by the early 1960s forced shipping companies not only to re-employ or sell existing passenger liners but also to think radically about the future. An immediate response was to redeploy existing vessels to cruise destinations, but ships designed for the North Atlantic were not suitably ventilated for hotter routes, and also lacked the open deck space needed to make such climates really enjoyable for passengers. Since then the cruise vessel has developed in ways, and at a pace, that make it indisputably the flagship of passengers at sea, but a host of other passenger-transporting vessels have come into being to serve the specific needs of widely differing routes and passenger markets, but all with the demanding reconciliation of speed with overall efficiency a requirement for operators. In some cases, though, technical developments that initially provided these qualities have had to be modified in order to enhance ship and passenger safety, a consideration that is increasingly important.

The triumph of Boeing on the North Atlantic was a dramatic demonstration that a new era of international passenger transportation had arrived, though in Britain such initiatives were too often met with conservative doubt which led to inventions being developed abroad. As early as 1891 experiments had begun with adjustable underwater 'wings' which at speed would lift a relatively small craft large clear of the water, thus greatly reducing drag, and the Italian Enrico Forlanini attained a speed of 38 knots with such a craft fitted with ladder-type foils on Lake Maggiore in 1906. Alexander Graham Bell also experimented with the ladder foil in the period after the First World War, and his experimental craft *HD-4* reached almost 70mph. Such hydrofoil technology was not commercially applied until 1953, with probably the first hydrofoil in international service being the Italian-built *Sirena*, which cut the run from Stockholm to the Finnish Aland Islands from over six hours to two hours and thirty minutes and led to the successful deployment of hydrofoils on sheltered waters world-wide. Sheer speed aside, hydrofoils can ride above wave turbulence and cause minimal wash even at high speed, a factor which is important on waters where this would cause annoyance or damage. Italian builders have retained a high profile in this field, with 35-knot passenger craft serving as ferries from the Mediterranean and Adriatic to the China Sea, as well as on lakes and rivers world-wide. The relative vulnerability of the surface hydrofoil's protruding foils has excluded it from more open sea work, although fully submerged foils operate in deeper and less turbulent water. Alongside recent hydrofoils, a new generation of fast passenger ferries with Mono Deep Vee (MDV) hulls is now in service on short sea routes world-wide; the *Aries* and her three sisters, which operate between Olbia and Civitavecchia, are among the largest and fastest in the world, and can carry one thousand eight hundred passengers and four hundred and sixty cars at 40.5 knots. Propulsion is by four Kamewa waterjets aft.

Other developments have drawn on aviation technology in different ways. Boeing itself developed the fast 'jetfoil' vessel, powered by two gas turbines giving some 43 knots, and these provided fast passenger short sea services for a time. An even more original invention was the Air Cushion Vehicle, first patented by John Thornycroft in 1877 and realised as a prototype in 1950 by the British engineer Sir Christopher Cockerell, who died in 1999. More popularly know as the

— ✥ THE HERALD OF FREE ENTERPRISE ✥ — AND ESTONIA DISASTERS

The price of safety at sea is eternal vigilance, and these two incidents illustrate in different ways the potentially tragic consequences of any slippage; they also demonstrate that, although some aspects of roll-on roll-off ferries had given experts concern for some time (not least because there had been great loss of life through sinkings) it took high-profile media coverage of these two disasters in Europe to effect change. The *Herald of Free Enterprise* vehicle and passenger ferry sank in calm weather on the evening of 6 March 1987, just after leaving Zeebrugge harbour; in just over a minute the ship was on its side on a sandbank and nearly six hundred people on board were fighting for their lives. Of these, one hundred and ninety-three were to lose that battle, and had the vessel sunk in deeper water the loss of life would certainly have been much higher. The official enquiry established that the vessel had its bow loading door still open as it left harbour, and that water taken in very quickly caused loss of stability and capsize. The *Estonia* sank in rough weather during the night of 28 September 1994 on passage from Talinn to Stockholm, and of the one thousand and forty-nine persons on board only one hundred and thirty-seven survived; eight hundred and nineteen bodies are still missing, and the wreck itself has been officially declared a grave site. The

'hovercraft', after government support for research and development this craft, neither ship nor plane, (which caused some legislative problems) was finally introduced as the car and passenger carrier *SRN-4* on the cross-Channel route in July 1968, and ten years later the two craft then in use were 'stretched' to enable them to carry fifty-five cars and three hundred and ninety passengers; in 1995 and 1999 the 60-knot craft were completely refurbished. Powered by four gas turbines, the hovercraft was propelled by four air propellers and supported by air pressure from twelve centrifugal fans; it had a cruising speed of 55 knots. In the 1990s hovercraft have seen competition on cross-Channel routes from Australian-built wave-piercing vessels that employ a sophisticated twin- and triple-hull design and offer greater space, together with the enhanced control and reduced noise levels important for cost-effective twenty-four hour operation. The largest wave-piercer in the world, *Condor 11*, operates between Weymouth and the Channel Islands, and such vessels are often deployed commercially elsewhere in the world (for example, the River Plate estuary) during the European winter final cause of the sinking is still disputed by several parties, but the official enquiry found that failure of the bow visor securing mechanism had allowed water to reach the vehicle decks; the vessel sank within twenty minutes of damage first being noticed on board.

The striking speed with which these vessels sank rendered meaningless many safety provisions; clearly the design of such ships, and especially the extended and unrestricted space needed for speedy vehicle turnaround, raised pressing design issues. Even those previously resistant now came to accept the need for drastic revision of the guidelines covering both the design and the operation of such ships. New international safety amendments progressively introduced from April 1990 address the safety of ro-ro vessels in a damaged condition, as well

as stricter standards for bow door securing mechanisms (and their maintenance and checking) and enforcement of overall regular scrutiny of overall safety provision. These amendments mean that much of the world's ro-ro fleet will have to be progressively modified between 1994 and 2001.

Although ro-ro ships are not statistically more liable to accident than other vessels, research shows that any accident involving them tends to result in considerable loss of life. Ship design is an inevitably compromise between efficiency and safety, and the highly public debate triggered by these two tragedies suggests that the risks of a faulty judgement are still high, especially as new ship designs present previously unforeseen technical challenges.

season, which demonstrates their full seagoing abilities. The hovercraft design solved the problem of hull resistance at high speed by keeping the craft itself clear of the water altogether. Other experiments have employed a variety of hull shapes and combinations to achieve maximum carrying capacity (a generous flat deck area) while reducing hull immersion to a minimum, and one solution widely adopted from Sydney Harbour ferries to the revolutionary 1992 cruise vessel *Radisson Diamond* has been the catamaran hull, a design borrowed from traditional sailing craft of the South Pacific islanders, and initially applied to fast sailing yachts. The *Radisson Diamond*, like some modern passenger ferry craft, also employs underwater pontoons for buoyancy and so avoids surface turbulence. Catamarans and trimarans have the advantage of speed and of shallow draught, making them ideal for a network of services world-wide where convenience and rapid connections are a priority, while their excellent seagoing qualities make it possible for them to operate even across relatively exposed stretches of open sea.

Urgent wartime needs produced innovations which found wide application in peace; indeed, the revolutionary jet airliners of the late 1950s themselves owed much to development of long-range bombers in the Second World War, and to the invention of the gas turbine engine late in that war. One maritime development to facilitate the seaborne landings of troops and their motorised equipment was the LCT (Landing Craft Tank), a vessel which could rapidly load and unload large motor vehicles across its lowered bow ramp, and the post-war boom in private car ownership brought a new demand for just such seagoing vessels to provide links for international car travel. Some such vessels (for example, car ferries with lifting bow sections) had first been introduced as early as the early 1920s on limited routes, but in the period after the Second World War modified wartime vessels operated directly on short sea routes between London's Tilbury docks and near Continental ports, as well as on cross-Channel and North Sea routes. The late 1950s saw the introduction of purpose-built vehicle and passenger ferries incorporating features which have since become familiar to millions of holidaymakers and commercial vehicle drivers world-wide: hydraulically operated loading doors with drive-on loading, spacious interior vehicle decks uncluttered by dividing bulkheads, and modern restaurant and accommodation facilities for passengers. Initially such vessels operated alongside an earlier, and more specialised, application of the 'roll-on, roll-off' principle (or 'ro-ro') dating from the last two decades of the nineteenth century, namely the train ferries, usually operated between countries by railway companies, in which train carriages were taken directly onto the vessel's ferry decks. Successful on routes where there was minimal tide, such ships had the drawbacks of having to carry the extra 'dead' weight of the railway coaches, of needing matching rail gauges at each end of their journey, and of being vulnerable to bad weather. Progressive post-war lack of investment in rail transport world-wide led to their demise, it was with car and commercial vehicle ferries that the future lay. Interestingly, though, it was the vehicle ferry *Princess Victoria*, introduced on the Irish Sea Stranraer-Larne run in 1938 by the London, Midland & Scottish Railway, which incorporated innovations (such as an unobstructed car deck, and a vehicle turntable) pointing to post-war developments – and problems. She was lost in the war, but her namesake successor of 1947 was lost in a storm in 1953 with great loss of life, an incident which prefigured the disasters which were to overtake (among others) the ro-ro ferries *European Gateway*, (UK, 1982) *Herald of Free Enterprise* and *Dona Paz*, (Belgium and Philippines, 1987) and *Estonia*

(Baltic Sea, 1994). These disasters, and especially the media coverage they attracted, caused major rethinking of the design of such ships, and especially the need to ensure the security of large vehicle-loading doors and to prevent the rapid movement of any water shipped across open cardecks.

Where once ferries were quite spartan vessels, the increasing trend has been to offer facilities on board more akin to a cruise liner than a mere ferry; passengers are now more demanding, and a ferry that offers a better all-round service has a competitive edge. In this field very high standards have been set by the modern superferries that ply the Scandinavian routes and, more recently, the new generation of fast ferries operating in the Mediterranean from Genoa, and in the Adriatic from Ancona providing passenger and vehicle crossing between Italy and Greece; similar vessels also operate from Japan. The larger Scandinavian vessels of the Silja fleet (which includes the world's largest passenger ferry, the 1993 *Silja Europa*) pioneered the idea of onboard 'streets' with a high transparent atrium roof, and shops and balconies fronting onto this interior area, while in 1977 the gas turbine-propelled *Finnjet* (1977) set new standards both in speed and in passenger accommodation in her operation from Helsinki. Gas turbines also power the 1996 Finnish-built *Stena Explorer*, giving cleaner and quieter power for the vessel's water-jet propulsion; unlike many fast ferries, this craft retains an extensive open deck area for passengers at sea, a once-traditional feature now increasingly hard to find as operators concentrate on money-earning interior facilities.

The dramatic increase in world-wide cruising can only be fully understood in the light of wider social and economic factors in the 'Western' world of which the already-noted rise in travel by air is but one: others include a general rise in living standards, and hence mobility; a growing category of people with disposable income retiring early for one reason or another; and an increasing desire in Western society to see foreign peoples and places already familiar from film, television and travel brochures, combined with a need to feel reassured about food, language, hygiene and day-to-day security. These latter concerns are met very successfully by the self-selecting and isolated community of the cruise ship. This allows passengers to see (and, if they wish, to visit) foreign ports while in important ways still staying 'at home'. Many of the most exotic destinations (and attractive climates) are found in areas such as the Caribbean, where average incomes are dramatically lower than those of passengers on board visiting cruise ships. When it is considered that some modern cruise ships carry some three thousand five hundred passengers and have a crew of some one thousand five hundred, it is no surprise that the total 'population' of cruise vessels at anchor off a palm-fringed island can exceed that of the island itself. The possible negative effects of such disproportion of scale require careful management if the tourism market is not to self-destruct, and some cruise companies have acquired (either through outright purchase or on long-term lease) holiday islands which they operate so as to meet their passengers' expectations.

In 1998 a major new player entered the cruise and entertainment business in the shape of the Disney Corporation, which had commissioned two passenger cruise vessels of highly original design from the Italian shipbuilders Fincantieri at Marghera (Venice); *Disney Magic* (1998) and *Disney Wonder* (1999). The trend with modern cruise ships has been for them to become increasingly box-like in hull form: this makes for efficiency of building (cabins fit more easily into a squarish hull, which is also cheaper to fabricate) and of operation, especially if passage through the Panama Canal is a factor in the ship's intended operation. The Disney liners completely broke with this trend, not only in a deliberate wish to have a very distinctive corporate image, at sea and in port, but also because the company had a very clear idea of how these vessels should fit and operate within their already-extensive holiday and entertainment sites in the States, including the nearby Disney island of Castaway Cay, to which the ships will sail from the company's new purpose-built terminal at Port Canaveral. Long and sleek, with two funnels in traditional style (the forward one is a dummy containing a passenger observation lounge), the Disney vessels are painted in the traditional North Atlantic colours of black and white, with red funnels (carrying the Mickey Mouse logo) but also feature an elegant clipper-type bow and unusual cruiser-type type stern, both carrying gilded decoration such as that on traditional sailing vessels, and with gold-coloured bow anchors exposed rather than recessed. Windows in the public rooms are of an exaggerated 'porthole' format, and innovation also characterises the overall design of the vessels, whether in the idea (later abandoned, much to the relief of the shipbuilders) of having the engine control room open to the public (the bridge still has a viewing gallery, with a glass rear wall giving onto the ship's fitness centre) to that of passengers eating a different restaurant each day, but served by the same waiters. At a purely technical level, the sleek hull of these vessels necessitated very long and exposed propeller shafts, and Fincantieri had to draw on its experience of building fast warships in designing these. The Disney vessels are also an original and highly sophisticated exercise in 'retro design'; that is, their form, detailing and paintwork deliberately evoke and rework features from 'classic' (North Atlantic) liners of an earlier era. The ships represent a new challenge on the contemporary cruise scene, and demonstrate its importance in the eyes of a major international player that has never operated ships before. New vessels from rival operators, including the 1998 *Grand Princess* (with its distinctive 'spoiler' containing a disco) and Royal Caribbean Cruise Lines' 1999 *Voyager of the Seas* (which boasts an ice rink and rock climbing wall) will certainly offer fierce competition; *Voyager* is the first of three sisters, while P&O alone ordered five new cruise ships in June 1999.

Cruise liners exist solely to offer enjoyment, of whatever kind, and this is typified by their super-streamlined exterior profiles and their extravagant interior decor; Joe Farcus aptly describes his shipboard environments for Carnival as 'entertainment architecture'.[1] From expensive round-the-world cruises lasting several weeks and costing thousands of pounds per person to four-day cruises from Miami, and from adventure cruises to Iceland to specialist-staffed 'classical' cruises in the Mediterranean, modern cruising offers a dazzling range of vessels, destinations and patterns of life on board. And whereas originally a cruise began and ended at the same port, today the cruise passenger can fly out and back, and can take advantage of pre-planned stopover packages at various resorts on the cruise route. More and more the cruise vessel presents itself and operates as a floating resort, and pampers its passengers accordingly.

Finally, comes news that an idea already discussed for several years is, it seems, actually to be built: a vast floating residential, leisure and entertainment complex which will bear more resemblance to a holiday resort than any previous 'ship'. As planned, this will be built by an international consortium and offer fully-furnished private apartments for sale to the super-rich at prices from two to six million US dollars each. This vast vessel would spend only some one hundred days each year at sea, locating itself mostly at ports convenient for major international sporting and other events, and with this development the traditional division between life at sea and life ashore would be even further blurred. Not for the first time, the whole concept of 'passengers at sea' may soon need rethinking.

---

1 For more detailed discussion of these and other designs, see my book *Building on the Sea: Form and Meaning in Modern Ship Architecture* (1996).

Destroyers armed with the uncanny Tomahawk missiles were surgically taking the heart out of Iraq's infrastructure and command network hundreds of kilometres distant. There was a spectacular incident one night late in January when HMS Gloucester *succeeded in destroying with her air defence missiles a long-range Iraqi Silkworm aimed from the Kuwait shore at the battleship USS* Missouri.

Alan Munro, *An Arabian Affair* (1996)

CHAPTER NINE

HIGH-TECH AND HIGH TENSION

Norman Friedman

WHEN THE SECOND WORLD WAR ENDED in 1945, the US Navy and the Royal Navy effectively controlled the world's seas. Their wartime experiences, and therefore their reactions to the way the war ended, were radically different. For the US Navy, the key part of the conflict had been the war against Japan, the defeat of a great seapower. For the Royal Navy, the key had been the defeat of the German attack on Allied shipping, the only battle that Winston Churchill admitted might have cost the Allies the war. Both navies had, of course, participated in the great D-Day landings that had brought the Allied armies back to the Continent after the disasters of 1940.

With the war over, both Western governments looked uneasily at the Soviet Union. Although badly bloodied, it was clearly hostile. Stalin's ambitions seemed to threaten a new war. Unlike Japan, Stalin lacked an effective surface navy capable of challenging US seapower. However, he already had a large, if obsolescent, submarine force. In 1945 he acquired the technology with which the Germans had hoped to renew the battle against vital Allied shipping, and began to rebuild the naval industry that had provided his big pre-war submarine fleet.

The other reality of postwar life was the atomic bomb. The most radical advocates of air power in both the United States and Britain argued that a future war might be fought exclusively with atomic (later hydrogen) bombs. There would be little or no place for classic armies and navies. This argument became particularly cogent in the United States in 1949, when the defence budget was badly squeezed. The United States had begun to finance the reconstruction of Europe under the Marshall Plan, and new weapons (particularly aircraft) were consuming an increasing fraction of the overall budget. There just was not room enough for substantial fleets and armies. For a short time it seemed, moreover, that given its monopoly on the atomic bomb the United States might be able to fend off the Soviets without fielding expensive mass forces.

That happy situation did not last long. In August 1949 the Soviets tested their own atomic bomb. The United States could no longer imagine defence on the cheap; a government study urged rearmament, including naval rearmament. However, the reality of a very tight budget remained. Ship retirements actually accelerated during the latter part of 1949 and the early part of 1950. Advocates of atomic-armed air power argued, moreover, that once the Soviets had the bomb much of classic naval warfare was no longer possible. For example, it was difficult to imagine a future D-Day, should the Allied armies once more be forced from continental Europe. Moreover, some argued that surface fleets in general were obsolete, since a single bomb might destroy several ships. The response was that moving ships might be difficult to find and that they could be dispersed to survive, whereas one bomb could certainly wipe out any fixed land base.

The central reality was that, once both sides had substantial atomic arsenals, atomic war itself was less and less plausible. Both sides planned for it, but in fact they were not likely to risk a big war. Instead, their basic conflict was reflected in a series of limited wars, beginning in Korea, around the edges of Eurasia. The issue for the Western navies was how to build forces capable of fighting both the limited wars of reality and the possible major war which might occur should the atomic stalemate somehow collapse.

Usually it was argued that any force capable of fighting the Soviets could certainly function effectively in a limited war. That was hardly the case. A major war against the Soviets would be marked by large-scale anti-shipping operations (a sort of Battle of the Atlantic revisited) and, perhaps, by air strikes against key Soviet targets. For example, a nuclear strike against a Soviet submarine base might drastically reduce the enemy submarine capability in the open ocean. On the other hand, anything resembling D-Day was apparently ruled out. A limited war would be very different. The enemy probably would not be able to challenge Western sea control, except on a coastal basis. Carrier air strikes would be a vital means of supporting friendly troops, particularly if the war began unexpectedly and the country had few air bases. It was very much an open question whether nuclear weapons would be used, but amphibious landings could be extremely useful as a means of getting to an enemy's rear.

The only way to unite the two kinds of war was to depend heavily on carrier strike forces to fight a particular kind of central war. In this style of warfare, carriers would seek to destroy as much of the Soviet anti-shipping force as possible by striking at Soviet bases. Hopefully the Soviets would have to challenge any such attacks, thus bringing their anti-shipping forces into contact with the carrier and her escorts. By operating on the flanks of a Soviet advance into Western Europe, naval strike forces might also hope to slow or even reverse that advance. For example, the Soviets might be forced to dilute their attacking force in order to deal with the threat of landings on their flanks. In that case, D-Day would indeed have a post-war echo.

This was very much a large-navy view of naval strategy. During the Cold War, and with the decline of the colonial empires, European NATO governments lost interest in limited warfare and rejected it. They concentrated on the main threat, a possible war against the Soviets. One consequence was that they emphasized a very different sort of shipping protection, building large numbers of specialized convoy escorts. At the time, the US Navy argued that the escort was unlikely to be very effective against the growing threat of nuclear submarines. A great irony was that after the Cold War all the Western navies found themselves employed in limited wars, such as the Gulf War and the peacekeeping operation in Bosnia. The US view was vindicated.

There was one other very important fact of Western naval life. The Second World War ended with both the US and the Royal Navy in possession of large numbers of modern warships, particularly aircraft carriers. In the British case, several ships were left incomplete at the end of the war; construction was suspended, and it was not resumed until the 1950s. The new jet aircraft demanded major modifications to existing ships. It happened that US war-built carriers were amenable to reconstruction; for the Royal Navy the most important resource left over from the war was the incomplete ships, which could be heavily modified before completion. In both cases it was obvious that wartime numbers could not be replaced on anything like a one-for-one basis. Moreover, new ships were generally quite expensive.

Ships last about twenty to thirty years. The fleet on hand in 1945 could be expected to survive through about 1965-1970. At that time governments would suddenly have to choose between a crash in the number of warships or an expensive replacement program. For different reasons, neither of the two main Western governments could afford large new fleets. Their navies tried to compensate by improving the capabilities of their individual ships. However, the collapse in numbers had to be very significant.

In the case of the Royal Navy, the British government decided in 1966 that it could not replace the existing carrier fleet. Although the last large British carrier, HMS *Ark Royal*, survived in service through to 1978, the British were forced to abandon the sort of power projection that had been so important since 1945. A more limited sort of carrier aviation was restored in the form of three light carriers (the Invincible class) capable of operating vertical take-off and landing aircraft (Sea Harriers). By way of contrast, the US Navy kept building and operating very large carriers. Although, at first, size was prized because it allowed the ships to operate long-range bombers capable of delivering nuclear weapons, later large and powerful catapults were vital because they allowed the ships to operate very high-performance fighters, such as the F-14 Tomcat.

Stalin seems to have wanted a pre-war style large-ship fleet, but his main success was – as expected – in rebuilding his submarine fleet and in developing a powerful naval air arm. His armies captured not only German U-boat technology, but also much of the new missile technology that the Germans had applied to anti-ship operations. A missile-armed bomber could attack a ship from well beyond anti-aircraft range. The allied navies developed anti-aircraft missiles in response, but relied largely on carrier-based fighters to defeat the bomber threat. Missile-armed bombers were so important to the Soviets that once they were perfected, in the late 1950s, between a quarter and a third of medium bombers were devoted to naval missions. As it happened, in estimating the Soviet bomber threat to the United States (which helped decide the size of the US bomber force), the US Air Force tended to ignore the naval roles of many of the Soviet aircraft.

For the Western powers, navies became indispensable. They offered global reach. They could bring national power to bear even when no nearby country offered bases. In emergencies, which proved all too common, they could offer support before bases could be built up. Perhaps most important of all, because ships could remain offshore for a protracted period, they could project their power without actually attacking. That is, a naval presence might make an unfriendly ruler think twice, whereas bloodshed might make him even more unfriendly.

Often the mere presence of powerful naval forces helped defuse a situation, encouraging friends and keeping enemies at bay. For example, in 1946 the Soviets pressed the Turks for bases. Many in the US government feared that, were the demands to be met, Turkey would soon pass under Soviet control. The entire

Anglo-American position in the Middle East would crumble. The battleship *Missouri* was sent to Turkey, bearing the body of the Turkish Ambassador who had died during the Second World War. Her presence carried a powerful message of US support. Similarly, a Mediterranean voyage by the new heavy carrier *Franklin D Roosevelt* helped encourage Western friends in France and Italy, at a time when both countries were under Communist threat.

In June 1950 the Communist North Korean army struck South Korea, achieving almost complete surprise. The US government of the day had assumed that Stalin and his communists would not risk a conflagration in so secondary a place. It seemed unlikely that Stalin would risk exciting the United States to re-arm, and thus triggering an arms race he could not win, with his smaller and less developed economy. That was exactly what happened. It now seems that Stalin calculated that if his forces won, the US position in the entire Far East (including Japan) would collapse. If the United States intervened successfully, the Chinese would enter the war to prevent their buffer state, North Korea, from collapsing. In that case China and the United States would fight, and Stalin's nightmare, a US-Chinese pact, would be precluded.

The North Koreans were initially quite effective, overrunning much of South Korea – including its airfields. Without those airfields US Air Force jets based in Japan could not spend very long over the battlefields; they could not provide the retreating South Koreans and US allies with effective close air support. However, British and US carriers could stay much closer to the battle area, so even the jets launched by the US carriers could spend longer over the battle. They, and a heavy influx of US and allied troops, eventually stopped the North Korean advance.

That left open the question of how to push the North Koreans out of South Korea. Any direct assault on land would have cost dearly in lives. The sea offered a way around the North Korean lines. In September 1950 the US Navy staged an amphibious landing at Inchon, up the Korean coast. With strong US forces at their backs, the North Koreans had to retreat. Later, however, there was a grimmer lesson. An attempted landing at Wonsan, further up the other Korean coast, stalled because the North Koreans had mined the port. It became clear that a very small primitive navy, equipped with modern mines (by the Soviets) could sometimes block operations by a much larger and more modern navy. On balance, though, the lesson of Korea was that despite the existence of the bomb (and of a modern air force to deliver it) local warfare was possible – and navies were an essential way of fighting it.

The US Marines drew the conclusion that they might have to repeat Inchon in the face of tactical nuclear weapons. They could not afford to concentrate valuable transports, as they had done during the Second World War. If the transports were dispersed, they needed some very quick means of getting troops to the beach. They found it in the helicopter; by the mid-1950s they had conceived a doctrine of 'vertical envelopment'. Troops would fly in, but the helicopters had limits. Heavy equipment and supplies still had to come by slow landing boat, over the beach. Ships, though fewer in number, would still have to congregate offshore.

A few years later the Royal Navy, which had fought in Korea, was in action again. In 1956 President Nasser of Egypt nationalized the Suez Canal, which was owned by an Anglo-French company. To the British, this act was part of Nasser's larger campaign to eject them from the Middle East, where they had several important allies. To the French, Nasser was deeply involved in the war they were fighting to keep control of Algeria. During the autumn of 1956, both governments agreed to attack Egypt in hopes of overthrowing Nasser. Meanwhile the Israelis also planned an attack, as Nasser had just bought massive amounts of Soviet weaponry that they suspected he planned to use against them. The British and French decided to use the Israeli attack as a pretext; they would claim they were seizing the vital Canal to protect it against both sides. For them, this was the largest amphibious operation since the Second World War – supporting forces included the French battleship *Jean Bart*. For the occasion, the British deployed the first helicopter-borne assault group in history.

The assault was a great success, but the war was a failure. The US government weighed in against the British and the French; it wanted to retain influence in the ex-colonial world. It enforced a truce and then the withdrawal of the British, French, and Israeli forces. The Suez Canal itself was blocked, so vital oil tankers were kept out of Europe. The British and French economies suffered. Nasser survived. Moreover, the vital NATO alliance was badly strained. The British and French could not have acted without sea power, since Nasser had ejected the British from their bases near the Canal. However, the freedom that the allied navies offered had been misused, with serious consequences. For example, the government of Iraq, before the war a British ally, was overthrown.

The United States was luckier. When it seemed that the Lebanese government needed armed help, US warships quickly landed Marines, who, as it happened, soon found that there was no war (the enduring image of the operation is of combat-loaded Marines trudging ashore past bikini-clad women bathing in the peaceful Mediterranean sun). In the Far East, at about the same time, US warships helped defuse a crisis by patrolling the Taiwan Straits, preventing the Communist Chinese from making good on their threat to seize Taiwan. In both cases, what mattered was that the US ships could operate freely, without needing bases in the area.

By this time, Nikita Khrushchev ruled the Soviet Union. He well understood that in a nuclear age, a big war was essentially impossible. He could, therefore, safely take chances, supporting Communist revolutionaries abroad. However, unlike the British and the Americans, he lacked a powerful fleet to back his friends. That became most obvious in the 1962 Cuban Missile Crisis. By the spring of 1962 Khrushchev knew that his own missile force was depressingly inferior to that of the United States. He lacked the long-range missiles he needed to threaten the United States directly. To make up for that, he placed his own shorter-range weapons in Cuba, within range of American targets. US President John F. Kennedy was outraged, and pressured Khrushchev to remove the missiles. To avoid the risk of landing troops or directly attacking the missile sites, he imposed an embargo, a blockade. Now Khrushchev faced a similarly unpleasant choice. He could either back down or he could try to force his ships through the embargo. Because he lacked an effective fleet, he had to back down. He might have tried to use his submarines to sink the US warships around Cuba, but that would have brought on the war neither he nor Kennedy wanted.

Western navies were busy elsewhere. Iraq had long coveted the oil-rich sheikdom of Kuwait, which was under British protection. The presence of a British aircraft carrier helped calm the situation there in 1961. Further east, President Sukarno of Indonesia tried to destroy the new Malaysian Federation, feeding in guerillas. Malaysia, a collection of former British colonies, was under British protection. In 1964-66 the Royal Navy supported an undeclared war against Indonesia, the 'confrontation'. It included an unusual large-scale night amphibious landing. The British victory in the confrontation would have been impossible without the Royal Navy, which concentrated much of its fleet in the Far East. Victory helped to unseat Sukarno, and thus to guarantee the future of Malaysia. Moreover, Sukarno's defeat protected other countries in the area, particularly Australia, which Sukarno had coveted.

By the time the confrontation was over, the United States was heavily committed in Vietnam. Although the war is commonly considered mainly an air

⚓ ANTI-AIRCRAFT MISSILES ⚓

For the US Navy, operations around Vietnam were largely updated versions of those it had conducted two decades earlier in the Second World War. There was one important exception. In the late 1940s, the US Navy had developed anti-aircraft missiles. By the mid-1960s it had converted many ships to fire them, and it had gone through a major upgrade programme to fix the defects of the first generation. It had three weapons in service: the short-range Tartar (being replaced by Standard Medium Range), the medium-range two-stage Terrier (being replaced by Standard Extended Range), and the long-range ramjet Talos. Missile cruisers off the Vietnamese coast used Talos to shoot down North Vietnamese MiG jets, in some cases over land. In 1972, when US carrier aircraft mined Haiphong harbour, the missile cruiser *Chicago* defended the bombers by shooting down two MiG-17s which tried to intercept them. For the first time, a surface ship was able to take over duties previously performed exclusively by carrier-based fighters. In another incident at about the same time the missile cruiser (actually large destroyer) *Sterrett* shot down a pair of North Vietnamese aircraft using her Standard (Extended Range) missiles.

and ground struggle, the US Navy was involved in four quite distinct ways. First, American aircraft carriers were used against North Vietnam, in hopes of convincing the North Vietnamese to stop supporting the communist guerillas (the Viet Cong) operating in the south. In this they supplemented land-based aircraft. They enjoyed an important advantage. The Viet Cong were well aware that US aircraft flying from South Vietnam were badly damaging the north. They therefore worked quite effectively to attack aircraft on the ground. Carriers at sea suffered no similar assaults. Second, US forces off the South Vietnamese coast stopped and searched boats suspected of smuggling arms to the Viet Cong, in Operation Market Time. Third, much of South Vietnam, particularly in the Mekong Delta, used rivers as roads. US naval (and army) forces therefore fought a riverine war in the south. Specialized riverine craft were built or converted from standard medium landing craft for this purpose. Finally, through much of the war a US amphibious force was maintained off the North Vietnamese coast. Simply by its presence, it threatened an amphibious invasion of North Vietnam. To deal with that very real threat, the North Vietnamese held troops back from combat in South Vietnam. The invasion was, as it happened, impossible because the US government feared that the Chinese would enter the war (as they had in Korea) in the event that the United States threatened to overthrow North Korea altogether.

This extensive naval effort helped keep the North Vietnamese from winning their war against South Vietnam; the war ended in a cease-fire in 1973, with thousands of victims on both sides. When the North Vietnamese attacked and won in 1975, US forces were not involved. That is another, non-naval, story.

While the United States was engaged in Vietnam, the Soviets created a revolution in naval warfare by deploying effective anti-ship missiles (P-15, which NATO called SS-N-2 'Styx') which even a small attack boat could launch. The Soviets were already transforming their surface fleet by arming ships with larger missiles, deploying numerous missile-armed heavy bombers (mainly Tu-16s, which NATO called 'Badgers'), and building nuclear submarines, many of which were also missile-armed. However, the new missile boats were probably more significant. The Soviets saw them as equalizers which could be widely distributed to allied states in the Third World. At a very low price they could, in theory, negate very expensive investments in conventional forms of seapower, at least near coasts. This was analogous to the earlier proliferation of torpedo boats, but the missile could strike at a long enough range to give the boat a realistic chance of success. Really important client states[1], such as Egypt and Indonesia, also got missile-carrying bombers.

During the confrontation the Royal Navy had faced a combination of Indonesian missile boats and bombers, but fortunately was already deploying helicopters on board its frigates, mainly to attack submarines. After the confrontation, it equipped the same helicopters with short-range missiles.

Soon this issue became much more than theoretical. In 1967 Egyptian missile boats, supplied by the Soviets, sank the Israeli destroyer *Eilat*. Although the missiles had been in service for some years, they had never before been fired in anger. Suddenly the possibility that the Soviets could supply a real equalizer against Western sea power seemed very real. NATO navies began urgent work on anti-missile weapons such as Seawolf and Sea Sparrow.

In December 1971 the point was reinforced. As India and Pakistan fought, the Indian Navy raided Karachi. En route, Styx-armed Indian missile boats sank the

1 The designation 'client state' includes but is not limited to formal allies; it indicates countries that receive significant assistance from larger powers. Thus during the 1960s Egypt was a client state of the Soviet Union, receiving significant military and economic assistance in return for political support; but she was not part of the Warsaw Pact headed by the Soviet Union, and the Soviets made no agreement to fight to save Egypt in the event of a war.

Pakistani destroyer *Khaibar* and the minesweeper *Muhafiz*. Similar missiles badly damaged a vital oil tank farm at Karachi and sank or damaged several merchant ships. The Indians found that they could tow their missile boats into position to strike, a dangerous but effective tactic. For its part, the Pakistan Navy submarine *Hangor* sank the Indian frigate *Khukri*.

In 1972 the US missile cruiser *Sterrett* claimed to have shot down a Styx anti-ship missile, but that seems unlikely; it does not appear that Styx had been provided to the North Vietnamese before the end of the Vietnam War. If the ship did in fact destroy the missile, it was the first occasion in history of a naval missile shooting down another naval missile.

For the Israelis, the *Eilat* incident was a terrible shock. They had paid heavily to build a kind of miniature Western navy, equipped with Second World War-built destroyers and submarines. Now the destroyers seemed worthless. The Israelis urgently developed their own boat-fired missile, Gabriel. Much smaller than Styx, it had a shorter range but could be carried in greater numbers. Having deployed their own boats, the Israelis got considerable insight into missile tactics.

There were two essential points. First, the missile boats had to fire at maximum range if they were to be effective. They were both devastating in attack and extremely weak in defence. Second, they carried too few weapons to be able to afford to waste them on false targets. When war broke out in the Middle East in October 1973, the Israeli Navy was ready. Its boats probably detected their Arab enemies by listening to their radar and radio signals. Once within range, they fired decoy rockets. The Arab crews suddenly saw large targets popping up on their radars. They assumed that they were under attack by major warships (later it became an article of faith in the Arab world that the US Sixth Fleet had been involved), and they fired their missiles. Many went wild, since there had been insufficient time to run up their gyros. Most of those that did guide locked on to the decoys and thus missed the Israeli boats altogether. The one that approached an Israeli boat was knocked out by its cannon. Once they had fired their weapons, the Arab boats were defenceless. The Israelis closed in, attacking first with their own missiles and then with their guns. They won resoundingly.

By this time Styx missiles had been sold very widely; eventually the Chinese produced a modified version of their own, which the Western navies code-named Silkworm. Thus the Chinese used Styx during a 1974 confrontation with the South Vietnamese over the Spratly Islands in the South China Sea. The Spratlys were considered important because it was widely suspected that beneath them lay enormous oil deposits. The area was (and is) claimed both by China and by several smaller countries: Brunei, the Philippines, Thailand, and Vietnam. This time Styx proved less effective; one damaged, but did not come close to sinking, an old US-supplied 1800-ton seaplane tender, the largest ship in the South Vietnamese fleet. On the other hand, the Chinese found a ready market for their Styx copy, providing it to both Iran and Iraq a few years later.

By the mid-1970s it seemed that a first-line Western warship had a reasonable chance of beating off a missile attack, using a combination of jammers, decoys, and anti-missile guns and missiles. However, big valuable amphibious ships were a very different proposition. They could not be heavily armed. They could not move very fast while discharging their landing craft and amphibious vehicles, and they had to do so quite close to the beach. They would be well within missile range. Moreover, the effect of discarding the war-built amphibious ships was dramatic. Fairly large numbers of ships were replaced by a smaller number of much larger ones, which were not much more battleworthy than their predecessors. The US Marines needed some equivalent to vertical envelopment that could move their heavy loads to the beach. They came up with air-cushion landing craft (LCACs), which could bring in cargo at 40 or 50 knots and move it not only over the sea but also across the beach. Moreover, they could cross beaches much steeper or shallower than those suited to conventional beach landing craft.

For the future, then, the Marines envisaged a dual assault by helicopters and by LCACs. The big ships would remain beyond the horizon, reasonably safe from coast defence missiles. Moreover, because they could use a much wider selection of beaches, they could attack in places an enemy would not expect. That enemy might not be able to put defenders (or mines) in position.

For the two big Western navies, the 1970s were a time of retrenchment. The US defence budget was cut drastically in the wake of Vietnam. All but two of the surviving Second World War-built carriers were retired without replacement, so that fewer ships had to cover more crisis areas. The Vietnam experience also discouraged US activism in the Third World. In 1976, for example, Congress vetoed any US involvement in a growing civil war in Angola, in which the Communist side was backed by Cuban troops. In the Soviet Union, the fleet commander, Admiral Sergei Gorshkov, took this opportunity to claim that the presence of his ships had precluded US involvement. It seems far fairer to say that any Soviet naval presence had had no particular effect on Congress; the legacy of

⚓ AUTOMATIC DATA LINK ⚓

Since the early 1960s, US and then most NATO warships have had computerised combat direction systems connected together by standard data links. In the nets formed by the links, each aircraft detected by any ship's radar is assigned a track number, so that its position can be updated by any ship that sees it. The computers on board the ships automatically reassign track numbers so that targets are not duplicated; they use the first number any ship in the group assigns.

Vietnam was reason enough to steer clear.

On the other hand, it did seem to many Americans that the Soviets were gaining some key naval positions as they moved into the Third World. By the mid-1970s they were firmly entrenched in Yemen, at the outlet of the Red Sea. Across that sea, they gained a base (a weapons depot) in Somalia. In theory, this position would have made it possible for Soviet forces to attack tankers headed south from the Persian Gulf, and around Africa to Europe. Sympathetic regimes in Mozambique, Angola, and Guinea-Bissau provided bases on both African coasts, again on the vital tanker route to Europe. At the other end of Asia, the Soviets were gaining influence in Vietnam (at the expense of the Chinese). Once they had a base there, they could attack tankers en route to Japan. If the Suez Canal resumed its former importance, the Soviets could rely on friends in North Africa, particularly in Algeria and in Libya (Egypt ejected Soviet advisors in 1972, before the Middle-East War). For example, the Libyans allowed Soviet crews to operate naval reconnaissance aircraft in Libyan colors, a practice called 'wet-leasing'. The clear implication was that, in wartime, Soviet naval strike forces would operate from Libyan airfields. In wartime, then, the Soviets could starve the West of oil.

To make matters worse, the US Administration of the time, led by President Jimmy Carter, rejected any argument that developments in the Third World could be important in the US-Soviet rivalry. For Carter, the confrontation with the Soviets was limited to Europe and to strategic missiles. The army fighting in Europe did need supplies, but that meant merely that anti-submarine escorts were essential. Carriers and the power they could project seemed to be outdated. One defect in this concept was that the Soviet threat to shipping embraced not only submarines but also land-based bombers carrying long-range missiles. Western convoy escorts did carry anti-aircraft missiles, but the bombers outranged them.

They might be able to beat off some attacks by shooting down the missiles, but they could not shoot far enough to destroy the bombers and thus to turn off the threat. Only carrier-based fighters could do that.

As in Korea, the world did not always match the US Administration's expectations. In 1979 the Shah of Iran, a major US ally in a crucial area, was overthrown, and it seemed important to be able to place US power within striking range of Iran and other parts of Southwest Asia. The remaining major US ally in the region, Saudi Arabia, rejected any attempt to base US forces on its territory. That left the sea. The United States leased the island of Diego Garcia from the British and developed it as a base. The main striking power in the area was provided by a carrier, on station in the northern Arabian Sea.[2]

The US Navy also raised questions about the course of a possible war in Europe. In peacetime the Soviets maintained very large forces on the Chinese border, because over the past two decades the Chinese had become increasingly hostile. The US Navy argued that powerful naval forces in the Western Pacific could help tie down those Soviet forces, and thus could help limit any threat the Soviets might direct against NATO. If the Pacific fleet were withdrawn in time of crisis, the Soviets could quickly transfer bombers and submarines to the Atlantic, where they could threaten the vital sea routes supporting a NATO army. The navy also argued that carriers could provide vital air support on the flanks of NATO, for example in the Mediterranean.

Once Ronald Reagan was in office, in 1981, the navy was able to elaborate its preferred strategy, as Reagan favoured a much more aggressive approach to the Soviets. Championed by John Lehman, Secretary of the Navy, the new Maritime Strategy extended the ideas the Pacific fleet was already proposing. The fleet could win sea control by forcing the Soviets into a series of major battles. For example, it could head north into the Norwegian Sea, its carrier-based bombers threatening the main Soviet naval bases in the Arctic. To deal with this threat, the Soviets would have to launch their missile-carrying bombers. The fleet's own carrier-based fighters could then destroy the bombers. No other Western naval force would have much of a chance of doing so; if they were left alone, the bombers could destroy vital NATO shipping. Similarly, the Soviets would feel compelled to use their submarines against the advancing carrier battle group, which would include anti-submarine forces far more potent than those around a convoy.

2 This was due to the concern that the revolutionaries might well try to expand their power; or that the Soviets might take advantage of disorder in Iran to expand South. The Soviets were, at this time, just beginning their long unhappy war in Afghanistan, and there was a real fear that their motive was to gain direct access to the oil-rich Persian Gulf.

Another element of the strategy was that US submarines would threaten the only naval asset the Soviets really valued, their ballistic-missile submarines. To protect that asset, the Soviets would deploy most of their own submarine force; the US submarine offensive, then, would tie down most of the Soviet anti-shipping force.

Proponents of the Maritime Strategy pointed out that it was a reversion to classic ideas of naval warfare. At the time, however, it seemed startling. From the early 1970s on, many had distinguished power projection from sea control. The US maritime strategists argued the opposite, that sea control could be won by a force projecting naval power into the enemy's homeland.

While US strategists theorized, the Royal Navy found itself fighting a naval war in, of all places, the South Atlantic. Having abandoned the 'East of Suez' role in 1968, the British Government argued that in future the Royal Navy should concentrate on the battle against Soviet submarines in the Greenland-Iceland-UK (GIUK) Gap north of the British Isles. This war would be fought largely by British submarines and by Nimrod anti-submarine aircraft cued by British frigates employing towed arrays to detect any submarines that got through. As for the Soviet naval air threat, land-based interceptors should suffice. The Royal Navy argued that it needed sea-based aircraft, partly to support a planned role in helping to defend northern Norway. As finances got tighter, the British Government saw less and less point in maintaining an expensive carrier capability. Arrangements were therefore made, in 1981, to sell one of the two new light carriers to Australia, and also to sell off the two specialized amphibious ships.

However, in April 1982 the Argentines seized the Falkland Islands, one of the few remaining British overseas territories; the British Prime Minister Margaret Thatcher decided to eject them. The naval campaign that followed was in many ways a small-scale version of that envisaged by the US maritime strategists.

The Argentine naval force consisted of submarines, missile- and bomb-carrying aircraft, and a small surface force, some of it equipped with anti-ship missiles. Against it the British could array submarines, a battle force (carriers plus escorts), and merchant ships carrying the invasion force. As in a future major war, there were never enough escorts to protect the vital merchant ships. Before any decision had been made to deploy a major naval force to the South Atlantic, the British had sent five nuclear submarines there. The submarines were essentially invisible to the Argentines, so their presence did not affect any attempt to negotiate an end to the crisis. When negotiations failed, the submarines were in place well before the battle force could arrive from Britain.

For their part, the Argentines hoped to use their own surface fleet to beat off the British attacking force. However, a British nuclear submarine, HMS *Conqueror*, torpedoed and sank the Argentine cruiser *Belgrano* (a planned parallel attack by another submarine against the carrier failed). The Argentines knew that their anti-submarine capability was insufficient to deal with such a threat, and for the rest of the war their surface fleet remained in port. A British submarine threat had tied it down, much as the US Navy hoped to tie down the main Soviet submarine threat in a major war.

That left the Argentines with land-based aircraft and submarines (only one of which was fully operational). The land-based aircraft were handicapped in that they had to fight at nearly the limit of their range, hence could not manoeuvre freely over the defended target area. Had the Argentine carrier been usable, the situation would have been quite different. Even so, they managed to sink several British warships. Perhaps the most notable Argentine success was a missile strike against the destroyer *Sheffield*. Eventually it became clear that the only really effective defence against Argentine air attacks was a combat air patrol over the ships, mounted by the two British carriers, *Invincible* and *Hermes*. This was not too different from the US perception that the aircraft threat to shipping was best dealt with by fighters rather than by missiles.

In some cases Argentine aircraft managed to get close enough to British warships to hit them with bombs which, in theory, should have been impossible; the Royal Navy had invested heavily in anti-aircraft missiles which should have kept air attackers well out of bombing range. However, the warships were close inshore and many of their radars could not distinguish aircraft from ground clutter (the improvements that would have solved this problem were among those not funded in the 1970s and early 1980s). The destroyer *Coventry* and the frigates *Ardent* and *Antelope* were lost to bomb attacks (*Ardent* was also hit by air-launched rockets). However, other ships survived because the bombs that hit them failed to explode. That was probably an indirect benefit of the British missile air defence. To evade the missiles, the Argentine attackers had to fly very low. Low-flying aircraft can be destroyed by the explosions of their own bombs, so the bombs have to be delay-fused, and the delay mechanisms did not always work (in some cases the delay was so long that the bomb bounced *through* its target before going off).[3] The irony was

3 The bomb fuse would be started by the initial impact with the ship, the time running as the bomb penetrated the ship. The bomb hit with considerable momentum, and the ship structure was quite light, so unless it went off a bomb might well pass through both sides of a ship. Much the same thing happened with armour-piercing shells (which also have delayed-action fuses) fired at unarmoured warships, such as destroyers, during the Second World War.

that the Argentines were already familiar with the main British system, Sea Dart.

The Argentines were certainly well aware of the importance of the carriers, and made considerable efforts to deal with them. For example, HMS *Sheffield* was fatally hit while screening HMS *Hermes*, and there is reason to believe that she was mistaken for the carrier (her design made for an unusually large radar cross-section). The lone Argentine submarine in the area made a special effort to attack HMS *Hermes* (she apparently failed due to an improperly installed torpedo fire control device).[4] In doing so, she attracted the attention of British helicopters, which nearly sank her. American strategists would have seen in this episode confirmation that the battle force could be expected to attract attackers which might otherwise destroy vital merchant shipping, and that any attack on it would bring the submarine into contact with particularly effective anti-submarine forces. As it happened, the British counterattack failed, and the submarine eventually escaped.

More generally, the attacking Argentine aircraft concentrated on the British warships. Only one amphibious ship and one converted merchant ship were hit and sunk. Presumably the Argentine view was they could not successfully attack such targets until the protecting warships were stripped away.

The Royal Navy made possible the reconquest of the Falklands. Carriers were clearly essential, and the radical cuts envisaged in 1981 were rescinded. Moreover, the Falklands War emphasized that Britain still had world interests, and that the Royal Navy had to be able to support them. This point was further proven by an ongoing war on the other side of the world, between Iran and Iraq. The war had broken out in 1979, and was fought mainly on land. However, it had a very important maritime dimension.

For both combatants, oil was the main source of income. In the case of Iran, it came by tanker out of the oil port of Abadan. Before the war, Iraq had shipped oil out of Basra, but the Iranians effectively cut the sea route, and the pipeline through Syria was cut because Syria supported Iran. At this time several of the Gulf states, such as Kuwait, supported Iraq as a bulwark against Iran, which had just undergone a fundamentalist revolution. Their economies were also based on oil, and their tankers also used the Persian Gulf.

---

4 The Argentine submarine had been used intensively to train crews for the expected next-generation TR 1700 type submarines about to be delivered. Reportedly her computer fire control system broke down, and in the emergency an extemporized system using a joystick was installed. Also, two wires were supposedly interchanged, so that when the stick was pushed in the direction of the target, the torpedo was accidentally directed 30 degrees off-course. This account is somewhat controversial.

By 1980 it was clear that the war had reached a stalemate, yet neither side was interested in a truce. Naval warfare offered a way to gain decisive results. The Iraqis obtained Mirage fighter-bombers and Exocet anti-ship missiles from France, and began to attack Iranian tankers; they also struck Abadan itself. For their part, the Iranians tried to stop oil traffic from Gulf states supporting Iraq. Lacking effective anti-ship aircraft, they used mainly small attack boats and land-based anti-ship missiles, which they bought from China. They also had some ship-launched missiles, and they mined parts of the Persian Gulf.

The Royal Navy instituted an 'Armilla Patrol' to protect tankers in the Gulf. Later the United States joined, and began to convoy Kuwaiti tankers (which were transferred to US registry), and US and British warships began to patrol the Gulf to discourage air attacks. The unstated theory was that no one would try such attacks if they risked sinking a Western warship, and thus inviting Western intervention.

One interesting lesson of the war was that modern anti-ship weapons were much less lethal than had been imagined. Many tankers took Exocet (and other missile) hits without being sunk. It turned out that a missile exploding deep in a full oil tank had remarkably little effect (and some early Exocets turned out to have defective fuses). When the Iranians hit a tanker in Kuwait City with a much larger Silkworm, the missile burned out the ship's superstructure, containing her crew quarters, but it did not set the oil tanks on fire. A supertanker that was mined suffered only limited damage, merely spilling some oil. For that matter, a ship carrying liquid natural gas, which many had supposed could be equated to a floating bomb, merely burned after being hit numerous times by small anti-tank weapons fired by Iranian fast attack boats.

After a series of incidents, the US Navy in 1986 seized an Iranian minelayer and, in a night missile battle, Operation Praying Mantis, destroyed much of the Iranian fleet. US and British mine countermeasures craft were sent into the Gulf to keep the shipping lane open.

The missile war against tankers continued. In 1987 an Iraqi Mirage mistakenly attacked the US frigate *Stark*, almost sinking her with two hits. The aircraft that made the night attack was clearly vectored to the ship; it did not search for targets. It was carrying two Exocets rather than the usual one. After the attack, the pilot returned to Iraq to be greeted as a hero, but the next morning, when it became clear which ship had been hit, he disappeared. It now appears that this incident was triggered by the Iranians, who were aware of US support for Iraq and

⇒ THE GULF WAR ⇐
AUGUST 1990 - FEBRUARY 1991

In August 1990 the Iraqi army occupied Kuwait, a small Western-oriented Gulf state. The Iraqi dictator, Sadaam Hussein, announced that any Arab government that co-operated with Western attempts to eject him from Kuwait was betraying Arab nationalism, and deserved to be overthrown. On the Kuwaiti border, the Saudis dithered. The Saudi royal family claimed the right to rule because it protected Mecca from, among others, unbelievers, meaning, in this instance, Westerners. Allowing Western troops on sacred Saudi soil might well endanger that claim.

Here seapower showed its value. The United States immediately moved carriers into the area. Their aircraft could help protect Saudi Arabia without requiring any intrusions on Saudi soil; in effect, they could protect Saudi Arabia whether or not its government agreed. The Saudi government could thus argue that the decision to accept Western help was out of its hands; it then agreed to accept Western armies and air forces on Saudi soil. Had the carriers not been present, the Saudis might well have found it far more difficult to ally themselves with the West.

The Western navies were also able to take more immediate action against Iraq, by enforcing an embargo in the Arabian Sea. That helped deny Iraq vital spare parts for the air defence system the allies faced the following January. Given an enforceable embargo, the Soviets and others supporting Iraqi defence systems could reasonably recall their personnel. Again, that drastically reduced the capability of the Iraqi system.

hoped that they could win the war if that support were withdrawn. Possibly the Iranians let the Iraqis imagine that they could achieve a decision in the war if only they destroyed a ship in that place that night. The ship was ultimately saved and US support for Iraq continued.

It seems clear in retrospect that the ship's commander had no expectation of being attacked. He was aware of the Iraqi Mirage almost from the moment it took off, thanks in part to radar coverage by a Saudi AWACS aircraft, and he regarded the Iraqis as friendly. In any case, the ship was unprepared for the attack, to the point that her decoy (chaff) ammunition was locked up and her anti-missile gun turned off. The captain was, inevitably, dismissed for having made no effort to defend his ship. The message to other US commanders in the Gulf was that the area really was a war zone, and that attacks might be sudden and misdirected. Later it would be suggested that the *Vincennes* incident was caused in part by her captain's fear that he might lose his ship due to inaction.

Once war broke out, US carriers contributed heavily to the air offensive, attacking from both the Gulf and the Red Sea to hit Iraqi defences from two sides. US surface ships and submarines hit Iraq with Tomahawk missiles, in the first combat use of this weapon. Tomahawk proved particularly valuable when Baghdad was covered in cloud; at such times manned aircraft were prohibited from attacking.

Much of the value of seapower lies in its mobility; the enemy must array forces to face a variety of challenges. In the Gulf, the US Navy mounted a credible threat of an amphibious assault. To meet that threat, the Iraqis placed a very large force facing the sea – which was ultimately irrelevant as the main allied attack came overland. To keep the threat credible, and to forestall any Iraqi attack on the carriers further down the Gulf, the allied navies had to operate at the head of the Gulf, close to Iraqi coast-defence missiles. In the course of these operations HMS *Gloucester* shot down a pair of Silkworm missiles headed for the US battleship *Wisconsin*. If the Sterrett incident is discounted, this was the first time in history that anti-ship missiles had been shot down by self-defence missiles (in this case, Sea Darts). It was an impressive demonstration that the main 'equaliser' bought by Third World navies, the anti-ship missile, was being mastered by newer technology

The Iraqis tried to mount a minor amphibious operation in support of an early (and abortive) ground offensive. The craft involved were caught and sunk by British missile firing Lynx helicopters. Several were missile-firing boats, lineal descendants of those which had prompted the original British interest in arming frigate helicopters with anti-ship missiles.

The Western presence helped stalemate the tanker war at sea, denying either side decisive results. As it happened, the war ended on a naval note. The US missile cruiser *Vincennes*, on patrol off the Iranian city of Bandar Abbas, mistakenly shot down an Iranian Airbus airliner on 3 July 1988. The Iranians presented this unfortunate incident as the intervention of the United States, the 'Great Satan', into the war. Given this sudden change in circumstances, it was honorable to seek an end to the war.

As it happened, the destruction of the Airbus had nothing to do with any US decision to intervene. The ship had been alerted to Iranian plans to attack the 'Great Satan', and the alert seemed particularly realistic on the weekend of the US national holiday, July 4th. Moreover, the ship had been alerted that Iranian F-14 fighters, which might have been fitted with anti-ship missiles, had been moved to Bandar Abbas airfield. The situation seemed particularly menacing since an Iranian P-3 patrol plane was orbiting near the ship, in what might have been interpreted as a 'targeting' pattern. Some small Iranian craft were nearby. Armed with rockets, they might have been intended to damage the ship's radars so as to open the way for a missile attack. All this, it should be emphasized, was supposition.

The key failure seems to have been in the ship's use of her automatic data link. In the case of *Vincennes*, the accompanying frigate *Sides* saw the Airbus first, so the track number assigned by the cruiser was dropped in favor of the earlier number set by the frigate. That change was not immediately obvious on board the cruiser.

Well to the south, but within radio range, was another group of ships, including a carrier. There was always a possibility that the two groups would accidentally merge their radio link nets. To avoid confusion, each group was supposed to use a distinct block of track numbers. Here the problems began. The group to the south, which included a carrier, used the same block as the *Vincennes* group. An airplane approaching the carrier to land was assigned the track number that *Vincennes* had initially assigned to the Airbus.

As the Airbus flew towards the cruiser, her commander kept asking it to identify itself, but the Airbus pilot was too busy climbing out of his take-off to notice the call, which was on the rarely-monitored International Distress channel. On board the cruiser, the ship's captain kept asking what the Airbus was doing. The display in front of him was two-dimensional: it showed that the Airbus was coming, but not whether it was climbing or diving or flying level. The captain asked in terms of the track number that his ship had assigned, not realizing that the number no longer referred to the Airbus. The link system, designed to share information among many ships, correctly reported that the airplane with the queried tail number was diving – it was landing on the carrier about a hundred miles away. The captain thought that the Airbus was diving at his ship, that it was a Kamikaze attack. He shot it down.

The captain already expected an attack. In fact, he had used his helicopter to trigger a battle with the fast, rocket-armed boats. He probably saw that as a spoiling attack, to prevent the Iranians from making the sort of coordinated attack which seemed to be developing. Perhaps the key problem was that *Vincennes* had only recently arrived in the Gulf and her captain did not know that the Iranians constantly announced that they would attack and destroy the 'Great Satan' – but that they never did. For example, in the unsettled conditions in Iran, it was most unlikely that the Revolutionary Guards (who controlled the small fast boats) would have cooperated with the regular forces (who controlled the P-3 and the F-14s). To further complicate matters, an error in using the ship's IFF system[5] made it appear that the Airbus was actually an Iranian F-14 (the Iranian aircraft was on the runway at Bandar Abbas, and its IFF emissions were picked up).

The tanker war was, in effect, a transition from Cold War operations, from operations centered on the Soviet threat to those centered on local emergencies. In the tanker war, for example, the West backed Iraq, which in the past had been a Soviet client state, against Iran, formerly a Western ally. This was entirely a matter of national interests; there was nothing inherently friendly about Iraqi policies.

That was soon demonstrated, as, in August 1990 the Iraqi army occupied Kuwait, a small Western-oriented Gulf state. America and several other Western powers intervened, and the Gulf War ended in February 1991. However, Western navies are still hard-worked in an uncertain world. Major operations have included the arms embargo and peace-keeping patrol off the former Yugoslav coast; a series of retaliatory strikes against Iraq, executed mainly with Tomahawks; and a US operation in the Formosa Strait to counter Chinese demonstrations (mainly naval) intended to cow the Taiwanese electorate (1996). Indeed, one of the lessons of an aborted retaliatory strike against Iraq (1998) was that naval forces are more important than ever. The Saudis denied the West the use of airfields, probably precisely because, as Sadaam Hussein predicted, their population would look askance at supporting a Western assault on an Arab government. Carriers would have provided a viable alternative, had the US and British governments decided to strike.

It had been lucky indeed that the Western governments had decided that victory and the bomb did not make navies obsolete after 1945.

---

5 The Gulf area is affected by 'ducting', a phenomenon which causes some electromagnetic signals (like those emanating from aircraft IFF transponders) to carry beyond the horizon. IFF works by a combination of interrogation (by the ship) and answer (by the transponder on board the aircraft). The time delay between interrogation and response indicates the range of the aircraft. In the case of *Vincennes*, reportedly the ship's crew mis-set the range of the IFF set, so that they did not realize that they were seeing a response from a relatively distant aircraft. Ducting made it possible for them to interrogate the aircraft on the runway, and to receive its replies. The ranging error made it seem, apparently, that the replies were relevant to the aircraft the ship's radar was tracking, the unfortunate Airbus. The Airbus itself was not sending out any military IFF signals. Because the displays were two-dimensional (range and bearing only) they could not easily distinguish between an aircraft on the ground (providing the misleading IFF signals) and a climbing airliner. The Aegis radar on board the cruiser did detect altitude, but the ship's IFF system could not have done so.

I was given to rhapsodizing on the potential of the Solent area, stressing its importance as a focal point for shipping of some sort for at least 5000 years. Many vessels, I argued, must have been wrecked and buried in the preserving mud to lie there forgotten, including the ship whose name had preoccupied me for so long.

Alexander McKee, *How We Found the Mary Rose* (1982)

CHAPTER TEN

THE GLOBAL SEA

Alison Gale

MODERN SHIPS COME IN ALL SHAPES AND SIZES; their design fits them for specific tasks. Each one is a tool used by seafarers to exploit particular resources from the global seas. The ocean offers: an efficient means of transport; an aid to defense; a playground for leisure; a source for extraction of fish and other animals, minerals and power; and a place for waste disposal. In addition the sea is a crucial life source for the planet. All of these activities have been carried on for centuries. The extraction of the mineral salt by the Phoenicians, for example, is recorded as far back as 1200 BC.

The technological developments of the twentieth century have revolutionized the use of the sea's resources. In particular, the scale and range of extractive activities have increased. The larger fishing vessels and freezing have enabled fish catches to rise exponentially, while scientific exploration of the seabed has discovered new sources of hydrocarbons and metals which provide energy and raw materials for the modern world. At the same time there has been growing awareness and knowledge of the importance of the oceans to the welfare of the planet, and concern over the adverse effects of waste products, especially of industrial and industrializing countries, reaching the sea. There has, therefore, also been a rise in national and international regulation of the use of the sea. The international fora that only evolved in this century have facilitated agreement on innovative regulation based on the entirely new concept of the sea as a global resource.

The sea has a surface area of about 361 million km^2 and covers 71% of the earth. With an average depth of 4.6km, the volume of seawater is about 1370 million km^3. This accounts for nearly all the water on the planet, as only 1.2% of the earth's water is locked in the ice caps, just 0.002% in the rivers and lakes, and only 0.0008% is vapour in the air. The cycle of water – evaporation and precipitation as fresh water – from the world's oceans is essential to the life of the planet. To live, humans need only two litres of fresh water a day. In developed urban societies consumption rises to over eight hundred litres per person a day, with industrial processes requiring huge quantities. The sea also has an aesthetic quality and recreational value. While flat coastal land can be at a premium for industry, most coastal dwellings are chosen for the delight of living by the sea rather than for their job opportunities. It was estimated that three out of four people in the USA would live within fifty miles of the sea by the end of the twenty-first century.

The seabed is not featureless. In deeper water, like dry land, it has mountains, valleys, escarpments and plains. Its general topography divides into a series of natural zones. The continental shelf is immediately adjacent to the land and is commonly defined as the area with a water depth of less than 200m. It stretches seawards for a distance of roughly 65km. At this point the seabed begins to slope downwards. This continental slope is at an angle of about 4° and extends some 80km, dropping to 1400-3200m below sea level. At this point the gradient becomes less steep. It now takes the name continental rise and extends slowly downwards to a depth of about 4000m. The deep seabed beyond is called the abyssal plain.

In the centre of the abyssal plain, in mid-ocean, the earth's geologically youngest rocks are found. They occur in spreading zones, basically areas in which molten rock rises to the earth's surface where it forms new crusts. These mineral-rich areas are abundant with micro-organisms called phytoplankton, the first link in the food chain of sea life.

For centuries it was only possible to exploit the resources of the sea which were visible from the surface. Ships sailed to collect the riches of other lands, rubbish was dumped, fish and whales caught, shell-fish dived for, sand and stone loaded into boats at low tide, and small estuaries blocked by dams with mills built to harness tidal power. In this century sub-marine exploration has shown that the seabed, and seawater itself, are rich sources of minerals. Mines sunk on land have extended galleries under the sea to win coal, tin and other metallic ores from beneath the seabed. Near-shore surveys have mapped deposits of sand and gravel. These are often the relics of river valleys that existed as dry land when sea level was lower. Coastal sediments also contain useful concentrations of minerals and metals. Oil and gas fields tapped on land have been found to extend under the sea and exploration of the continental shelf has found new fields in deeper water. The continental slope also contains these hydrocarbons while the abyssal plain contains nodules and crusts rich in many metals. So many elements occur naturally in the water column that 'the oceans' most ubiquitous mineral resource is seawater'.[1] Magnesium is already commercially extracted and there have been experiments in extracting commodities such as deuterium which is used in nuclear fission reactors.

Winning the resources of the global sea depends on access to the oceans. Freedom of the seas, the right of everyone to navigate and trade across the globe, was expounded by Elizabeth I when her enterprising seamen challenged Spanish claims to the Americas. The Dutch took up this call for *mare liberum* when they confronted Portuguese dominance in the East. At times states have also argued for the right to reserve the resources of the sea for their own people. The idea of *mare clausum* is to close the sea to foreigners. It was usually applied to coastal waters to ensure a country's defense or to safeguard its fisheries. Freedom of the seas became the accepted principle while most states, when national interests demanded, also defended their territorial rights out to a three-mile limit.

By 1900 the three-mile limit was formally agreed by an International Convention. However several states claimed more extensive rights. In 1945 President Truman saw the opportunities for developing offshore oil and claimed two hundred miles of seabed around the USA. By the 1950s offshore oil production was a reality. The Geneva Convention (1958) recognized the new interest of coastal states in the seabed. It cited their ability to reach resources to a depth of 200m, the accepted definition of the continental shelf. However, the Convention left the door open to wider claims by stating that: 'outside the area of the territorial sea . . . to where the depth of superadjacent waters admits of the exploitation of the natural resources of the [seabed].' As technology advanced the deep-sea would be literally up for grabs.

As the deep-sea was explored it seemed possible that the few nations with sufficiently advanced technology might carve up the abyssal plain. This was an unpalatable prospect for undeveloped and coastless nations. In 1967 a historic speech to the United Nations asked for international control of the non-territorial seabed and made the unprecedented call for its resources to be treated as a 'common heritage of mankind'. Two decades later negotiation has achieved the consensus that may, in the twenty-first century, make this dream reality.

Weighing-in at no fewer than two hundred and forty pages, the United Nations

---

1 Earney, F, *Marine Mineral Resources*, 1990.

═ MARITIME ARCHAEOLOGY ═

Valerie Fenwick

Nineteenth-century archaeologists predicted that the deep oceans would preserve complete wooden hulls, with their structure undamaged by waves, shipworm and salvage. Twentieth-century technology developed for military purposes and for mineral exploration has proved them right. Unfortunately, the equipment which has taken archaeology under water has also brought the destruction of historically important sites worldwide. Just as on land the metal detector has enabled unskilled searchers to find ancient artefacts, so underwater magnetometer and side-scan sonar searches have enabled treasure salvors to locate ancient wreck sites and remove items with sale-room value.

The century opened with a discovery by Greek sponge-divers, who were accustomed to diving to great depths without any breathing apparatus. In the spring of 1900, off the island of Antikythera at a depth of 60m, they found a wreck carrying superb Classical statues. Hard-hat divers from the Greek Navy took over and the statues were placed on display in the National Museum in Athens. The scenario was repeated in 1907 near Mahdia on the coast of Tunisia, and the Tunisian Department of Antiquities then employed helmeted sponge divers to raise bronze statues from the first century BC wreck. In 1948 the wreck made history when the newly developed aqualung and water jet were used for archaeological exploration by a French team under Jacques Cousteau and Phillipe Taillez. Their techniques were extremely crude, but ten years later off the Côte d'Azur, Taillez applied for the first time careful excavation and recording techniques under water on the wreck of a Roman ship on the Titan Reef. Meanwhile in Italy the use of the underwater grid and photomosaic for recording were being

Convention on the Law of the Sea III 'is without doubt one of the most complex treaties in the whole history of international relations.' [2] It has three hundred and twenty articles with nine appendices. The Convention allows coastal states to claim two hundred-mile Economic Exclusion Zones with control over the seabed and seawater, though others have a right of navigation. If every coastal state and island claimed this area as much as 40% of the global sea would be under the control of individual nations. The deep seabed beyond these national zones has

2 Brown, E, *The International Law of the Sea. Vol 1 Introductory Manual*, 1994.

pioneered on another Roman merchantman found between Spargi and Sardinia.

The predicted survival of entire hulls was proved in brackish seas where teredo (a marine wood-borer) cannot live. In the Baltic in 1956 the Swedish warship, *Wasa*, was found at a depth of 30m in Stockholm harbour, where she sank on her maiden voyage in 1628. The hull was so intact that hard-hat divers were able to make six tunnels beneath it and attach straps to lifting pontoons. Five years later *Wasa* was brought into shallow water in a series of eighteen steps, before finally being raised and floated on her own bottom into a dry dock where she could be conserved. The ship had not yet been fitted out for a long voyage or naval campaign and so was comparatively empty. Without the difficulties of excavating many artefacts, the mud from the decks could be hosed away as she was lifted.

In England twenty-three years later, the task which faced the team who hoped to raise the sixteenth-century veteran warship *Mary Rose*, was very different and immensely complex. Though only half of her hull survived, it was buried in sediments and crammed with artefacts and equipment. Visibility was variable and made the task of recording difficult. A very large team of volunteers was trained on site, as it was important to ensure consistent accuracy. A computer programme was developed to record the position of objects in three dimensions. From measurements taken from at least three points it worked out the 'best-fit', immediately detecting inaccuracies or mistakes made in poor visibility by even the most experienced archaeological diver. Over twenty thousand artefacts were recovered and the careful recording and conservation has enabled this veritable 'time capsule' to reveal new aspects of Tudor maritime life.

Sport divers using the aqualung can only work in shallow waters – 60m is their usual limit. However, since most ships are lost close to the coast, amateurs have been able to locate many thousands of wrecks of all periods. The majority ⬎

been declared the Area where deep-sea mining can develop, regulated by an International Sea Authority. The principle of the common good has been accommodated; explained in simple terms this means that for every part of the Area licensed for mining by an individual state, a portion will be assigned to a body called the Enterprise to be mined for the community. This framework for the global seas is an innovation in the international economic order. How it works in practice depends on the technology for deep-sea mining becoming a commercial reality in the new century.

Across the world fish are caught using the millennia-old spear, hook and trap.

➤ have been denuded of interest for future visiting divers as they have been successively stripped for souvenirs. In many parts of the world it is now rare for archaeologists to find a historic shipwreck which has not been damaged in this way. Sometimes the seabed surface no longer shows any sign of a wreck; contemporary salvors may have reached its contents, the sea may have destroyed every trace of hull, or modern sport or archaeological divers may have lifted all the surface objects.

However, remote-sensing equipment can locate buried remains and even the pattern of scours made round a hull prior to its disintegration. Mapping such scours has provided new information from the *Mary Rose* site, even though the hull itself has been recovered. Equipment is becoming ever more sophisticated, capable of working in shallow water and even mapping the seabed right up to the water's edge by means of a wide-angle inferometer. Sensitive and rapid mapping of a wreck site, with its precise location accurately fixed by the Global Positioning System, are of the greatest help to maritime archaeologists, since they enable underwater recording to be carried out more quickly and accurately than ever before. Towed underwater bells and small submarines were developed by American university research teams and were successful in locating ancient wrecks along the coast of the eastern Mediterranean and mapping them much more quickly than could be done by conventional techniques. However, subsequent scientific investigations may still require many seasons of painstaking work, as in the case of the Bronze Age shipwreck excavated at Uluburun off the coast of Turkey by George Bass and a team from Texas A&M University.

Rocky coasts and wave-beaten shores are a high-energy zone, which easily break wrecks apart. In some cases large

These traditions, and the discovery of harpoons amongst the prehistoric tool-kits, show that fish were the first resource of the sea claimed by Man. So long as the hunters fed only themselves and their family groups the breeding cycle of fish ensured a plentiful supply. As populations grew, medieval and later fishers fed inland towns by salting, drying or pickling their fish. Catches increased but they were still won by man, oar and sail-power alone. The introduction of engines, sophistication of fishing gear and development of freezing have enabled twentieth-century fishermen to outstrip the reproductive capacity of their prey. The world demand for fish and fish products continues to increase but the supply will collapse unless catches are controlled so that fish populations have the right conditions to continually replenish themselves.

Fishing remained wind-dependent long after steam-powered ships were at work. North European boats used two basic techniques. Pelagic fish, such as parts of the hull have been buried in rock gullies or soft sand and mud. Recording and recovery of these often complex structures and the remaining artefacts require carefully controlled conditions to be implemented. Construction of a sheet-pile fence (known as a 'cofferdam') is one solution that enables fragile objects to be handled with the care possible on land. The cofferdam may be drained, as in the case of five Viking ships excavated in the 1960s in Roskilde Fjord, Denmark (and now on display there), and in the more recent case of *La Belle*, a seventeenth-century French explorer's barque found in Matagorda Bay, Texas in 1995. Alternatively, the cofferdam may be flooded to provide a volume of still water with good visibility, as at Yorktown, Virginia, for the excavation of the brig *Betsy* in 1982.

The dream of intact hulls in deep water was realized in 1980 when a manned submersible filmed the schooners *Hamilton* and *Scourge* sitting upright and virtually intact in the near-freezing fresh waters of Lake Ontario where they had foundered in 1813. In 1990, Dr Robert Ballard of the Woods Hole Oceanographic Institute used *Jason*, his ROV, to transmit 3-D information and digital images from an electronic still camera (ESC). These could be sized and added to a mosaic picture of *Hamilton*. In addition to well-publicized explorations of *Titanic*, the Woods Hole Institute has also searched the deep waters crossed by the trade routes of ancient Rome. At a depth of 818m and around 120km west of Sicily, the first Classical wreck to be investigated with ROV technology was examined in 1989. The operation was watched on television by 250,000 children in North America as part of an educational programme. Nicknamed *Isis*, the wreck scatter visible on the soft seabed proved to be a small Late Roman merchantman with a ➤

herring, mackerel and pilchards, feed near the surface and were caught in drift nets. These hang like a wall from floats on the surface and fish swimming become entangled in the mesh by their gills. Demersal fish, including cod, halibut, haddock and plaice, which live nearer the seabed were caught in a trawl net, dragged along the bottom.

In 1881, *Zodiac*, the first purpose-built steam trawler showed how fishing would develop in the twentieth century. Launched in Grimsby, she and her sister ship *Aries*, brought home catches four times as big as those of the sailing trawlers. By the beginning of this century steam trawlers had almost completely replaced their sailing counterparts. The steam trawler fleet soon numbered one thousand four hundred vessels, typically 120 x 20ft with a triple expansion engine. Engines allowed them not only to work local waters in spite of tides and wind, but to make quicker passages to distant fishing grounds off Iceland, Newfoundland and

➤ mixed amphora cargo from North Africa. Subsequent expeditions using a nuclear submarine and an ROV, which trundled along the seabed on wheels, have located further ancient shipwrecks in this area of the Mediterranean.

The apparent ease with which shipwrecks can now be located in deep waters renders this, the last, greatest and most dramatic place for contact with the past, very vulnerable. It makes all the more urgent international agreement to protect and manage historic shipwrecks outside territorial waters. The International Council on Monuments and Sites (ICOMOS) has, since 1987, been the lead organization and advises member states on appropriate legislation to provide protection in national waters. In practice protection is proving difficult to implement and some small or undeveloped countries have chosen to exploit this resource for short-term revenue by entering into profit-sharing arrangements with treasure-salvage companies.

For the professional underwater archaeologist, modern commercial diving apparatus is replacing the aqualung. Instead of cumbersome cylinders of air strapped to a diver's back, a light umbilical supplies an oxygen mixture from the surface vessel. More importantly the umbilical carries a two-way voice communication system and transmits to the team on the surface the image on the diver's video camera. This makes it possible to record sites rapidly in even short windows of visibility.

Lack of funds and facilities preclude the conservation and display of many important ship remains. Full recording has sometimes been followed by careful reburial of the timbers so that they are available for future generations. In Red Bay, Labrador, about three thousand timbers from a sixteenth-century basque whaler have been reburied in sand,

Greenland. Steam also powered winches to haul larger trawls.

The industrialization wrought by steam-power affected more than the fishing boats. The coal for their engines was most readily available in larger ports linked by rail to the collieries, and the railways also provided fast routes to distribute fish to inland towns. Individuals, often the master, owned the sailing trawlers and drifters which worked out of any small harbour or quay, but they were now replaced by companies in major ports such as Grimsby with the capital to operate fleets of steam trawlers. The wet fish shop was no longer the only outlet for the increasing catches. Britain's fish and chip shops were the 'fast food' restaurants of the early years of the century, with some twenty-five thousand opened before the start of the First World War.

Fishing was a tough job. It took strength and stamina to withstand the hazardous conditions on the fishing grounds where the trawls were worked covered with sheeting weighed down by concrete-filled tyres. Reconstructed sections and models are easier to display than the original remains, and computer-modelling of the data obtained from study of the ship structure is increasingly used to discover the capability of the original hull and the probable form of missing portions. Nevertheless, the construction of a full-scale copy, using the materials, tools and methods identified from study of the timbers, allows a great deal more to be learned about the social and technological context in which the ship was built.

At the end of the nineteenth century the voyage across the Atlantic of a copy of a Viking ship found in a burial mound in Norway served to inspire twentieth-century historians of exploration, such as Thor Heyerdahl and Tim Severin, to recreate other ancient voyages; one such voyage was that of the balsa raft *Kon-Tiki* across the Pacific, another was the skin boat *Brendan* across the Atlantic. These craft were based on ethnographic and historical, as opposed to archaeological, research. Similarly there was no archaeological find upon which the experimental trireme, *Olympias*, could be based. Instead, all of the indirect ancient evidence had to be carefully interrogated. A benefit of building reconstructions is that the end product can be sailed and used to test theories, different rigs and actual performance. However, where the timbers of shipwrecks survive, they can provide hard information on form, scantlings, type of timber, fastenings and building techniques with which to test historical information. Reconstructions based on all the available evidence and using contemporary materials and tools advance specialist research and understanding, and at the same time provide opportunities for enthusiasts to help to build and sail them.

twenty-four hours a day. Before acetylene, and then electric, lamps, the decks were illuminated by paraffin-soaked wads. Crews hauled the nets on pitching decks, awash with icy seawater, and often had only four hours rest in every thirty. Time ashore was short, often only as long as it took to unload and refuel the vessel; many fishermen left the sea prematurely worn-out.

In the 1930s marine diesel engines made smaller boats, used for drifting, more versatile. In Britain these motor boats, under 80ft in length, were officially classed as inshore vessels but they could easily work as far afield as the Norwegian coast. Refrigerated lorries were an important advance which enabled motor fishing vessels (MFVs) to work out of any port.

When, in the 1950s, compact diesel engines replaced steam machinery on larger trawlers it created space for bigger fish rooms. While these accommodated greater catches they increased the difficulty of keeping fish fresh until the holds were full. Refrigeration only became successful after design changes created even more space by having the trawl handled over the stern rather than the side of vessels. The first British-built 'factory' stern trawler was the 2605-ton *Fairtry* built at Leith in 1953. Initial trials proved uneconomic, as large crews had to be carried to gut and fillet the fish aboard ship. The answer was found in only gutting before freezing, leaving the filleting to be completed ashore.

Electronic fish-finding equipment and navigational instruments made trawlers even more efficient. The former USSR, Japan and Korea, in particular, developed long distance fishing fleets based on factory ships. These were capable of taking 100 tonnes of fish a day.

Today the Netherlands are renowned for building large deep-sea freezer-factory trawlers. The *Helen Mary*, launched in 1996, is 116.7m long with a flush deck and three-tiered superstructure. Fish and water are pumped from the nets into twelve refrigerated seawater tanks. In four hours these can cool 660 tonnes of fish from 20°C to -2°C ready for freezing. The fish are sorted by machine and frozen in blocks, wrapped and packed in cartons to be stored in the refrigerated and insulated cargo hold that has a 6903m capacity.

In the 1940s a new style of net was developed. The cylinder-like purse net enclosed a shoal of fish. Measuring 300 fathoms in length and some 90 fathoms deeps they took catches of up to 200 tons against the old-style drift net's capacity of 30 tons. Purse seine nets are used by modern vessels catching tuna. The *Albacora Uno* is one of a new generation of tuna seiners. Launched in 1996, she is 105m long and carries an engined 12m skiff which assists in laying her nets. To haul in the nets and handle the catch she has a main winch and eighteen auxiliary winches. Her cargo freezing and storing capacity is 2800m³.

Over-fishing was noticed soon after steam trawlers came to dominate the North Sea fisheries. A greater proportion of the catch was made up of smaller, less mature fish. The fish sizes, and so fish population or stock, increased during the 1914-18 hostilities which kept boats off the fishing grounds. The 1939-45 war repeated this phenomenon. When shortages again became apparent some countries acted unilaterally to safeguard the livelihood of their home fleets. Iceland, for example, declared a national twelve-mile limit in 1958, and a fifty-mile limit in 1971. Each claim precipitated a 'cod war', with Britain's navy upholding the rights of her trawlers.

Despite clearly declining stocks and catches the 'world catch' continued to increase. Between 1945 and the 1980s it grew by as much as 7% a year. This was possible because as one species became depleted, fishing fleets targeted another. A much wider variety of species now appears in supermarkets and on restaurant menus.

A major use of fish is the production of meal for agricultural fertilizers and animal feeds; supplied to developed countries with high population densities and intensive farming methods. The Norwegians and Danes, for example, took immature herring from the North Atlantic for fishmeal. When the supply declined they moved to mackerel, sprats and sand eels. The Norwegian mackerel catch rocketed up from 20,000 tons in 1963 to 870,000 tons five years later. Meal can be made from fish low in the food chain and the Norwegians also experimented with krill. Much of the world catch comes from less developed regions. Anchoveta from Peru comprised 28% of the world catch in 1980. However, hopes that fishmeal used as a protein supplement would reduce malnutrition on a global scale has not become a reality as the demand for fishmeal in developing countries has held the prices at high levels.

The world catch cannot continue to rise because the number of species is finite. Taking creatures from low down in the food chain affects species that are their natural predators. Options for managing fisheries are threefold: access to fisheries can be limited by zoning and the two hundred-mile Economic Exclusion Zone places many areas under national controls; regulation of gear, for example the mesh size of nets, is intended to ensure that only certain species, or fish of certain maturity, are taken; and measures such as closed seasons, quotas and licenses aim to limit the overall catch.

There are many problems with regulations to limit catches: they are difficult to enforce; a control of mesh size is only readily effective in fisheries when catching a single species; and there is not always agreement on the current levels of fish stocks or the outcome of controls. Fishing is an important economic activity that provides employment and a major source of protein. For governments conservation of fish stocks is not an end in itself but the route to a healthy fishing industry.

Unfortunately action to safeguard fish stocks can, in the short term, injure the fishing industry. Interpretation of European Community policies has meant that many British fishing boats have been deliberately rendered unseaworthy. While foreign vessels take up the quotas, the British fishing communities lose their livelihood. This is not only an economic injury, as fishermen and fishing communities have the same fierce loyalty to their dangerous way of life as is found

REMOTELY OPERATED VEHICLES (ROVS)

SCUBA divers are safe to depths of about 40-60m but time-consuming ascents limit their seabed work. Since the 1970s divers have worked three times as deep to maintain offshore rigs. Their tasks are identified by camera-carrying ROVs, piloted via umbilicals. Heavily manned, and specially equipped, Diving Support Vessels (DSVs) lower bells from which divers work, tethered by pipelines supplying breathing gas, warming water, and communications. Underwater work costs around £1000 an hour. Cost-cutting dreams of maintenance robots were partly answered by ROVs designed to increase diver efficiency. *David* was trialled in the North Sea. Piloted from a DSV, it clamped onto the rig to provide a stable working platform complete with pneumatic power and winch, hand tools, lighting, close-circuit television and cleaning equipment.

ROVs were glamorised by Ballard's searches for famous shipwrecks. In 1988 *Argo*, with video cameras and sonar, located the shipwreck known as *Isis* in 818m. It was investigated by the 3000lb *Jason* but tethered to the ship via the larger ROV *Medea*. *Jason*'s robotic arms salvaged objects. The *Lusitania* and *Titanic* expeditions used ROVs tethered to manned submersibles. Following the 1997 Mediterranean project, Southampton University is designing tools for ROV pilots to replicate the sensitivity of human excavation. Salvage

in mining communities. The end of fishing severs important links with the past. In Britain the proliferation of heritage centres in fishing ports reflects the attempt to embrace the tourist industry but some are also an important focal point for communities to continue to express their relationship with the sea and with past generations.

Dredging followed trade as ports kept their quays open by removing mud, sand and gravel from river channels. Early methods included digging at low tide, and scoops and rakes mounted on boats. Horses, and later steam engines, were put on board vessels to power grabs and chains of buckets. Dredgers ('dredges' in the US) were essential to deepen navigation channels for the huge draft of modern ships. Many twentieth-century dredgers serve another function; they are purpose-built to win seabed materials.

Dredgers excavate in four ways: a hydraulic arm, like a land excavator, only useful in very shallow water; a chain of buckets travelling round a ladder whose length limits working-depth; a suction pipe, with a cutting head, worked by water jets or high pressure air; and a dragline with a grab.

is a commercial operation where recovery is the principal aim; archaeology is the science of interpreting the past from surviving physical remains. Excavation destroys evidence and is avoided where possible, and excavated objects are carefully recorded so that the maximum information can be retrieved.

ROVs are used for seabed monitoring, checking pipelines, and recording geological features and marine life. Routine deployment in advance of seabed construction can prevent destruction of the natural and man-made heritage. Norway's Statoil funded an archaeological survey prior to constructing a pipeline from the North Sea. In 1997, from depths of 200m, ROVs located and recorded the scattered shipwreck, *Jedinorog* (sunk circa 1760), and then lifted vulnerable timbers.

Deep-sea mining projects have intensified hopes of building untethered ROVs. The Japanese ROV *Kaiko* took the record for deep-sea exploration. In 1995 it reached the bottom of the Mariana Trench in the Pacific recording a depth of 10,911m. The research ship *Kairei* lowers *Kaiko* from an A-frame crane at 75m per minute.

Not all ROVs operate in deep-water or for exploration. Since 1992 students at the US Naval Academy have designed and built ROVs for routine tasks such as cleaning marine growth from ship's hulls. ROVs save the time and cost of docking, and cleaner-heads that capture the effluent, prevent anti-fouling from polluting the ocean.

Urban development and roads consume vast quantities of aggregate, sand and gravel. The world contribution of marine aggregate is currently small. It is likely to increase as land deposits are worked out, built over, or their use constrained by environmental controls. Since the early 1960s Japan has won sand and gravel, initially from depths of less than 30m. By the mid-1980s new deposits were targeted in 45-50m with survey exploring depths of 70-80m. There were two hundred and seventy-nine firms operating five hundred and sixty-six small dredgers to produce fifty-seven million tonnes of aggregate a year. At that time Great Britain, which also has a major dredging industry, had just twenty companies operating sixty dredgers.

British dredgers are focused on London and the southeast. Aggregates are high bulk and low value so it is uneconomic to transport them over large distances. For this reason dredgers use many small ports, but this limits the size of vessel which can be operated.

Cement is also essential to the construction industry. It is made with calcium carbonate usually obtained from rocks like chalk. Lacking such rocks, Iceland dredges enough shells from the seabed to meet its total requirement for cement and the supply of lime for agriculture.

On land artificial lakes are made so that dredgers can recover ores such as tin and gold. The same geological processes that created those deposits were at work in areas now drowned by the sea. They have been added to by material eroded from the land. Tin is one of the most ubiquitous. It has been dredged off Great Britain, USA, the Philippines, Thailand, Malaysia and Indonesia. Suction dredging off Cornwall, in Britain, recovered tin some of which was 'lost' into the sea during early mining on land.

Whereas tin markets can be depressed, other dredged materials have a more predictable return. Nome beach in Alaska yielded gold worth $100 million. To recover the same gold from just offshore a refitted tin dredger was put to work raising 11,000 tonnes of sand a day. The famous diamond-bearing sands and gravels of South Africa are also found on the beaches and in the surf zone. Dredging proved so dangerous and expensive that great bunds were built to protect excavators reaching 12m below sea level.

Dredging has been limited by economics, the sale price of aggregates, for example, is not high enough to repay money spent on developing vessels for deep-water excavation. However, metal ores have prompted investment of millions of pounds. The metals were first discovered in 1868 in the Kara Sea and then in 1879 by the British exploration vessel *Challenger*. Her grab samples showed how little was known of the under-sea world, bringing up four thousand four hundred and seventeen new species of marine organism. They also lifted manganese nodules, which, in addition to manganese, contain copper, nickel, cobalt and molybdenum. These are the prizes whose commercial exploitation for use in modern manufacturing processes will reward the successful development of equipment to mine the seabed in depths of over 4km.

The nodules have the size and irregularity of potatoes. Their formation, which is of course measured in millions of years, has challenged geologists. The composition and metal content varies in different sea areas, and sometimes they are thinly scattered and sometimes lie thickly like a cobbled street. It is generally accepted that they form by accretion drawing on the mineral elements of both seawater and sediments. Where there is little sediment, manganese and iron minerals form crusts rather than nodules.

Black or white smokers are another source of newly formed metallic minerals. These are chimney-like structures along spreading zones. They are formed by heated seawater, which has been drawn into the earth and is driven back to the surface through vents. While underground the seawater dissolves minerals, which precipitate onto the seabed when the water is forced back up. The vents are thus built of material containing sulphides including zinc, copper, iron, silver, cobalt and gold.

The viability of exploiting manganese nodules depends on the seabed topography and geology, and the content of the nodules. Comprehensive surveys are essential. These require the most accurate satellite-based navigation systems. Many of the survey instruments have been developed from those used for oil exploration: echo sounders and side scan sonars, grab samples, towed dredges and video or still photography from towed fish.

Early efforts to collect commercial quantities of nodules used bucket-dredger principles with the buckets on a continuous cable between two ships. This tended to tangle and lose contact with the seabed, whilst scooping too much mud with only a few nodules. Other projects copied suction-dredgers and used water or air pumps to lift nodules to the surface. Not surprisingly such surface-to-bed pipes place a huge drag on the towing vessel. Remotely operated vehicles are another option.

Huge investment is needed for research and to build the mining vessels, the processing plants to extract the metals and the systems for waste disposal. Forecasts show costs in the order of $1000 million so feasibility depends on projects with long life spans and leases for large areas of seabed.

Oil tankers appeared on the oceans in the nineteenth century but oil production only moved into the sea after 1900. Early steps followed onshore oil fields into the sea: on America's west coast wells were drilled from piers along the shore. In 1923 platforms supported above the sea on wooden piling were used to drill in Lake Maracaibo, Venezuela. It was twenty years before drilling moved out of sight of land and the first purpose-built, offshore, mobile drilling rig went into service in 1954 in the Gulf of Mexico. The USA produced the first jack-up drilling rig in the following year and in 1957 surveys began in the North Sea.

Seismic surveys use a variety of instruments to examine the seabed and the rocks beneath. Most follow a simple principle: shock waves are emitted which, depending on their frequency and wavelength, are reflected back from either the seabed or the rock layers deep below. The delay in their return is measured. The interfaces between rock layers diffract the waves and alter the speed of their travel. Modern systems output a digital record from which information can then be

⊷ TORREY CANYON ⊶

Modern navigational aids are not fail-proof, and hazards which have caused shipwrecks for centuries still take casualties. Historical shipwrecks often carried valuable cargoes whose loss caused economic shock waves. Today, however, the cost is counted not only in terms of the capital cost of ships and cargoes but in the impact on the environment.

The Isles of Scilly, a group of one hundred and forty-five islets and rocks, lie in the Atlantic entrance to the English Channel. They have wrecked more than eight hundred ships. Many were lost before instruments were developed to measure longitude: coming from the Atlantic, the Mediterranean or Africa, eighteenth-century masters could not be certain of their position until land was sighted.

In 1967 the world's thirteenth largest merchant vessel, the oil tanker *Torrey Canyon*, was bound from Kuwait to Milford Haven, Wales. After passing the Canary Islands, the automatic pilot was set to carry her five miles to the west of the Isles of Scilly. The Islands were still one thousand four hundred miles away. At 06.30 on 18 March they were sighted on radar just twenty-four miles off. Tide, currents or wind had fractionally shifted the ship's course so, over the great distance, she was now headed east of the Islands. The precise events of the next eighty minutes are disputed. The officers and captain adjusted course to pass between the Seven Stones Reef and the main islands. They had difficulty in identifying landmarks to confirm their exact location while fishing boats added to the problems of manoeuvring the 974ft 5in vessel travelling at over 15 knots.

At 08.50 *Torrey Canyon* struck Pollard Rocks. Her cargo of 100,000 tons of crude oil began spilling into the sea. Within a week it washed onto British and

formed into two- or three-dimensional images of either the seabed or underlying rocks.

Surveyors look for rock formations that are likely to contain hydrocarbons. Over three hundred million years ago the area that is now the North Sea was a swamp in which generations of plants grew and decayed. They were buried and compressed, later to become coal. Climate change brought desert conditions and the wind covered the layer of coal with sand. By two hundred and twenty-five million years ago a shallow sea had once more formed and became cut-off as a saltwater lake. Evaporation left salt as a rock layer above the sand. When the sea again filled the area more sediments and the bodies of tiny marine creatures were deposited, building up for hundreds of millions of years. Under pressure and with then French beaches. Eleven miles off Lands End the stricken ship lay outside Great Britain's three-mile territorial waters. As marine salvage was then organized on the principle of 'no cure, no pay', salvage teams were paid only for saving ships and cargoes. There was no incentive to contain oil that had already leaked from the vessel. This task fell to the Royal Navy whose tugs sprayed detergents to break up floating oil slicks.

On 27 March the tanker broke up and salvage was abandoned. There was only one option left – aircraft bombed the tanker to burn-off the remaining cargo. The ship had been insured for $16.5 million and the cargo for a further $1 million. The French and British clean up cost $14-16 million.

The disaster galvanized world opinion to demand protection from accidental oil spills. International law changes slowly, but in the last three decades changes have been made to reduce the risk of accidents, to enable seaboard countries to take immediate action even outside territorial waters, and to provide funding for the clean up.

Twenty-nine years later the measures came dramatically under scrutiny. On 15 February 1996 *Sea Empress* grounded outside Milford Haven, spilling about 73,000 tonnes of oil. This time the British government had responsibility for coordinating salvage and clean up. With oil affecting fisheries, holiday beaches and two of the UK's three Marine Nature Reserves, conservation groups, such as the World Wildlife Fund, called for an ecological disaster to be declared. The Welsh Office committed £250,000 to environmental impact monitoring, especially to study long-term effects on, for example, shellfish and bird populations. For the first time monitoring included archaeological sites, such as submerged prehistoric land surfaces, fishtraps and shipwrecks. The Marine Accident Investigation Bureau blamed inadequate training of pilots, poor coordination of salvage operations and the absence of a double-hull.

the right temperatures, bacteria acted on the buried sea creatures and on vegetable matter in the coal to form hydrocarbons – combinations of hydrogen and carbon. Sometimes liquid, oil, and sometimes gaseous, natural gas, the light hydrocarbons travel upwards through porous rocks until an impervious layer blocks their progress. At this point they spread sideward until progress is similarly blocked, perhaps by folds or faults in the rock layers.

These reservoirs often hold both oil and gas but some contain almost exclusively one or the other. The principal constituent of natural gas is methane, the fuel burnt by cookers and central heating boilers.

Only drilling can prove the surveyors' theories. About one in fifteen of the test holes drilled in the North Sea found oil and gas in commercially viable quantities.

A stable platform makes drilling possible. The drill bit is supported on a pipe that is rotated through a rotary table. As the bit penetrates deeper into the seabed, drilling is halted and additional lengths of pipe added at the surface. The whole assembly, with a pipe some 3km long, is suspended from a derrick. The pipe carries a lubricating and cooling mud solution to the drill bit, and returns rock particles to the surface.

Jack-up drilling rigs are floating platforms, sometimes self-propelled and sometimes towed. They are cumbersome and require good sea states. Once over a drill site, their legs are lowered either by electricity or hydraulics. They rest on the seabed or occasionally sink through soft sediment to harder rocks, perhaps 9m below. The platforms 'jack-up' to about 20m above the waves and are extremely stable but the legs limit their working depth to about 110m.

Semi-submersible drilling units are more mobile. They have a series of hulls or caissons that support the deck with its drilling equipment. The most common have parallel rectangular caissons with thrusters to assist in position holding. Under tow they are ballasted to 6-8m but when drilling this depth is increased to 20-25m. The need for mooring equipment limits them to depths of about 500m.

Drill-ships are essentially mobile drilling platforms in the form of a ship. Their profile is characterized by the centrally placed derrick as the drill assembly works through their centre of gravity. They remain over a borehole by using dynamic positioning systems. These use transducers on the seabed whose signals are received by hydrophones along the ship's side. A computer calculates the angles between the two sets of devices and, if the position has altered, adjusts it automatically by starting on-board propulsion units. Drill-ship operations are not limited by legs or mooring equipment. They also have sufficiently large capacity to be relatively independent and can, therefore, operate a greater distance from shore. The technology of the drill-ship has been adopted for some of the prototype, deep-sea mining vessels.

Production involves drilling sufficient wells to allow an oil or gas reservoir to empty. Special platforms or subsea units are positioned to manage the flow of hydrocarbons and their transfer ashore by either pipe or ship. Ships also perform the specialist production role. The 211m *Balder FPU*, completed in 1996, is a purpose built floating production, storage and off-loading vessel (FPSO). She is designed to work medium-sized oil fields and has facilities for separating oil and gas, and ten tanks for storing crude oil which can then be off-loaded via pipelines to shuttle tankers moored 75-95m astern. Continuous production is helped by the pipes that lead to the wellhead passing via a turret. This remains stationary, suspended on a roller bearing, while the ship rotates about it to keep head-to-wind in all weathers. She has ten mooring chains.

Shuttle tankers carry crude oil from production units to the refinery thus overcoming the need to build pipelines to small, remote or difficult fields. The new generation of these vessels are called MSTs (multipurpose shuttle tanker), they can provide a conventional shuttle service, act as floating storage and off-loading vessels connected to a production unit, and take on the role of an FPSO.

When gas is piped ashore, methanol is injected to prevent it forming an ice-like substance called methyl hydrate, which has now been discovered trapped in the seabed. When methyl hydrate reverts to gas its volume is hugely increased, and accidental release of it causes huge blowouts of gas, which bubble violently to the surface. Some people see this as the cause of previously unexplained disappearances of ships. It could be a vast source of power for the twenty-first century.

The frontiers for conventional oil and gas production lie in deeper water and the arctic regions. Brazil led the way into deeper waters where floating drill and production units are used. Ice is the major arctic challenge. The hostile environment demands special equipment, and the cost means that only very large fields are worth developing. Conventional rigs were replaced in the 1970s with islands built of aggregates. Then ice-islands took their place. These are made by spraying seawater over an area of ice. It builds up in frozen layers until it becomes so heavy that it sinks to the seabed forming an island. Floating ice-islands have also been used. Off Canada a full drilling operation, reaching the seabed 300m below, was supported on floating ice 300m in diameter and 6m thick. Ice, however, has unpredictable qualities and the Japanese have built an island drilling system using concrete.

The 'ocean is not pure water, but a toxic mixture of practically every element known to man'.[3] Many minerals can be usefully extracted but high concentrations are dangerous. Pollution is defined as the introduction by man, directly or indirectly, of substances or energy to the marine environment resulting in such deleterious effects as to harm living resources; cause hazard to human health; hinder marine activities; or impair the amenity.

Oil was one of the first pollutants to cause public concern. In 1925 the Isle of

3 Nelson, L, *Stream, Lake, Estuary & Ocean Pollution*, 1991.

Wight presented an eighteen thousand signature petition to the British government complaining of oiled holiday beaches. The Island lies in the mouth of Southampton Water, near Fawley oil refinery. Its concern was shared by coastal towns between Hampshire and Kent, whose beaches overlook the busy shipping route of the English Channel. Their problem was very much the result of a misguided attempt to stop oil pollution inside ports. In 1922 the Oil Pollution Act banned the discharge of oil inside territorial waters. As the ports had no waste disposal facilities ships cleaned their tanks at sea and the oil drifted ashore. The USA passed similar legislation, though with stiffer penalties.

Despite early environmentalists being charged with 'an intensive campaign of an offensive nature'[4] the problem of oil discharge continued. Thirty years later an international treaty, OILPOL 1954, again resorted to prohibitive zones.

The *Torrey Canyon* disaster focused world attention on the threat from accidental oil spills. Coordinating change fell to the International Maritime Organisation that was formed by the United Nations and first met in 1959. They tackled both accidental and routine oil losses. Change has taken time because environmental needs had to be balanced with the economic complexities of world shipping industries. Designs to improve safety could only be introduced as existing ships were replaced. Environmentally friendly working methods could not impair tankers' wage-earning by, for example, requiring time in port or carrying extra equipment which would take cargo-space.

Washing oil tanks with water caused routine oil discharges. They were reduced by using slop tanks to hold the waste. The water separated out and was pumped off at the next port, crude oil was then put on top of the residue. This load-on-top practice was introduced, as an addition to OILPOL 1954, in 1969. In the next ten years the use of water as ballast was confined to dedicated ballast tanks so its discharge contained no oil, and the problem of oily cleaning water was overcome by using crude oil to wash tanks. However only waste disposal facilities in ports could eliminate oil loss from routine operations. In 1995 a special manual provided the necessary guidance; and Associated British Ports, for example, launched an initiative in 1998 to increase the use of waste disposal points in their twenty-two ports.

From 1975-1995 shipping accidents caused less than a quarter of recorded oil spills. However, their scale and impact has maintained pressure to improve tanker

4 Pritchard, S, *Oil Pollution Control*, 1987.

safety. The time taken to upgrade fleets means that many measures only came into force in the 1990s. Larger tankers have double holds, so the outer can rupture without spillage; and, like crumple zones on motor cars, ballast tanks placed in the vulnerable parts of ships can suffer impact while oil tanks remain intact. New tankers, in excess of 20,000dwt, are fitted with special towing gear so that assistance can be given more easily.

Enhanced safety inspections are expected for tankers. There are extra training requirements for their crews and, in regulations aimed to reduce collisions, special measures exist to take account of their draught and reduced manoeuvrability. To help monitor tanker movements, national governments can demand Mandatory Ship Reporting in areas of environmental or navigational concern.

Since 1996, new insurance arrangements allow 'special compensation' payments to salvors when there is an environmental threat. They can receive expenses plus at least 30%, and possibly as much as 100%, if damage is minimized or prevented.

Anti-pollution measures can bring returns. The slop tanks of the 1960s, for example, saved as much as 800 tons of oil on a voyage. Norway's state oil company, Statoil, have joined engine-builders to develop a system to save gases emitted from cargoes. These volatile organic compounds (VOCs) are normally lost into the air as inert gas is put into the tanks to prevent explosions. By collecting and condensing the VOCs they obtain fuel for the ship's engine. Most VOC is emitted during loading so one problem is how to store the gas so it is available throughout a voyage. The other is to produce an engine capable of running on both VOC and conventional diesel. The partners were ready to patent the new equipment and ran vessel trials in 1999.

Oil is only one marine pollutant. The sea is a sump receiving wastes from many sources. These have included: solid wastes such as colliery spoil; outfalls, especially from urban and industrial sites on estuaries and coastal plant such as nuclear power stations; sewage, particularly from coastal towns; rivers containing agricultural pesticides and phosphates as well as petrol run-off from roads. Offshore industries also cause pollution, for example: oil escapes during production; and sediment plumes from dredging can blanket and kill marine life.

Apart from oil discharges and spills, ships also contribute to marine pollution through exhaust gases, by losing deck cargo, jettisoning litter especially plastics and discharging sewage. They also effect the environment on land. Ports are essential to passenger and freight cargo. Since only a small proportion of inland transport is now by water these have to be served by rail, and more than ever, by road. Containerization increased the area of land that ports require, and with the need for deep water berths, they have migrated from more urban areas to the open land of estuaries. Such marginal lands are wildlife habitats and an important feature in the 'unspoilt coast' expected by leisure users. These adverse effects of shipping have to be weighed against its advantages. Carriage of freight by sea remains far more energy-efficient than road or air transport.

GENERAL BIBLIOGRAPHY

Published references more specific to subject matter may be found in chapter footnotes.

Alderton, P M, *Sea Transport,* 1980 (London).

Amundsen, R, *My Life as an Explorer*, 1927 (London).

Bannerman, G, *Cruise Ships: The Inside Story*, 1976 (Sidney, British Columbia).

Bass, G F, *A History of Seafaring Based on Underwater Archaeology*, 1972 (New York).

Bathe, B W, *Seven Centuries of Sea Travel: From the Crusaders to the Cruises*, 1973 (New York).

Beesly, P, *Very Special Intelligence*, 1977 (London).

——, *Room 40*, 1982 (London).

Bekker, C, *Hitler's Naval War*, 1974 (New York).

Bennett, G, *Naval Battles of World War II*, 1975 (London).

Bixby, W, *The Track of the Bear: 1873-1963*, 1965 (New York).

Brennecke, J, *Tanker*, 1980 (Hereford).

Bridgland, T, *Sea Killers in Disguise: Q Ships & Decoy Raiders*, 1999 (London).

Brigham, L W, (ed) *The Soviet Maritime Arctic*, 1991 (London).

Brown, D K, (ed) *The Eclipse of the Big Gun: The Warship 1906-45*, 1992 (London).

——, *Warrior to Dreadnought*, 1997 (London).

——, *The Grand Fleet*, 1999 (London).

Bruce, W S, *The Log of the Scotia Expedition 1902-4*, 1992 (Edinburgh).

Burrell, D, *Scrap and Build*, 1988 (Kendal).

Campbell, N J M, *Jutland: An Analysis of the Fighting,* 1986, reprinted 1998 (London).

Chichester, F, *Gypsy Moth Circles the World*, 1967 (New York).

Compton-Hall, R, *Submarine Boats: The Beginnings of Underwater Warfare*, 1983 (London).

Cooke, A, *Liners and Cruise Ships: Some Notable Smaller Vessels*, 1966 (London).

Couper, A D, *The Geography of Sea Transport*, 1972 (London).

——, (ed) *The Times Atlas of the Ocean*, 1983 (London).

——, (ed) *The Shipping Revolution: The Modern Merchant Ship*, 1992 (London).

Cowin, H W, *Conway's Directory of Modern Naval Power 1986*, 1985 (London).

Dawson, P, *British Superliners of the Sixties*, 1990 (London).

——, *Canberra: In the Wake of a Legend*, 1997 (London).

——, *Cruise Ships: An Evolution in Design*, 2000 (London).

Dear, I, *Enterprise to Endeavour: The J-Class Yachts*, 1999 (London).

——, *The Royal Ocean Racing Club: The First 75 Years*, 2000 (London).

Delgado, J P, *Across the Top of the World*, 1999 (London).

Dequng, P, *Ships of China*, 1988 (Beijung).

Desmond, K, *Power Boat Speed: Racing and Record Breaking 1897 to the Present*, 1988 (London).

Dunn, L, *Passenger Liners*, 1961 (Southampton).

Earney, F, *Marine Mineral Resources*, 1990 (London).

El-Sayed El-Shazly, N, *The Gulf Tanker War: Iran and Iraq's Maritime Swordplay*, 1998 (Basingstoke).

Everett, M, *The Story of the Wreck of the Titanic*, 1912, reprinted 1998 (London).

Falconer, J, *Sail on Steam 1840-1935*, 1993 (London).

Fenwick, V & Gale, A, *Historic Shipwrecks: Discovered, Protected & Investigated*, 1998 (Stroud).

Fox, R, *Liners, The Golden Age: Photographs from The Hulton Getty Picture Collection*, 1999 (Cologne).

Friedman, N, *Battleship Design and Development 1905-1948*, 1978 (London).

——, *Modern Warship Design and Development*, 1980 (London).

——, *Carrier Air Power*, 1981 (London).

——, *The Postwar Naval Revolution*, 1987 (London).

——, (ed) *Navies in the Nuclear Age: Warships since 1945*, 1993 (London).

Garrard, A C, *The Worst Journey in the World*, various editions.

Gold, E, *Maritime Transport: The Evolution of International Maritime Policy and Shipping Law*, 1981, (Lexington, Massachusetts).

Goss, R O, *Studies in Maritime Economics*, 1968 (Cambridge).

Greenhill, B, (ed) *Sail's Last Century: The Merchant Sailing Ship 1830-1930*, 1993 (London).

—— & Hackman, J, *The Grain Races: The Baltic Background*, 1986 (London).

—— with Morrison, J, *The Archaeology of Ships and Boats*, 1995 (London).

Greenway, A, (ed) *The Golden Age of Shipping: The Classic Merchant Ship 1900-1960*, 1994 (London).

Griffiths, D, *Power of the Great Liners: A History of Atlantic Marine Engineering*, 1990 (Sparkford).

——, *Steam at Sea: Two Centuries of Steam-Powered Ships*, 1997 (London).

Grove, E, *Vanguard to Trident*, 1987 (Annapolis).

——, *The Future of Sea Power*, 1990 (London).

——, *Sea Battles in Close Up: World War Two*, 1993 (Annapolis).

Hamer, D, *Bombers Versus Battleships: The Struggle between Ships and Aircraft for the Control of the Surface of the Sea*, 1999 (London).

Hardy, A C, *The Book of the Ship*, 1947 (London).

——, *History of Motorshipping*, 1955 (London).

Hastings, M & Jenkins, S, *The Battle of the Falklands*, 1983 (New York).

Heaton, P, *Yachting: A History*, 1956 (New York).

Hocking, C, *Dictionary of Disasters at Sea during the Age of Steam: Including Sailing Ships and Ships of War Lost in Action 1824-1962*, 1969 (London).

Hooke, N, *Modern Shipping Disasters 1963-1987*, 1989 (London).

Hope, R, *A New History of British Shipping*, 1990 (London).

Horlaftis, G, *A History of Greek Owned Shipping*, 1996 (London).

Hornsby, D, *Ocean Ships*, third edition 1986 (London).

Howarth, D & Howarth, S, *The Story of P&O*, 1986 (London).

Hughes, T, *The Blue Riband of the Atlantic*, 1973 (Cambridge).

Hughes, W P, *Fleet Tactics*, 1986 (Annapolis).

Huston, J, *Hydraulic Dredging*, 1970 (Centreville, Maryland).

Hunt, W R, *Stef: A Biography of Vilhjalmur Stefansson, Canadian Arctic Explorer*, 1986 (Vancouver).

Huntford, R, *Shackleton*, 1985 (London).

Hutton, W M, *Cape Horn Passage*, 1934 (London).

Hyde, F E, *The Cunard Line*, 1975 (London).

Hynds, P, *World High Speed Ferries*, 1992 (London).

Ireland, B, *Jane's Naval History of World War II*, 1998 (London).

James, N, *Alone Around the World: The First Woman to Sail Single-Handedly around the World*, 1979 (New York).

Jane, F T, et al (eds) *Jane's Fighting Ships*, annually since 1898 (London).

Johnson, P, *The Encyclopedia of Yachting*, 1989 (London).

——, *Yacht Rating*, 1997 (London).

Kåhre, G, *The Last Tall Ships*, 1990 (London).

Keble Chatterton, E, *Q-Ships and their Story*, 1972 (London).

Kemp, P, *A Pictorial History of the Sea War 1939-1945*, 1995 (London).

Kendall, L C, *The Business of Shipping*, fifth edition 1986 (Centreville, Maryland).

Knox-Johnston, R, *A World of My Own: The Single-Handed, Nonstop Circumnavigation of the World in Suhaili*, 1970 (New York).

——, *Beyond Jules Verne: Circling the World in a Record-Breaking Seventy-Four Days*, 1995 (London).

Konstam, A, *The History of Shipwrecks*, 1999 (New York).

Lambert, A, (ed) *Steam, Steel & Shellfire: The Steam Warship 1815-1905*, 1992 (London).

Landstrom, B, *The Ship: An Illustrated History*, 1961 (London).

Marcus, H S, *Neither Guns, nor Butter: A Look at National Maritime Policies*, 1983 (Seattle, Washington).

Mariott, J, (ed) *Brassey's Fast Attack Craft*, 1978 (London).

Marsden, P, *Ships and Shipwrecks*, 1997 (London).

Massie, R K, *Dreadnought: Britain, Germany and the Coming of the Great War*, 1991 (New York).

McKee, A, *How We Found the Mary Rose*, 1982 (London).

McKee, E, *Working Boats of Britain*, 1983 (London).

Miller, D, *U-Boats: History, Development and Equipment 1914-1945*, 2000 (London).

Miller, W H, *The Last Blue Water Liners*, 1986 (London).

Morris, C F, *Origins, Orient and Oriana*, 1980 (Brighton).

Munro-Smith, R, *Ships and Naval Architecture*, 1973 (London).

Nelson, L, *Stream, Lake, Estuary & Ocean Pollution*, 1991 (London).

Ohrelius, B, (trans Michael, M) *Vasa: The King's Ship*, 1962 (London).

O'Sullivan, P, *The Lusitania: Unravelling the Mysteries*, 1998 (Doughcloyne, Cork).

Packard, W V, *The Ships*, 1984 (London).

Paine, L, *Ships of the World: An Historical Encyclopedia*, 1998 (London).

Paloczi-Horvath, G, *From Monitor to Missile Boat: Coast Defence Ships and Coastal Defence 1860 to the Present*, 1996 (London).

Preston, A, *Battleships of World War I: An Illustrated Encyclopedia of the Battleships of All Nations 1914-1918*, 1972 (New York).

——, *Sea Combat off the Falklands*, 1982 (London).

——, *Submarines*, 1982 (London).

——, et al (eds) *Warship*, quarterly 1977-88, annually since then (London).

Pritchard, S, *Oil Pollution Control*, 1987 (London).

Quartermaine, P, *Building on the Sea: Form and Meaning in Modern Ship Architecture*, 1996 (London).

Rinman, T & Brodefors, R, *The Commercial History of Shipping*, 1983 (Gothenburg).

Rousmaniere, J, *America's Cup*, 1984 (London).

Rule, M, *The Mary Rose: The Excavation and Raising of Henry VIII's Flagship*, 1982 (London).

Sadler, D H, *Man is not Lost*, 1968 (London).

Sawyer, L A & Mitchell, W H, *The Liberty Ships*, 1970 (Newton Abbot).

Savours, A, (ed) *Diary of the Discovery Expedition to the Antarctic Regions 1901-1904*, 1966 (London).

——, *The Voyages of the Discovery: The Illustrated History of Scott's Ship*, 1992 (London).

Schofield, B B, *The Russian Convoys*, 1964 (London).

Scott, R F, *The Voyage of the Discovery*, 1905 (London).

Sekula, A, *Fish Story*, 1995 (Dusseldorf).

Slader, J, *The Fourth Service*, 1995 (London).

Sowinski, L, *Action in the Pacific: As seen by US Naval Photographers during World War 2*, 1981 (London).

Stanley, J (ed), *Bold in Her Breeches: Women Pirates Across the Ages*, 1995 (London).

Stopford, M, *Maritime Economics*, 1988 (London).

Sturmey, S G, *British Shipping and World Competition*, 1962 (London).

——, *Shipping Economics: Collected Papers*, 1975 (London).

Sturton, I, (ed) *All The World's Battleships: 1906 to the Present*, 1996 (London).

Sweetman, J, *Tirpitz: Hunting the Beast*, 2000 (Stroud).

Swithinbank, C, *Forty Years on Ice: A Lifetime of Exploration and Research in the Polar Regions*, 1998 (Lewes).

Talbot, F A, *Steamship Conquest of the World*, 1912 (London).

Throckmorton, P (ed), *The Sea Remembers: Shipwrecks & Archaeology*, 1996 (London).

Traung, J-O, (ed) *Fishing Boats of the World*, 1955, 1960, 1967, three volumes (London).

Tunstall, J, *The Fishermen*, 1962 (London).

Vernon Gibbs, C R, *The Western Ocean Passenger Lines and Liners*, 1970 (Glasgow).

Villar, R, *Merchant Ships at War: The Falklands Experience*, 1984 (London).

Watson, M H, *Disasters at Sea*, 1987 (Wellingborough).

Wilson, E, (ed King, H G R) *Diary of the Terra Nova Expedition to the Antarctic 1910-1912*, 1972 (London).

Ward, D, *Complete Handbook to Cruising*, 1989 (Lausanne).

Warner, W W, *Distant Water: The Fate of the North Atlantic Fisherman*, second edition 1983 (Boston, Massachusetts).

Watts, A, *The U-Boat Hunters*, 1976 (London).

Whitley, M J, *German Destroyers of World War Two*, second edition 1991 (London).

Williams, D L, *Liners in Battledress*, 1989 (London).

Woodman, R, *The Arctic Convoys 1941-1945*, 1994 (London).

——, *The History of the Ship: The Comprehensive Story of Seafaring from the Earliest Times to the Present Day*, 1997 (London).

——, *Malta Convoys 1940-1943*, 2000 (London).

INDEX

PICTURE CREDITS

All photographs reproduced in this book appear courtesy of the Conway Picture Library, with the following exceptions:
Plates 1, 2 and 21, courtesy of The Chrysalis Picture Library;
Plates 14 and 15, courtesy of Ian Dear.

LITERARY CREDITS

The opening extracts from each chapter are quoted from the following books:

Chapter 1
Erskine Childers, *The Riddle of the Sands*. 1903, this edition 1986 (London), page 80.

Chapter 2
Marshall Everett, *Story of the Wreck of the Titanic*. 1912, this edition 1998 (London), page 19.

Chapter 3
C S Forester, *Brown on Resolution*. 1929, this edition 1978 (Bath), page 240.

Chapter 4
H W Tilman, *Mischief Among the Penguins*. 1961, this edition 1988 (London), page 140.

Chapter 5
C S Forester, *Hunting the Bismarck*. 1959 (London), page 109.

Chapter 6
Stanley, J (ed), *Bold in Her Breeches: Women Pirates Across the Ages*. 1995 (London), page 256.

Chapter 7
Miles Smeeton, *Because the Horn Is There*. 1970, this edition 1985 (London), page 66.

Chapter 8
Joseph Conrad, *Typhoon and other stories*. 1903, this edition 1990 (Harmondsworth), pages 109-110

Chapter 9
Alan Munro, *An Arabian Affair: Politics and Diplomacy behind the Gulf War*. 1996 (London), page 257.

Chapter 10
Alexander McKee, *How We Found the Mary Rose*. 1982 (London), page 141.